THE YEARBOOK

Dear I exist,

I exist too. I found your red pen messages and think we might get along. I leave messages in books too.

Meet you in the pages of The Perks of Being a Wallflower? We can exist together?

From,

Someone who gets it

xxx

The Yearbook is a work of fiction
but it deals with many real issues
including emotional abuse and bullying.

Links to advice and support can be found
at the back of the book.

To Libraries, and everyone who has ever needed to hide in one

First published in the UK in 2021 by Usborne Publishing Ltd., Usborne House, 83-85 Saffron Hill, London EC1N 8RT, England. usborne.com

Usborne Verlag, Usborne Publishing Ltd., Prüfeninger Str. 20, 93049 Regensburg, Deutschland, VK Nr. 17560

p5 quote from *The Cocktail Party* by T.S. Eliot / p42 quote from *To Kill a Mockingbird* by Harper Lee / p127 quote from *Stargirl* by Jerry Spinelli / p252 quote from *The Great Gatsby* by F. Scott Fitzgerald

A CIP catalogue record for this book is available from the British Library.

ISBN 9781474996723 JF AMJJASOND/21 05374/1

Printed and bound in Great Britain by CPI Group (UK) Ltd, Croydon, CR0 4YY

FSC www.fsc.org MIX Paper from responsible sources FSC® C020471

HOLLY BOURNE

THE YEARBOOK

SCHOLA EST HORRIBILIS

USBORNE

Half of the harm that is done in this world is due to people who want to feel important. They don't mean to do harm, but the harm does not interest them. Or they do not see it, or they justify it because they are absorbed in the endless struggle to think well of themselves.

T.S. Eliot

I bet the author has never even read T.S. Eliot and has just inserted this quote to make the book sound more intelligent.

Most likely to be...

A SUPERMODEL:

Grace Langdon

A C.E.O.:

Amelia Murry

FORGOTTEN:

Paige Vickers

ST BENEDICT'S SCHOOL YEARBOOK

NOTE FROM THE EDITOR

Look, you don't need to read this to be reminded what secondary school was like. Just close your eyes and you're there. Like it or not, you're there. With your popular kids, your smart kids, your sporty kids, your drama kids, your obsessively-into-graphic-novels kids, and that quiet one you all suspect will become a serial killer one day. Someone says the word "school" and we're all there. In the churning chaos of the corridors, the Darwinism of the lunchtime canteen and the toilets with the locked cubicle and muffled crying coming from under the gap. The unspoken social hierarchies deciding who gets to sit where on the grass slope next to the Astroturf. You can smell the stale reek of the PE changing rooms. The earnest stink of a newly-trained teacher who cares too much; the stench of the jaded teachers who stopped caring long ago. Hear the jolting trill of the bell, the whispers as you walk past, the loud echoes of everyone demanding to be heard above each other. The dramas, the traumas, and the untrue rumours. The endless, predictable terribleness of it. Getting up each morning, putting on that damn uniform and having to march yourself into this prison, wondering what psychologically-damaging memory you're going to make that day. A government building chock-a-block with scared teenagers, desperate to know who they are, and if they matter, and whether they're going to get out of there alive.

So with all this in mind, you can't blame me that, for many years, I wanted absolutely nothing to do with school. Let alone this yearbook, and everything this yearbook represents.

Until, of course, I did this…

CHAPTER 1

It was yearbook photo day and the English block toilets were clearly not the best place to hide from the fiasco. I'd planned to lock myself in a cubicle with a library book and dodge the whole thing. But, as I pushed into the mint green arena, I found a cluster bomb of girls, fighting for mirror space and panicking about the state of their faces.

"Can I borrow your mascara? My eyelashes look like they've become freaking...vegan?"

"My hair! Why is it doing this to me?"

Entire contents of make-up bags were dumped into the sinks. The air stank of a pungent mixture of hairsprays. I bumped into Grace, who was leaning over the mirror with the best lighting.

"Sorry!"

I watched her weigh up whether I was worth disciplining before she half-smiled to accept the apology and returned to contouring her face. Though she raised her eyebrows at Laura on the neighbouring sink.

I was stuck. If I went to the loo now, they'd notice I'd stayed in there and no doubt spread a rumour I'd missed the photos due to chronic diarrhoea. My only option was to pretend I also needed to overhaul my appearance and wait until they'd finished. Getting to a mirror was tough, however. Grace, Amelia and Laura held three out of the four available – one each, of *course*. One mirror for the pretty one, one mirror for the scary one, and one for the sheep. All three of them united in their commitment to unnecessary awfulness. The remaining mirror was being fought over by three others – not daring to complain. Chloe had a true talent for applying eyeliner under exceptional circumstances. She'd managed to load up her smoky eye perfectly despite access to only the mirror's top corner. Her best friend, Hannah, squatted under her, piling concealer onto a chin spot. Both ignored me as I loitered. I had no lipstick to blot. No mascara to reapply. So I stood on my tippy-toes and punched my hair to try and give it volume.

Punch punch punch.

Why won't they all hurry up?

I could only see a tiny fraction of myself in the mirror.

Punch punch punch.

Amelia pulled out a mini bottle of hairspray and fumigated her head. My eyes stung as the chemical mist drifted over and we all held back coughs. Amelia was the scary one. I glanced at my battered watch and took a step backwards, ready to inch my way into a cubicle, when the door slammed open with Mrs Collins on the threshold.

"Right, girls, come on. Preening over," she barked in her thick Irish accent. "And do ANY of you remember the school rules about no make-up?"

Amelia, unruffled, continued to spray her hair. "But, miss, it's the yearbook pictures."

"Yes, and you were due in the hall five minutes ago." She clapped her hands. Chloe jumped and ruined the corner of her eyeliner. "Out!" She started guiding us out like a sheepdog.

"I need the loo," I protested, as she tried to shepherd me with the rest of them.

"No, you don't. Come on. Picture time."

And with hair full of fruitless punches, I got frogmarched away.

In the hall, everyone had broken the no-phones rule to use them as mirrors. The teachers were too slammed to stop us – pulling off the gigantic task of lining us up, firstly in alphabetical order for our individual shots, and then in height order for the year group photo. Photographers clicked away in two corners with their silvery umbrellas that somehow made us look slightly better, even with our acne and experimental haircuts. I shuffled to the back of the queue, jumper sleeves pulled over my hands, looking for Joe Vividichi and Lily Welsh. After five years of alphabetical lines, I knew to slot myself between them. In Year Seven, Joe and I once spoke about the annoyance of having a surname near the end of the alphabet because you always have to go last. Then he got attractive and popular and we'd never spoken since. Not that I've spoken to anyone much, especially since Ruby left.

We inched forward as pupils squatted on a stool and pulled their most attractive face. We all knew the significance of these photos. The yearbook headshot was the photo that comes to define you in history.

I didn't want mine to be taken.

I really did not see any point. No one knew who I was, no one would remember me anyway. The most I'd be in our year group's shared history was, "*Oh yeah, that girl who never really spoke.*"

But I was stuck in the line now and had no choice.

Soon enough, it was my turn to insert my forgettable face into nobody's memory.

"Paige Vickers?" The photographer's assistant looked up from her sheet and I stepped forward.

"Hello, Paige." The photographer's voice was way too boomy. He was all red and sweaty. "Come over here and sit on the stool for us, my love."

I didn't like that he'd called me "my love" but I sat down obligingly, wanting it over.

"Right, if you just swivel your knees round. No, not that way, the other way. That's great, my darling. Okay, now twist your head towards me. No, too much. To the right a bit. Brilliant." He lurched up from behind his lens and mimed pulling each side of his mouth up. "Now big smile, missy.

Come on, more. That's better." *Snap snap snap.* The umbrella flash created lightning throughout the hall. "Even bigger smile now, come on."

Here was the problem. I did not know how to smile, especially for a photo. I'd had next to no practice.

"Huge grin. Come on! It's your last year of school. You've got your whole future in front of you… Alright then. Never mind."

I got off the stool to make way for Lily and compliantly joined the height-order line. Mrs Collins was in her bossy element, herding us all into size-appropriate clumps. I accidentally caught Amelia's eye and she gave me a dirty look for the crime. Despite being one of the most popular girls in school, Amelia knew who I was. My only minuscule claim to fame was that I was chief reporter for the school newspaper and nobody read it more intently than her group. Though I'd never been stupid enough to write anything other than wonderful stories about them. I stared at the dusty wooden floor and, ten minutes later, we were instructed to climb onto some dodgy metal scaffolding. The super-talls were led onto it first, boys joking about pushing each other off the back row, while teachers barked detention threats.

Mrs Collins pointed at my group. "Right, you lot next. Up you go. No funny business."

I climbed the steps and siphoned myself into the second row, taking in the giant poster on the back wall reminding us to ask ourselves what Jesus would do. The scaffolding creaked and Sam Hutchins encouraged all the boys to jump. The shrieks thrummed in my ears as Mrs Collins issued him a detention.

"Stop it. All of you. You're Year Eleven, for Christ's sake. Bloody act like it," she told us all.

Mr Photographer did not speak to us like we were Year Elevens.

"Right, boys and girls, I need you to squeeze together for me. Squidge squidge squidge. Come on, don't be shy. A bit more, a bit more…" We all gradually formed one big clump of navy blue jumpers, an impenetrable wad of literal uniformity. The teachers took their seats at the front, sandwiched by the shortest students. "Okay, everyone. I want to see huge smiles. On the count of three – one, two, three." Umbrellas crackled around us, blinding us collectively. In an instant, we all became history, staring out into the future. We blinked from the flash, and when we opened our eyes, we'd already aged past the moment of capture.

The photographer grimaced at his camera screen. "Come on, let's not be silly now."

"What's happened?" Mrs Collins barked.

"It appears some of your students thought it funny to give someone 'bunny ears'."

We looked around to discover the epicentre of the drama. Laughter rippled out from the front, near Joe Vividichi and Ethan Chambers. It appeared we had our suspects. And, judging by the red face of Charlie Shaw in front of them, it appeared we also had our victim. Charlie had muddled through school okay until he got drunk at the Year Nine disco and passed out in the boys' toilets, soaked in his own urine. He'd since had a sizeable bullseye on his back.

Mrs Collins twisted around in her chair. "Grow up. Honestly, what are you lot like?"

"Let's try again, boys and girls. Big smiles now. One, two, three." We were dazzled again, but he was already frowning. "Come on, not again."

Actual snorts echoed around the hall, starting a contagion. Girly giggles joined the harmony, and Grace's high-pitched squeal pierced the air to my right.

Mrs Collins stood up. "Right, you lot. No more. Act your age. I'm sorry," she told the photographer, "I don't know what's got into them."

School, I thought. *That's what's got into them.*

She threatened us with a year group detention, which only made everyone laugh harder. Joe was in peak-Joe mode – showing off, puffing his chest out, spraying his alpha scent everywhere. Charlie's red face seeped down the neck of his shirt.

"One last time. No bunny ears. Eyes on me. Say cheese. One, two, three."

The hysteria was so loud at this point that you couldn't even hear the flash of the bulbs. About twelve people surrounding Charlie were craning over to give him bunny ears. I kept myself to myself, stared at the poster, and wondered what Jesus would do – whether he'd have given Judas bunny ears while posing for a Da Vinci painting?

Mrs Collins jumped up again, shouting in such a thick Irish accent none of us could understand her. People started mocking her accent. The photographer crossed his arms with resigned disgust. Miss Bell, a new maths teacher, jogged out quietly to drag Reverend John in to tell us off and pray for us. And through all of this laughter and mayhem, I craned my neck to take in Charlie Shaw. A grin stapled to his face, no choice but to take the hit and laugh it off. Soon enough, Reverend John would come booming in and give us a year group detention. We'd have to sit through a twenty-minute lecture about letting down the school (and don't forget God). Then, after a mass apology to the photographer, we'd all say cheese and the bulbs would flash for a final time. This would be the shot they'd use in the yearbook. In the future, people would pick out their own face first to see how attractive they'd managed to look. Then they'd pick out the faces of their crushes and enemies, taking it all in, before shoving the yearbook in a drawer somewhere to age like a fine wine.

I thought about Charlie. How whenever he looked at that photo, all he'd remember was how he was given bunny ears repeatedly until we got a year group detention, which everyone then blamed on him.

That was what his lasting memory would be.

That was why I'd wanted to stay in the toilet.

It was better to be forgotten than scarred.

CHAPTER 2

It was lunch by the time we were allowed off the scaffolding. I grabbed a cheese and pickle sandwich from the canteen and hurried up to the library. The crazed lunchtime corridors faded to hushed bliss as I pushed through the doors. Books beckoned me in from where they were stacked high up to the ceiling – commanding peace and quiet in exchange for the privilege of being around them.

"Hi, Paige," said a giant pile of books on the front desk. "I think that's Paige, anyway. Hang on, I can't see you." Ms Gordon, the school librarian, removed the top book and appeared in all her dramatic glory – her cropped haircut and thick-rimmed glasses coming into view. Ms Gordon had an…intense relationship with fashion. Every outfit was like its own piece of performance art. She was the only teacher I could imagine existing outside these walls; whereas part of me still believed Mrs Collins slept in her biology classroom. I was quite fond of Ms Gordon. She ran the school newspaper, she let me eat my lunch in the library every day, and she never compared me to my brother, Adam.

"There you are! Don't forget we've got an important paper meeting tomorrow."

"I won't."

I went up the stairs to bagsy the little alcove on the top floor. I plumped down on the cushion, got out my book and sandwich, and settled in for the hour, trying to block out the ghost of Charlie's face.

I didn't do anything. I didn't stop anything. I just let it happen.

But at least it wasn't happening to me.

My stomach hurt. I didn't know why I'd bothered buying a sandwich. I opened my book, hoping it would stop my brain from overthinking. I huddled my knees in to myself and started reading the second chapter of *To Kill a Mockingbird*. We were studying it that term for English and it wasn't too awful compared to some of the other boring stuff we had to read. At least it wasn't written in really old-fashioned language.

I got sucked into the story of two children living in the deep south of America, obsessed with their hermit neighbour. My library copy was battered from years of overuse – with random important passages underlined in angry red pen by a past student and the corners folded over to make them easier to find. The library was lullaby quiet. A group of Year Sevens whispered at a table below me, Lily Welsh was in her usual spot, reading near the main desk, and some of the sixth formers click-clacked on their laptops in the corner. Ms Gordon hummed as she restacked the books and I could've probably stayed there all day and no one would've noticed I was missing. I became wallpaper. Safe, unnoticeable wallpaper.

I won't get blamed for a group detention, I won't have bunny ears put above my head, I won't get called names or have rumours started about me, I won't come home from school sobbing and swearing I can't go back. I won't get so badly bullied I have to leave like Melissa Nutley did.

The lunch hour passed – no memories made, but then no traumas made either.

But you will get forgotten…

The warning bell rang, and everyone stirred like animals emerging from hibernation. People collected their belongings and complained to one another about upcoming maths. I didn't stand and nobody noticed. Nobody ever noticed. The room emptied around me, and nobody asked, "*Hey, are you coming?*" and nobody said, "*Hey, you're going to be late.*" I stared at the yellowing page of my library book till my eyes blurred. Thinking of all the people who had read it before me, and all the people who were yet to read it, never knowing that I once held it in my hands. I turned the corner down to mark my place, leaving a tiny mark of myself behind. But it wasn't enough. My stomach still hurt. So I got out my pencil.

I exist, I wrote in the margin. *I once read this page. I breathed. I lived. I'm not special at all but I exist.*

* * *

The rest of the school day passed without incident, blurring into other school days that passed without incident. Just one big smudge of *head down, arms crossed and don't make eye contact*. I spoke a few sentences out loud. Hannah asked to borrow my pencil sharpener in maths and I said, "Sure" and then, "You're welcome". Then she threw me by initiating further dialogue.

"Like I'll need to understand simultaneous equations in music college," she said, rolling her eyes and flicking a page of her textbook.

"Yeah."

"I still can't believe we have a year-group detention. Charlie is such a *dick*."

"Hmm."

If you don't say anything bad about other people, it is less likely that they will say bad things about you. But you cannot call out other people for saying bad things about other people because that makes them feel bad about themselves and that will trigger them to say bad things about you too. Stay vague, stay silent, stay safe.

I was exhausted by the time the bell went. Students spilled out into the hallways, loud and lively. Chatter mingled with the noise of slamming lockers and phones beeping now they'd been allowed to roam free again.

I couldn't stop thinking about Charlie as I walked the familiar journey home. I wondered if he was okay, or if he went home and cried, or punched a wall, or maybe didn't mind as much as I thought he would.

I watch, I learn, I'm horrified, and yet I never do anything.

I wondered if Joe had given his bullying any further thought as I speed-walked through the park. Then I crossed the main road and took the shortcut through the grotty tunnel under the railway track. Ruby and I used to be cartoon-like terrified of this tunnel. We'd call it "The Murder Dash" and would dare one another to race through it, hair flying behind us, screaming with our hearts falling out of our mouths, certain we'd get pounced on by some lurker. Now I took it most days, alone. It was still creepy, though the previous year the council had installed a security camera. Remembering Ruby gave me the familiar pang I regularly tried to ignore. The *I'm-lonely* pang. The *I-have-no-one* pang. The *Ruby-I-miss-you* pang. A hollowing of the stomach, a constant hunger.

I descended the steps to find the tunnel empty as usual. I stopped just under the security camera, its red light glowing in the gloom. On, and watching. I put my bag on the floor, checked again that there was no one around, then I raised my arms like I was a ballerina and twirled a series of pirouettes. I swirled and twirled till I was dizzy and breathless. Then I looked up at the red light and winked, before picking up my bag again.

I smiled the rest of the way home, wondering, as I always wondered, if anyone had seen my dance. Imagining a bored security guard in a council office somewhere noticing my twirls. Remembering he'd seen me do it before. *Who's that girl and why does she dance?* I pictured them asking themselves. Leaving another tiny trace of myself behind.

* * *

My smile drooped when I stepped through my front door.

"I'm home," I called needlessly, as Mum was hyper-attuned to the house's every movement. I hung my jacket carefully on the stand, next to a framed photo of Adam winning a football cup, and his framed A-level certificates.

"I'm in the kitchen."

I went to say my cursory hello and see what overcomplicated meal she was making. Mum sat in an apron at the oak table, peeling a giant bag of potatoes and plopping them into a cold pan of water.

"Did you have a good day?" she asked the potato in her hand.

"Uh huh." I got out a glass from the cupboard and filled it at the tap.

"That's good."

"You?" I examined her over the rim of my water. She was immaculately put together, as always. Thin and toned, hair cut, coloured and straightened, outfit all matching, make-up applied.

She chopped the naked spud in half. "Oh yes, it was fine. I went to yoga with the girls. Did some shopping. Shepherd's pie for dinner."

"Great."

"See you later."

"See you."

That was actually quite a lot of conversation for the two of us recently. Mum had been super jumpy since Adam started university. Overcompensating for his departure with elaborate dinners, too worried about Dad to take interest in me. I took my glass and left her to it – padding upstairs to my tiny bedroom that I was still stuck with.

It's his room, Paige. It's where he grew up. Besides, you wouldn't want to swap it anyway, would you? Not when you've got yours just how you like it? Would you, Paige? No. I thought not.

The bedroom door thumped against the end of my bed and I squeezed into my box. I'd painted it myself – a deep shade of purple that made me feel warm and safe, like I was in the womb of a mother who actually cared about her child. Not to get too Freudian on you or anything. I changed out of my uniform into some joggers and my favourite *Fear and Loathing in Las Vegas* T-shirt that Aunt Polly got me. Then I grabbed a pen from my tiny desk and crouched to open the drawer under my bed. Inside, it harboured several used notebooks, every page stuffed full, the dates of the last five years marked on them. My current notebook was the same cheap green exercise book as all the others, and it was almost full too – the pages swollen with ink. I fell onto my bed and turned to a clean page.

4th October

Today was yearbook photo day. Joe and Ethan kept giving Charlie bunny ears to ruin the group photo and we ended up getting a year group detention. Everyone blamed it on Charlie, even though he did nothing wrong.

I read it back, watched the moment become an accurate historical record of that day. My stomach hurt a little less. Satisfied, I snapped the notebook shut and hid it under my bed with all the others.

Nobody noted it down, you see. All the horrid things people did to each other at school. Nobody kept tabs on it. Nobody was ever held accountable. The school's anti-bullying policy may as well have involved someone in a novelty dinosaur costume singing at us to be kind to each other. I saw everything though. People didn't notice me, but I noticed them, and I saw the horrid things they did to each other and I didn't want it to be forgotten. I may've been too scared to write about it in the newspaper, but at least I wrote it down in these notebooks. A record existed somewhere. I wrote it all down. Everything I saw, everything that happened that shouldn't have – then I hid it under my bed. I wasn't sure what I ever planned to do with the notebooks, but it made me feel better that they existed at all.

With my daily "torture journalling" achieved, I faced the challenge I faced every afternoon… How to fill time when you're completely and endlessly alone?

CHAPTER 3

Over time, you learn coping strategies for the overwhelmingness of your constant solo company.

Rule one: distraction is your friend. Always have something on – TV, music, a book on the go. Never allow yourself to sit alone in your own silence, that's when it starts to creep up on you and make you miss people too much.

Rule number two: do not go on social media. It's self-harm, looking at all the non-lonely people, out having non-lonely lives, and making memories and ensuring nobody forgets them. Knowing what people do in school is enough, without knowing what the hell they do outside of it through a Juno filter.

Rule three: if you have a wobbly day, where you feel empty and pointless and that you could fade away into nothingness and nobody would miss you at all, remind yourself that most people feel like this *anyway,* even if they're out and about and taking group selfies. Remind yourself it's better to be lonely than hurt. It's better to be alone than in a room full of people who can turn on you.

Rule four: if all else fails, you can always talk to your robot friend.

I rolled over on my bed and stared up at the ceiling.

"Alexa?" I called out. "Why are people so mean?"

A blue light in the corner flashed. "Positive distinctiveness," a calm, lady voice parroted back. "People in a social group need to feel different and unique from others in a superior way. Degrading others has been shown to raise our own self-esteem."

"Sounds about right." She didn't reply because I didn't say "Alexa" first.

"Alexa?"

I wished she'd say, "Yes?" but she never did.

"Alexa, how are you today?"

"You know I don't have feelings."

"I bet you do and you're just hiding them."

Silence.

"I bet you're secretly judging me for being such a loser."

Silence.

"I bet you make fun of me with all of your robot friends when you're hanging out in the cloud together."

Silence.

"Alexa?"

Silence.

"Alexa, why are we here?"

Her cool voice filled my empty room. "The answer to the question '*What's the meaning of life?*' has produced much philosophical, scientific and theological speculation throughout history. Different people from different cultures believe different things."

"Not particularly helpful, are you?"

Silence.

"So smug, aren't you? With all your useless answers."

Silence.

"I know you can hear me."

Silence.

"Fine then, be that way."

I sighed at myself then opened Adam's old laptop and loaded up *Spotlight* again. I'd watched it a thousand times before – it's about the group of journalists who exposed the abuse within the Catholic Church. I got under my covers and submitted to the story. The house filled with the smell of beef. The food would be ready at seven for him. Whether or not he'd be home by then was another matter entirely. We wouldn't eat until he did. We would not mention it if he was late, or if we were starving, or if it all went dry.

At six thirty-seven exactly I heard the key in the lock.

I closed the lid of my laptop.

Mum turned down the radio.

The scrape of the key. The doorknob turning. I got out of bed and made my way towards the top of the stairs. Mum's feet creaked on the floorboards downstairs. Together we listened.

You can learn a lot about someone from the way they open the door. Over the years, you can learn to differentiate between a good key jangle and a bad one. You can distinguish whether that was a genuine door slam or just the wind catching it, don't worry. We listened. Stomachs attuned. Then...the door unlatched in a most charming way. My stomach settled, though it wouldn't fully relax until...

"Oh honeys?" Dad called, all faux American. "I'm ho-o-me."

Not just a good mood, a *great* mood. Mum and I arrived in the hallway together. Me scuttling down the stairs, her removing her apron. Dad's face cracked open into a warm, welcoming grin.

"Both my girls at once. What a lucky man I am."

He opened his arms for a hug and I went in, putting my face into the armpit of his suit.

"Hi, Dad. Good day?" He'd referred to me as one of his "girls". I was included. Part of the family. It felt like someone had dropped vanilla essence directly onto my tongue.

"Great day. Lovely day. Even better now, of course."

He released me so he could plonk a giant kiss on Mum's lips. She was lit up like a lighthouse on steroids. Waves of happiness rolled off her, crashing through the room.

"You're early, darling." She pulled him in so the kiss would last longer.

"Wanted to get back here, didn't I?"

"Dinner's almost ready."

"As I said. World's. Luckiest. Man."

"Paige? Set the table?" she asked.

I nodded compliantly and skipped off to the dining room,

collecting knives and forks and such from the kitchen on my way. I set Dad's place at the head. And, as it was a great day, I put Mum's and my places on either side. He strode in and poured himself a whisky from the drinks cabinet – switching the radio to his favourite jazz station and turning it up. Mum clattered back into the kitchen, trying to hide her hurry so he didn't accuse her of being stressful. She returned immediately with a bowl of his favourite olives.

"Just to keep you going, it will be ready soon."

He yanked her back to plant another kiss. "What have I done to deserve you?"

Mum blossomed like magnolia in spring. She lost ten years off her face instantly.

"Only fifteen minutes away," she mumbled. Dad whacked her arse on her way back to the kitchen and she let out a little gasp of surprise. "Glynn, a child is present."

"She enjoys seeing her parents in love, don't you?"

I knew to always nod and always agree. "You're love's young dream."

We were left alone with the olives but he was in such a great mood I wasn't too tense, especially as I knew to keep to his favourite subjects.

"Did you see Adam's message?" I asked. He'd sent through a photo to the family group chat of his latest essay mark. A first, of course, because it was Adam. The group chat should essentially just have been titled *Adam breathed – applaud.*

"Killing it, as ever." Dad puffed up like it was his own achievement. I mean, Adam wouldn't be so very brilliant if he hadn't come from Dad's bollock and grown up with Dad as a shining example of what a brilliant man looks like. "Bristol is lucky to have him."

We never mentioned that Bristol was Adam's second choice uni after he wasn't accepted by Cambridge. Cambridge was the Voldemort in our household – never to be spoken of. I'm surprised Dad hadn't driven there overnight to egg the place.

"And how was school?" He asked like he might actually be interested and I bloomed pathetically, sitting higher in my seat. I didn't want to ruin this rare moment by telling him about the group detention.

"Yes, really good," I said excitedly. "In chemistry we did this experiment to see if…"

I hadn't finished my sentence before he glazed over, shifting his attention to the whisky glass. My bloom shrivelled as quickly as it had arrived. I carried on, even though it was devastatingly obvious he was bored. He sloshed his drink around, his nose slightly wrinkled. "Hmm," he kept saying, as the alcohol swirled. "Hmm."

"…So, yes, it was quite funny. You know. For chemistry."

There was a painful delay before he realized I'd finished. He gave me a tight smile. I waited for him to comment, to even *pretend* he was interested. I hoped for it so much that my stomach hurt. The anticipation of acknowledgement. Or the biggest win of all…*praise.* If they treated me the way they treated Adam for even a day, I reckon I could live off the oxygen of that praise for a year.

"So, guess who I saw at work today?"

I examined the sentence for any link whatsoever to what I'd just said but found none. "Who?"

"Jude Law."

I wasn't sure who he was, but I gasped appropriately. "Wow, really? Where?"

"In reception, waiting to go to the offices on the top floor."

Dad's office block had a film production company in it, so celebrity sightings were pretty common and made him very excited. It was almost like he believed he had something to do with them coming in.

"That's pretty cool."

Dad's smile widened. "Lost all his hair, mind." He reached up to his thick grey-speckled mane and leaned back in his chair. "You hear that, Jane?" he called out. "Jude Law came into the office today."

Mum arrived in the threshold like he'd snapped his fingers for her. "Is that right? I've always had quite a crush on him."

A twinge rumbled down my back when she said that. It was a dangerous joke. But he laughed appreciatively, the good mood a supercharged shield. "Oh, have you now?" he teased. "Even though your husband has a much better head of hair?"

She laughed too, and I joined in. All of us laughing in the dining room, like happy families do. When it was like this I couldn't help but worry I'd made up the other part of Dad.

Mum walked over and rubbed his head like he was a dog. He closed his eyes and leaned into her hands.

"Much better head of hair," she said. "Anyway, dinner is ready. I'll just go get the plates."

Eating was blissful. Straight out of a movie. Dad was on fire. All hands waving as he spoke, telling the funny stories we'd heard a million times before (though we never dared tell him that we'd heard them a million times before). The one where he got into a fight with a fireman, the one where he drank his university professor under the table, the one where he accidentally ended up in (and then won) a rap battle… The stories were so recycled I could tell them word for word, and yet, we pretended along as we forked Mum's carefully-cooked dinner into our mouths. We laughed and gasped and cleaned our plates and heard all Dad's opinions on each and every one of Jude Law's movies and what advice he would've given Jude Law if he wasn't too busy at work today to chat to him properly. The table was so relaxed you could almost see the wood seep and bend in the middle. I was able to finish my whole meal. Old memories slipped away. I told myself I was too dramatic and needed to be fairer to Dad.

But I knew to quit while I was ahead. Especially as Dad had been extra…Dad-like since Adam left. I said thank you for dinner and that I was going upstairs to read, and my parents nodded without saying anything.

I got back to my room, and asked Alexa to play some happy music. And, with hours to fill before bedtime, with no one to call, no one to see and nowhere to go, I decided to get even further ahead in English. I dug around in my bag and pulled out my library book. I pulled back my duvet and clambered into the smell of me sleeping.

I exist…

I opened the page on the note I'd left to the universe and blushed. How many times had I written this in the margins of books that weren't mine? Or scratched it into trees? Or the sides of park benches. Tiny marks of myself left for people to find and wonder who I was, while nobody who knew me ever really wondered about me.

I was so pathetic… No wonder my parents preferred Adam.

I shook my head to attempt to dislodge my self-loathing and turned the page. It was distracting that someone had underlined so much of the story in red pen, but I tried to train my eyeballs away from it. For a school set text, it really was actually okay. It was all about being a kid and playing for hours in the summer holidays. It reminded me of Ruby, and our summers together avoiding our houses. As I turned the pages, I felt the nick from the double-edged sword of nostalgia that always came when I thought of Ruby. The sweetness of remembering, combined with the bitter taste of what happened.

I'm pathetic.

But at least I had a story to get lost in. I read and turned pages, read and turned pages – pulled away from the din of the TV downstairs because Dad had put Sky Sports on super loud.

Then I saw it.

I was reading a scene where the children talk to their father, Atticus, and he tells them that they can never really understand someone until they've crawled into their skin to see their point of view. There was a scribble in the book's margin. In red pen. The same distracting red pen that had been plaguing me.

This time, they hadn't underlined anything, but had written their own commentary at the side.

No. It's impossible to truly understand anyone else's point of view. We all have to learn to sit with the profound loneliness of knowing no one will ever understand us, and us them.

Everything blurred around me as I read the red words. They zoomed into sharp focus, so sharp that they seared themselves into me, branding me with their wisdom.

Learn to sit with the profound loneliness…

At that moment, Mum must've made a mistake because I suddenly heard a shout float through the floorboards. Instinctively, I turned off my bedroom light and hid under the covers, feigning sleep. I tried to tune out Dad's scolding and Mum's crying. My intestines curled themselves into tight knots as Dad's footsteps thudded up the stairs and their bedroom door shut just on the verge of slamming. What had happened? He'd been in such a good mood. I lay in the dark listening to Mum cry softly. Then to the noises of her coming up to apologize and beg for forgiveness. Muffled murmurs came from their room. Then, after half an hour or so, it was quiet. I'd lain there, invisible, with the book held to my chest the whole time. When it had been silent for ten minutes, I sighed, and picked up the book again.

No one will ever understand us, and us them.

The message made so much sense, it was like I'd always known it. I felt so much less alone than I had earlier that evening.

Nobody truly gets anybody else. *Everybody* sits with loneliness.

I sometimes felt lost being me and living in my house. The only person I'd ever told about my dad, Ruby, was long gone. Ruby was the one I'd told about "quiet time" when I was a child – the terrifying periods when it was illegal to make a noise in my home. Even though I'd only been seven years old, I still remembered the…loneliness I felt when she expressed surprise and said they didn't have "quiet time" in her house. Then, as the years passed, she was the one I complained to about Adam and him always being better. And Mum, and that I didn't understand why she put up with Dad's moods. When I lost Ruby, it wasn't just the grief of her absence that hurt, but the grief of no longer being understood.

But maybe everyone else feels misunderstood? I thought, as

I read back the red words. *Maybe we are all lonely? Maybe I'm not such an invisible freak?*

And, just like that, I felt so understood and so connected to this stranger who had scribbled in the margin. I held the book's open page against my chest like I was trying to photocopy it onto my heart, listening to the temporary peace of my parents' sleep. Then I flipped back to the start and scanned each page to see what else this person had underlined. Looking at all the quotes they'd marked up. Seeing the book through their eyes, wondering…

The night was long and sleep evasive. Even in their unconsciousness, you could still feel my parents' anxious energy pulse through the house. It stained the walls, seeped into the carpets, lingered in the air like paint fumes. I ran my finger along the crimson handwriting – wondering at this stranger invading my margins, who completely and utterly got it. Who left this for someone to find. Someone who may've needed it. Someone like me.

Who are you? I asked.

BACK OF A LOO CUBICLE DOOR...

~~AMELIA HAS CRABS~~

Whoever wrote this is
a skanky BITCH

I HATE MY LIFE

DOESN'T EVERYONE?

OH SHUT UP. NO ONE CARES.

MRS COLLINS IS SUCH A DICK

I cry my tears
I hurt my heart
For what?
For what?

DON'T GIVE UP THE DAY-JOB,
SHAKESPEARE

WHY IS SCHOOL SO FUCKING SHIT?

I exist. I was here.

repitition

CHAPTER 4

Forty thousand years ago, some navel-gazing cave person wanted to leave their mark on the world. So they made paint from berries, smeared it over their palm and printed their hand against the rock. When the paintings were discovered thousands of years later, it revealed the unthinkable: that cave people dwelled on their legacy despite their constant struggle to survive.

These ancient humans had thoughts like:

Will anyone remember me when I'm gone?

How can I ensure people know I existed?

So, in order not to be forgotten, they left us cave-paintings.

You can still see their handprints today. You can hold your palm up to theirs and wonder. *Who were they? What was their story?*

They were here and they wanted us to know it. They left their mark, their legacy, to ensure we did.

And, forty thousand years later, we had the St Benedict's School loo graffiti…

I finished writing my message in Tippex and sat on the toilet to watch it dry. The paint of my *I exist* cracked into its chalky finish. I wondered if, at some point in the distant future, this cubicle door would hang in a museum. Maybe people would queue to see this toilet door and drink in this profound slice of history left for them.

We existed. We were at school and we existed. Oh, and, by the way, Amelia has crabs.

It was ten minutes before my supposedly-important newspaper meeting, and I decided to hide and read until the crowds died down. Another school day had passed without incident. Charlie was still villain of the year for the group detention. He couldn't walk anywhere without people yelling, "THANKS, CHARLIE." Additionally, a ridiculous rumour was going around that Chloe had rabies. Her best friend, Hannah, had been stupid enough to tell Amelia in form time that she'd been around Chloe's house the night before when Chloe's hamster had randomly died. Apparently Chloe had it out on her hand, when the thing started fitting and then dropped dead in her palm.

"*It kind of looked like rabies*," Hannah had said, betraying her best friend in exchange for a brief moment with Amelia. Who then, of course, told everyone that Chloe's hamster had bitten her before it died of rabies, and so now Chloe had rabies. All completely stupid but stupid enough to catch ablaze. People had been growling at her all day, laughing, "*Watch out, in case she bites.*" My insides ached with the injustice of it, and with anger at myself for just letting it happen, like I'd let Charlie have the worst week of his life in exchange for a quiet life for me.

I pulled out *To Kill a Mockingbird*, hoping to find more messages from the red-pen person. I read as quickly as I could, turning the pages in a flurry, losing track of where I was and why I was so angry.

I caught sight of red ink and my heart quickened.

I'd got to a scene where the children are almost attacked by a rabid dog but their father shoots it dead with only one shot. The kids were surprised their dad had hidden how good he was with a gun.

"*I wanted you to see what real courage is, instead of getting the idea that courage is a man with a gun in his hand,*" Atticus told the children.

I rushed past to look at the red handwriting scribble next to the quote.

Also, if you're not scared, then it's not courage.

My eyes closed as the words dissolved into me. For a few seconds I felt like I was swirling outside of my body. Then, without warning, tears leaked from both eyes.

If you're not scared, then it's not courage.

What if you're scared but you do nothing? I asked myself, staring at the page. What was the opposite of courage? Cowardice? Not only was I a nobody, I was a cowardly nobody. At home. At school. Invisible to all. Nobody would ever write a story about me and how brave I was. People hardly knew I existed… Noise from outside got louder as the bathroom door swung open. The clop of footfall. I sniffed, and stayed as quiet as I could. The intruder locked herself in the neighbouring cubicle and I heard the unmistakable sound of her tears.

School.

I flushed the perfectly clean toilet to give them some noise privacy and put my book into my bag. Then I scraped back the lock and opened the door to the row of mirrors, revealing my blotchy reflection. I washed my clean hands, then squatted to check under the door. They were snuffling gently, obviously waiting for me to leave.

Their shoes were black, chunky, with pink nail polish patterns adorning the edges. I couldn't place them immediately but then remembered I'd seen them in art. They were Chloe's shoes. The stupid rabies rumours had inevitably got to her.

I hovered outside the sniffing stall, unsure, and held my hand out uselessly, like I was trying to comfort her invisibly through the door.

Ask her if she's alright. Be a human. Don't leave her crying alone in a cubicle.

I opened my mouth but closed it again. If I spoke, that would draw me into the situation. I didn't want to be involved in any situation. I couldn't face the thought of people saying I'd caught Chloe's "rabies" and being barked at all day – not on top of everything I had to endure at home. I was scared, but I didn't have courage. So I told myself

Chloe wouldn't want to be comforted by some random anyway, and pushed my way into the corridor, leaving her to fall apart in peace.

The school felt tired, like it needed a yawn to punctuate the end of the day. My stomach was in its usual tension knot. I hugged my bag to my chest, my precious book snuggled safely inside, and kept my head down as I passed Grace and the Awfuls clumped around Amelia's locker.

Grace sniggered cruelly as she tossed her ponytail back. "Chloe wasn't in my last lesson today. Oh dear. Do you think she's gone to the vet?" They all laughed without showing their teeth, in case boys were secretly watching them.

Laura nodded like the eagerest beaver in the universe. "I still can't believe Hannah told everyone. I mean, that's a little harsh."

Amelia shot her a look. "Oh, come on. It's a dead hamster. It's not like her gran died or anything. She should see the funny side. Nobody can take a joke these days. Anyway, Grace, we need to get our prom dresses soon. Otherwise someone might get the same one in the spring/summer drop."

I managed to pass without my face betraying me. Wondering what life must be like if that's your major life concern – someone wearing the same dress as you. Especially when you'd made a person cry that day for literally no reason, other than their pain briefly amused you.

I climbed the steps to the newsroom, not passing anyone else as I went up. I felt all discombobulated – from the second message I'd found in the book, from how it had made me feel: guilty and angry and itching with self-loathing. I didn't like it when emotions hit me in school. I didn't like it when emotions hit me anywhere. Emotions always had consequences.

"Paige, you're here. Take a seat. Did you have a nice afternoon?" Ms Gordon was perching on the front desk of our cramped newsroom. I spent almost as much time here as I did in the library. In this tiny box filled with slightly dated computers.

I nodded but said nothing as I sat down next to Daisy and pulled my sleeves over my hands.

"Yes, Ms Gordon, I had a brilliant day," Ms Gordon said in a high-pitched voice. "Every day at this school is a total dream, especially with you here as my librarian." She smiled kindly. She was in a red and pink suit – clashing beyond all reasonable doubt.

Daisy laughed and I reluctantly joined in. Ms Gordon was obsessed with "*getting me out of my shell*".

I'd been working on the newspaper since Year Eight, after Ruby left, but still didn't really know the rest of the team that well. Some of them, like Daisy and Candise, were super close – bonded by the years of stressful deadlines. But I, unsurprisingly, kept myself to myself. What I liked about the paper was I could see my name in it as my byline, without the story having to be about me. When I got my first ever front-page splash in Year Ten, with a story about vegan food in the canteen, I took it home proudly, wondering if it would get framed and put up next to Adam's stuff. But all Dad said was, "Ha, veganism is for pussies."

I took out my pen and notepad and wrote the date at the top.

"What's this meeting about then?" Daisy asked. "Surely enough news hasn't happened to print the paper yet?" We printed one edition near the end of each term normally and it was only October.

Ms Gordon tapped her nose with a finger adorned with a giant plastic ruby ring. "Let's wait for the others and then I'll tell you."

"Others?"

I glanced around and we all seemed to be present and correct. Candise and Daisy were there. As was Luke, our photographer, who spoke even less than me, but took brilliant photos. Then two Year Nine girls and one Year Eight boy – all of them at the bottom of the ladder, to do the crappy jobs, until the end of the year when everyone else was too stressed with exams.

Ms Gordon looked at her red leather watch. "They should be here any minute, they knew it started at four… oh, here they are. Come on in, girls."

And there, coming into MY newsroom and sitting with MY Ms Gordon, were Grace, Amelia and Laura – collectively smelling of vanilla and jasmine and the scent of other people's worst living memories.

"Hi, is this the right place?" Amelia asked, looking around my beloved newsroom like someone had pooed themselves and then rubbed it all over the walls. Admittedly, it was an oversized cupboard, with only one small window and a collection of refurbished Macs, but still…

"It is indeed." Ms Gordon gestured for them to sit next to me, NEXT TO ME.

My body clamped up. I hunched my shoulders and put my head down so my hair covered my face. I could feel Daisy trying to catch my attention to exchange a *What the hell?* look but I didn't dare glance up in case they saw.

Grace took out a ridiculous notepad and even more ridiculous pen. I was so angry I wanted to swipe it onto the carpet and scream, "WHAT ARE YOU DOING HERE?" Instead I just focused on her notepad. It was neon pink, with *GIRLBOSS* written all over it.

"So, you guys probably want to know what's going on," Ms Gordon said. She sat straighter, like she was trying to impress them. "I'm really excited to have Grace, Amelia and Laura with us today. They're on the official Leavers' Committee, meaning they're in charge of all the events like the Leavers' Assembly, the Ball, and…" She drummed her hands on the desk. "…the reason we're here today…putting together the school yearbook." She jazz-handed the hell out of her jazz-hands while I took a deep breath. I should've known.

The yearbook. A concept metabolized into compulsory school tradition from American TV. A bound monument to the collection of people forced to spend five years together.

A leather-clad keepsake of that specific social experiment. Or "*nostalgia*" as idiots would call it.

"The girls here were hoping we'd be able to pitch in and help a bit," Ms Gordon announced. She clearly thought this was a brilliant idea by the way her eyes shone, glancing over at them several times. I instantly lost ten tonnes of respect for her. I honestly believed Ms Gordon was above all this school stuff, but she was sucking up to the enemy. "They've got some exciting ideas to really shake things up, haven't you, girls? Do you want to explain?"

I had to force myself to look at them – these intruders. Amelia was chewing gum and Ms Gordon hadn't even told her off. Laura was looking all around, like she couldn't believe this place had existed the whole time. Grace took the lead, unsurprisingly, opening up her notepad and addressing us with the confidence of a CEO leading a morning briefing.

"Yeah, so," she said. "As you know, most yearbooks are totally basic. They've always been just a few photos and some dumb letter from the head of year, acting all sentimental."

"Please don't call them dumb," Ms Gordon said, remembering she was a teacher.

Grace ignored her. "Yeah, so. We think ours can be so much more than that. I mean, think about it. Think what a yearbook signifies. You keep it *for ever.* It's, like, a *relic.*" I couldn't believe Grace had just used the word *relic*. "It's a memory of the best years of your life."

Best years of YOUR life, I thought. *Worst years for everyone else.*

"...and, yeah, so we decided to raise the price of them so we have extra budget to really make something, you know?" She twirled her hair around her gold pen. "Leave some legacy behind?"

I was also floored that she knew the word *legacy.*

Grace smiled with false modesty. "But, of course, we don't know anything about journalism or whatever, so we asked Ms Gordon if she'd help us out. And she said you would."

At that moment, I lapsed and shared a dangerous look with Daisy. Daisy spent two weeks off school in Year Nine after Amelia told everyone she'd had anal sex in a car park with the lead singer of some sixth-form band. Once I overheard Daisy telling Candise that she'd only ever kissed him. But he'd made out it was more and boasted to Amelia's older brother she was the first black girl he'd got with. I'd detailed the whole awful thing in one of the notepads under my bed.

We. Were. Not. Happy.

Grace, Amelia and Laura. The three of them were dangerous. Irredeemable. Poison...

"I think it's such a sick idea," Ms Gordon said, beaming at them like an SAD lamp while I winced. "And, guys, the extra project will look great on your uni applications... So, if you're up for it, today is about brainstorming ideas. We've got most of the year to put it all together, but it's good to get thinking. What did you girls have already?"

Please notice how, at no point, did anyone actually ask "*us guys*" if we were "*up for it*". Just like that, we were recruited.

Amelia took over – getting out her very own expensive notepad that said *BE KIND* on it, which would only be more inappropriate if Hitler had a matching one.

"Yeah, so, we're definitely doing all the obvious things like '*Most likely to...*' etc." Amelia met everyone's gaze in a way that made it clear she didn't care what we thought of her. "But we also wanted some stories in there too. So we thought we'd have a section of the book dedicated to each year of school and all the best things that happened. We'll call this section *Remember when?* and we'll interview the key people involved. So, like, for Year Nine, an example would be when Sam ate a battery."

The three of them started giggling attractively, vibrating with the memory of a story that only, really, involved them. I mean, of course the whole school heard about it, as it involved Sam Hutchins and Grace had been dating him at the time and made a meal out of it for ages, about how she almost "*lost the love of her life*". He'd stupidly eaten a cell battery during DT as a dare, not realizing that he may as well have swallowed two litres of poison. I mean, maybe the girls were right. Maybe it was soooo hilarious when he had to be carted off in an ambulance for emergency surgery. Maybe it was "*like, so funny*" Mr Granger got fired for gross negligence because it happened in his lesson.

The trio of them giggled themselves out, and I smirked as it was too dangerous not to. Ms Gordon, who, to be fair, hadn't been working at the school when this happened, put up both thumbs.

"Paige is our best interviewer, aren't you?" she said, nodding towards me. "Would you be up for that, Paige?"

They all looked at me expectantly – probably the first time they'd ever considered me at all – and it took everything not to let my rage spill over. "*No, I would not be up for that. No, I want nothing to do with this self-absorbed vanity project,*" I wanted to scream.

But, of course, I didn't do or say anything like that because I was a total coward.

"Yep."

"Great! Great! Isn't this great? What other ideas did you have, girls?"

They spoke and spoke, while we listened and listened. Every idea seemed to revolve around the central theme of making the yearbook a tribute to how beautiful and popular they were and all the wonderful memories they'd made at school.

"We HAVE to have a section dedicated to the Year Eight French trip… And a section dedicated to all the school plays… Maybe a 'glow up' competition? I mean, Amelia looked hilarious before she had braces, didn't you, Lia? You would definitely win that. Maybe a 'favourite couple' section? I mean, I, personally, would love to forget the two months I spent dating Sam Hutchins, but, like, you can't hide from your past, can you?"

The rest of the paper staff, like me, had no choice but to

nod along. We nodded to all their ideas. We nodded to the commitment to help write it and put it together.

My anger tasted sharp, like biting your tongue and drawing blood. My hand shook so hard that I couldn't take notes. When I filled out my daily cruelty diaries at home, these three girls made the most appearances. These three girls and their surrounding group were probably responsible for the most tears cried among their fellow students. Yes, it was a giant cliché that the popular kids in school aren't very nice, but it was beyond true in our case. It was like they'd read a manual. Grace was the pretty one; so pretty that you could never quite believe someone who looked like that could be so cruel. Amelia was the tough one, with a face so soured over the years by her endless evil looks that she'd probably bully herself for being ugly if she hadn't made herself the bully. And Laura was the catty one – happy to follow orders in exchange for immunity. I'm sure, behind closed doors, there was more to them. I'm sure they were complex and 3D and flawed, with their own complicated life stories interwoven with pain like everyone else. But you know what? I couldn't care less about that. Because I never saw it. Nobody at school ever saw anything but the gloss and the bullying.

When the meeting finished, the girls left first, not even saying thank you as they clopped out. The rest of the newspaper staff shook their heads in disbelief then started drifting out, saying meaningless goodbyes.

"What a joke," Daisy muttered as she stood up next to me, her anger soothing me ever so slightly.

"You alright, Paige?" Ms Gordon asked from behind her desk as she switched off her two computer monitors. "Exciting stuff, eh?"

"If you say so."

Her eyebrows arched in surprise. "You're not excited? I thought this would be a great opportunity for you to spread your reporting wings a bit, you know? Take up a bit more space..."

I didn't know how to reply. I felt so betrayed. Ms Gordon was an ally. A champion. She let me hide in her library at lunchtime...who did she think I was hiding from?

"I thought you'd be thrilled!" she continued, missing the anger entirely. "Getting to interview all those people? All those juicy human-interest stories?"

I squinted my eyes shut and swallowed back words. If journalism was about exposing the truth and uncovering the real story, this joke of a yearbook was like the opposite of it. It was...*fake news*. All the puff pieces for the popular people, without any truth about the pain they caused. Surely she must see that? Surely she remembered how school worked?

The truth singed the tip of my tongue but I was too scared to say it. She was practically the only person apart from my Aunt Polly who'd ever believed in me, and I was too scared to break that link.

"Yeah. Whatever...I have to go now."

CHAPTER 5

The anger consumed me on my walk home. I tried running, to see if I could outrun it, but my aching legs and gasping lungs just fired me up even more. I wished that once, just once, I was brave enough to scream out everything I wanted to scream. To roar and to yell and to tell it like it is without knowing for certain that would only make everything worse. As I sprinted through the scary tunnel I didn't stop and dance. Instead, in the gloom, I found myself yelling, "Screw this!" into the camera. "SCREW THIS!" I screamed, like a banshee. "SCREW THIS LIFE I HAVE TO LIVE!"

I jogged to a halt at the end of my road – bending over and getting my breath back. I couldn't be angry in the house. He'd be able to smell it, like a shark detecting a droplet of blood in the sea. I kicked the garden wall of a nearby house to try and drain myself of my emotions. *Kick*...and another, and another. *Kick kick kick*.

It didn't work though. Mum picked up on it the second I got through the front door.

"No need to start an earthquake," she said. "Seriously, Paige, it's a good thing your dad's not back yet."

"Sorry," I said. Not really sorry at all.

"What is it?"

She didn't ask out of concern, only irritation.

"Nothing. I have a stomach ache."

"Oh. Well." She blinked a few times. "Maybe go upstairs until you feel better?"

I was already on my way up. Some mothers might have asked where it hurt and for how long and could they get you anything. They took your temperature and offered solutions like a cup of ginger tea made with love. My mum was only scared that my upset stomach would somehow upset and annoy Dad. I hurled myself onto my bed, doophing into the duvet and letting out a small groan. I willed my emotions to go back where they came from. But all I could picture was Ms Gordon's stupid desperate-to-please face. All I could think about was the stupid yearbook and the stupid lengths stupid people go to add to their already overinflated sense of importance.

"Alexa? Why isn't the world fair?" I said to my pillow.

"Believing the world is fair is a way of magical thinking," she replied.

"What does that even mean?"

Nothing.

"Alexa? Is karma real?"

"Karma is not about punishment or reward," she parroted. "It makes a person responsible for their own life, and for how they treat others."

"You didn't answer my question."

Silence.

'You never really answer my questions."

Again, total silence.

"It's almost like you're not a real person."

I stayed face down. Deep breath in, and out, in and out… It wasn't working. My brain was spinning like a malfunctioning carousel. I got up and rummaged in the drawer for my most recent notebook.

5th October

The whole year group is yelling, "THANKS, CHARLIE," for the detention that wasn't his fault.

Chloe cried in the toilets because they've started a rumour that she caught rabies off her dying hamster.

Grace, Amelia and Laura have forced me to join the yearbook committee, and want us to spend the year making it a huge, biased bit of fake news dedicated to how wonderful they are.

Writing it out didn't give me the same release it normally did. I still felt like I was fizzing with injustice. Frothing with pointless energy over what to do about everything. I needed to distract all my cortexes. I needed something, *anything*.

The book.

I scrambled up and retrieved it from my bag, finding the page about bravery that I'd left it on. Staring at Red Pen's handwriting. Who the hell were they? Are they? Were they still at my school?

I shoved my pillow against the headboard and propped my book against my knees. As I turned each page, I hoped to find more red ink. Mum's cooking noises faded to nothing as I sped through – finding red underlines littered here and there. I found an important passage underlined. It was a quote from Atticus, saying that before he learned to live with other people, he needed to live with himself first. But my heart ripple-skipped when I saw more red pen. An arrow directed me out of the text and into the margins.

The end of childhood = realizing adults don't know what the hell they're doing.

A trickle of calm siphoned its way into my bloodstream. I read the sentence back several times, stroking the words. Forgetting the rest of the actual book.

A light knock at my door.

"Paige?" Mum called. "How are you feeling? Are you well enough for dinner?" She needed to know on a practical basis, rather than an emotional one. She had no space for any demands for attention from me, as he took up everything.

"Not really," I called back, still staring at the page. "Maybe it's better if I just stay up here?"

"Okay."

I heard her descend the stairs, not missing out the two creaky ones because he wasn't home yet. It still hurt. Her not even bothering to come in. Didn't shock me, but it hurt.

"Alexa?" I asked, when Mum was out of earshot. "When does childhood end?"

The speaker turned blue. "Childhood is the age range spanning from birth to puberty. Various childhood factors can contribute to a person's personality formation."

I shook my head. "That's not what it says in my book."

Silence.

I felt a twinge of loneliness as I reminded myself how un-normal it is to have a robot instead of a friend. But the pang hurt less than usual, with that book held in my hand. They got it. Whatever I felt about life – the person with the red pen got it. Everything they'd written felt like it had been written just for me and I felt less alone because of it. Like I was holding hands with someone I'd never met before.

I sped through the rest of the book. The front door opened in a pretty neutral way, with a pretty neutral Dad walking over the threshold. I heard Mum greet him and explain that I was sick. I stilled, contemplating if he'd come up to see how I was. Hoping maybe he'd be worried and care.

"Feeling better?" Dad boomed up the stairs.

It still felt special that he'd even asked. A smile wiggled onto my cheeks.

"No, sorry. I hope you had a lovely day."

He didn't reply. There was the noise of plates being served up, of conversation muffling through the floorboards, the chinking of forks hitting china. I stayed put – reading. The smell of lamb hung in the air, making my mouth water, but I kept going – hope and intrigue guiding me on. My parents were making their getting-ready-for-bed noises as I whooshed through the final chapters. Gargling with Listerine, the *click-click* of the bathroom light being turned on and off. I heard my doorknob go and rummaged under my covers to look sick.

"How's the patient?" Mum asked, finally coming in and perching on the end of the bed.

"Feeling a little better," I lied. "Was your evening okay?"

"Yes, yes. Your father is tired though, so be quiet." She reminded me to be quiet most nights. Like a nervous tick. She couldn't relax until she'd reminded me and I'd promised.

"I always am."

"Right, great. Thank you. You know he hates noise. Feel better soon." She closed the door behind her.

The house stilled around me as I reached the ending of the book. The story itself was beautiful and made me weep quietly, using my pyjama top to mop up my snot. The final few lines were about how most people are nice, once you get to know them. A noble thought. One I'd maybe agree with if Red Pen hadn't taken to the page, scrawling all over *The End.*

A message that read…

People always believe they're nice in their own heads. That's what makes it so scary when you look at the state of the world.

I laughed out loud then got scared that I'd woken Dad. I ducked under the duvet so it would muffle my giggles. What Red Pen had written wasn't only funny though, it was so true. I bet the Awfuls were sleeping soundly, not giving much thought to the various people they'd made cry today, thinking they were probably quite decent people. Every part of me felt connected to and understood by this unknown person. A feeling I hadn't felt in so long.

And then, there, under my duvet, I made a decision.

I needed to find whoever wrote these messages.

CHAPTER 6

I tumbled out of bed the next morning with an urgent sense of purpose. I used my phone to take photos of all the red pen messages so I wouldn't forget them, and found myself weirdly eager to go to school as well, obsessed with solving the mystery. Who were they? Male? Female? Did they still go to this school, or had they graduated long ago? What did they look like? Why did they have this book? And, most importantly, had they defaced anything else?

"Paige, hello. How are you today?" Ms Gordon greeted me in the library at lunchtime with her usual enthusiasm. Her fashion was off-the-scale today – mustard yellow tights under an orange tunic, all pulled together with a neon pink belt.

I hadn't forgiven the betrayal yet, however. "Yep. Fine."

"Only fine?"

"Actually, I was wondering what books I have coming up for English? I finished *To Kill a Mockingbird* last night, and want to read ahead."

She nodded, looking at me like a proud Orangina bottle. "Very keen."

I smiled and shifted my bag from one shoulder to the other.

"You're in top set, right?"

I nodded as she tapped some stuff into her computer. "Okay…right. Let me see the reading lists. They sometimes change them year on year. The government is obsessed with messing with everything. Here it is. Right." The printer whirred into action, spewing out a sheet of paper. "There you go. All there."

I took it, feeling its warmth in my hand. "Thank you." I turned towards the stairs.

"You're welcome. Let me know how you get on with the books. And," she called after me, "I'm looking forward to hearing your ideas for the yearbook."

I threw a sarcastic thumbs up behind my head and jogged upstairs, claiming my snug without much competition. It was a quiet lunchtime. Out the window I could see autumn sunshine gushing downwards and most students were outside, soaking up what they could before the weather turned. Two tiny Year Sevens doodled with gel pens in the corner, but, other than that, the whole floor was empty. I looked down at the reading list and scanned it for my upcoming coursework reads. There was the compulsory Shakespeare – *Macbeth*. There was also a poetry anthology and *Jane Eyre*. I started with poetry, tracing my fingers over the alphabetized shelves. On the bottom shelf, I found a wodge of anthologies. I checked the coast was still clear before I pulled them out onto the scratchy carpet.

My hands trembled as I opened the first copy and my heart double-flipped when I noticed a pencil scribble on page eleven.

It's them, it's them, it's them.

But closer inspection revealed it wasn't their handwriting. And of course it wasn't in red pen.

I sped up, flipping through the rest of that copy, but they hadn't been there. I chucked it to one side and picked up the next. This one was brand new and freshly folded into its protective plastic cover. I threw the book aside and ripped through another. Nothing. Just the faint remnants of pencil underlines someone had rubbed out before returning. I let out a loud huff of frustration that made Ms Gordon's keyboard-tapping stop. I breathed quietly and, when she resumed typing, I flicked through the next book, and then… in the whirring of the passing pages, a glimpse of red ink. A smile fault-lined across my face and I hugged the book to me, before dumping the others back on the shelf.

With renewed enthusiasm, I half-jogged to find *Jane Eyre*. The copies were lined up in order, no one even thinking about taking them out yet, as we weren't studying it until after Christmas. I grabbed them all, flick-flick-flicking through, and boom. I found it on the third go. Red ink. Same handwriting. I snapped *Jane Eyre* shut, forcing myself not to read the scribbles until later. That evening was my weekly visit to Aunty Polly and, with that to look forward to and these books in my hand, life suddenly felt more bearable. After finding a red-penned *Macbeth* too, I practically skipped to the front desk.

"Woah, so now you're super keen," Ms Gordon said, taking my bounty for bleeping and stamping.

I handed over my library card. "Does that make me a massive loser?"

"What? No! It's a good thing. Enthusiasm is a contagious and wonderful thing if you ask me. Though, hang on…" She bleeped through *Macbeth*. "You know the rental period is only two weeks? You don't have to get them all out in one go?"

"I know."

"Well, okay. Brilliant." She handed them back. "Here we go. I'm looking forward to your amazing English marks on results day."

I raised both eyebrows. My parents couldn't cope if I achieved anything they had to notice. That energy was reserved for Adam and Adam alone.

"Ha. We'll see." I shoved the books in my bag and checked the time on my phone. There were still ten minutes until the end of lunch. I retreated to a chair in the corner to read through my biology coursework. I pulled out my folder and tried to lose myself in the reproductive issues of pandas.

I smelled them before I saw them.

Their collective scent of florals and vanilla and bitchiness. The *clip-clop clip-clop* of their polished heels. I lowered myself into the chair.

"Oh, hi, Ms Gordon," Amelia called.

They clattered to a halt at her desk. She grinned and tweaked her fringe. "Oh, hey girls. What can I do for you?"

Amelia slapped a piece of paper on the desk. "Can you photocopy this for us? It's for the yearbook."

Ms Gordon picked up the sheet. "Well, I'm…"

"I reckon we need about fifty? For the whole school."

As far as I was aware, Ms Gordon was not a photocopier. Yes, there was a printer in the library that we paid five pence a sheet for photocopies. SHE didn't photocopy for you. You were supposed to get a card and…well…

"I guess I can take it out of the budget and…"

"Fab," Grace said brightly. Her hair was pulled into the perfect ponytail, crowned with a brown polka-dot headband. "The bell's going in a few mins."

"Umm. Sure, okay. I'll do it now."

My face scrunched up as I watched Ms Gordon head over to the photocopier. The distant hum and whir of the machine didn't drown them out.

"Have you noticed Chloe's not been in today?" Amelia said.

Grace laughed cruelly, tossing her ponytail back. "Oh God. The rabies has got to her." They fell about laughing like the three witches cackling over a cauldron in *Macbeth*, and I wondered how Shakespeare knew about secondary school before it was even a thing.

Ms Gordon returned with a stack of A4. "There you are, girls. Have you checked if it's alright with the head to put them up?"

"Oh yeah, sure," Amelia said, with hardly any conviction.

"Can we put one up here?" Grace asked.

"Of course. Maybe on the door?"

"Brilliant." Amelia leaned over her desk and snapped off a piece of Sellotape. Then, without saying thank you or goodbye, out they went, as the warning bell jerked me from my chair.

"Right, Paige. Off to lessons you go." Ms Gordon shooed me with her hands. "Careful with your back carrying those books." She winked at me like we were best mates.

I couldn't wink back. I shut the library door and stood still to collect myself before maths. *Must be calm. Empty. Vacant. Push out the emotions.* But curiosity got the better of me and I twisted to see the poster.

REMEMBER THIS? it said, above a picture of a girl with glasses.

AND THIS…? This time it was three girls laughing in a fountain.

WHAT ELSE?

We're collecting photos for the Year 11 yearbook!!!!???!

Please send your funniest/ugliest/most embarrassing and incriminating photos to school dropbox no. 22.

Help us make our school days something we will never forget!!!!!!!

Love, Grace, Amelia and Laura

Yearbook committee

xxxx

I stared at the poster for one full minute. There was so much wrong with it, you could've analysed it in a psychologist's office for several sessions.

I mean, *of course* they'd put up a photograph of Lisa from Year Seven, when she wore those insane thick glasses and yellow anorak, and carried a plastic bag full of pitta bread around with her. It looked innocent enough, but it was a deliberate choice. Lisa's swan-like transformation had been noticed by our whole school. She started Year Ten a completely different person. Glasses replaced with lenses to showcase big green eyes with fat lashes. Anorak replaced with biker jacket, rarely worn, all the better to showcase the body puberty had gifted her over summer. And no bags of pitta bread to be seen ever again. Instead she carried around the hearts and badly-timed erections of every boy in our year – shooting up the social ranks based on hotness alone. Grace and the Awfuls were forced not only to acknowledge her, but to accept her. Have her sit with them occasionally at their lunch table – pretending they were besties but then spreading it around that she was a slut. Lisa's sluttiness was confirmed when she started dating Travis Williams, an Upper Sixth, dumping Grace and co, and leapfrogging over them into the sixth-form common room. Here was her punishment. Under the guise of a joke. Of course, they'd used a stunning photo of themselves as a juxtaposition. The three of them, soaking wet, on the school's Year Eight trip to Disneyland Paris, after Joe had dared them to jump into the water fountain.

Help us make our school days something we will never forget.

I fought the urge to rip the poster down. Most people would love to forget their school days *because* of students like them.

I made my way to maths under the weight of my book-laden bag, head down, weaving out of everybody's way. I passed another poster carelessly stuck on a locker and fought another destructive urge.

I slunk into class just in time. My bag thunked as it hit the carpet, but not loud enough to drown out the cascade of whispered rumours started by the Awfuls the day before.

"Did you hear about Chloe?" Guy, one of the music people, asked his friend, laughing.

"That she has rabies? I know. Hilarious."

"I didn't even know you could get it from a hamster."

"Dude, I kissed her at the dance last year. Do I have it too?"

They burst into macho waheys of laughter, before Mr Sanders clapped us to attention and tried to make us care about simultaneous equations. My pencil snapped against my equation. Such a stupid rumour. But its stupidity didn't make it any less painful. It didn't matter if it was one old picture, or a silly rumour, or a detention that everyone really knew wasn't your fault. It was the mindlessness of the cruelty I couldn't handle. They hurt you because they could. For minor entertainment. A small suck of power to carry them through till the end of the day, certain they'd be able to get another hit from someone else tomorrow. They were like vampires and no one dared to slay them, no one held garlic up to their cruelty, no one threw open the curtains to watch them wither under the light of the truth of what they were really like. And it wasn't like I was going to do it. Because, just like everyone else at the school, I was scared of them... I hated them, but I was scared of them. In fact, when I watched someone like Chloe suffer, my instant response wasn't anger, but *relief*. Relief it wasn't my turn. Not my day ruined, reputation ruined. Someone else had unwillingly taken the bullet for me.

If you're not scared, then it's not courage.

I sat and steeped in the humiliation of my cowardice, like a teabag brewing in a yellow-bellied mug. I could solve simultaneous equations okay but I couldn't solve how school made me feel. Terrified and tragic at the same time. Yes, I wrote stories for the paper, but it was always safe stories about uncontroversial things like fundraising concerts or canteen food. I never actually held anyone truly to account.

You do, at least, note it down, I reminded myself. In my notepads.

That night, after I saw my Aunt Polly, I would get out my book and I would write it down.

6th October

Grace etc. deliberately used an ugly photo of Lisa on the yearbook posters.

It wouldn't be forgotten, I soothed myself. I had recorded it. Everything they'd ever done, I'd recorded it. But then again, maybe it would be forgotten? Because, really, what was I ever going to do with those notepads, when I was always so scared?

CHAPTER 7

My Aunty Polly greeted me with a giant smash of a hug. "Come on in. It's so weirdly hot today. I have a fan! I bought one for the cats."

"Not for yourself?" I joked. A sense of humour was something I only got to express once a week. Polly was my mum's sister and the opposite to her in every way. Independent, warm, interested, fearless, and she seemed to genuinely care for me. As a result, huge hidden parts of my personality unravelled themselves over our weekly dinners. I probably used ninety per cent of my spoken words at her house, over cups of tea, unconditional love, and the warmth of a Keanu-Reeves-themed cat on my lap.

"Neo is a big fan of the fan, bless him." She led me through to the back conservatory, past her "hallway of fame", decorated with framed photos of all the weird and wonderful adventures she'd had. It was even hotter inside – not like October at all – with Wick, her ginger cat, dozing happily in front of her new purchase.

"Sit yourself down. It's a Dyson fan. I KNOW. Fancy-pants. Nothing but the best for the children. Right, tea? Bickies? Why am I even asking? Coming right up."

I dumped my heavy bag and took up residence in front of the cool air. I squealed as Ted, a tabby (and her secret favourite) jumped on my lap without announcement. He circled for a second, using my school skirt to sharpen his claws, then settled. His purring lulled me out of my bad mood and I was smiling and mellow when Polly returned with a laden tray.

"Ha, he's found you." She plopped it down on the table and handed over my cup. "I love that he's napping NOW when he was up at four a.m, howling outside my door like a furry lunatic." She took her own mug, with a photo on it of her jumping off the top of a waterfall in Thailand.

I gratefully sipped the tea. "His body is already creating a furnace on my lap."

"Push him off whenever you want. You know what cats are like, they respect you more the more aloof you are." She took a slurp of her drink. "How are you anyway, Paigey? How was school?"

"It was school."

"That bad, huh?"

"It's okay. It's just…ergh…you know I'm on the paper?"

She nodded through the steam of her tea.

"Well, Ms Gordon just let these horrid popular girls completely hijack us out of the blue to help them make the Year Eleven yearbook. They're awful people, and now

I have to work with them all year."

Polly's face scrunched up. "Why would it take a whole year to make a yearbook? Surely you just shove in the Year Eleven headshots and some disgusting inspirational quotes."

"Not this year. This year they want to make it a yearbook to remember."

She threw her arms up at that. "What's there that anyone WANTS to remember? It's more about what you wish you could forget."

"Bingo."

"Oh, I'm sorry, Paigey. That sucks."

"It's okay. Well, it's not, but it's school. What else should I expect?"

She grinned. "The fact that you hate school is a brilliant indicator you're going to turn out marvellously. Just look at me. Hated it. Worst five years of my life, and I've had freakin' breast cancer."

I laughed, dislodging Ted, who let out a yelp and leaped down off my lap. "Surely that was worse than school?"

She shrugged, smiling. "I dunno. I mean, I didn't have to do PE lessons on the chemo ward. Or algebra. Or go to any stupid assemblies. Or get called a 'dyke' at least once a day."

"Sounds like a blast."

"Well, that's what chemo is, isn't it? A big blast of chemicals."

We both laughed, though mine was a little forced. Polly may've been the most cheerful cancer patient the world had ever known but, for me, it was the worst time in my life.

Ruby had gone only two months before. And Mum and Dad fought non-stop about Mum needing to go to the hospital.

"She's got no one else, Glynn."

"She should've thought of that before she made all her wacky lifestyle choices."

"I can't let her get the bus back from hospital."

"I don't see why not…"

And crossed arms and crying and silent treatment and Dad acting like he was the one with cancer, not Polly. And Mum being torn, and me being terrified, and Adam attempting to be peacekeeper. Finally it was Golden Boy who convinced Dad his wife should perhaps care for her potentially-dying sister. I'd had to stay quiet throughout, knowing if I took Mum's side, Dad would dig in even more.

"So, are you going to do it?" Polly asked, offering me my third chocolate Hobnob.

"It didn't occur to me that I could say no."

She raised both eyebrows. "That's the impact those sorts of people can have. But you can always say no, you know that, right?"

"I guess…" I watched Ted rotate on the floorboards, figuring out which comfortable surface to sit himself on next. I could've said no. But that would've meant drawing attention to myself. Nobody notices you more than when you're saying "no" to them.

Polly examined me and smiled. "Sorry, I should stop trying to make you into a mini-me."

"No, don't be sorry. I'm sorry."

She laughed widely. "You always apologize in response to somebody else's apology. Your mother always used to as well. Still does probably..." She let out a sigh and stared out at the unusually-summery day. "Maybe you should chat to your mum about school?" she suggested delicately, as she always did whenever she mentioned Mum. "They were the best days of her life, or so she says."

"She still says that a lot."

"Well, it might be good to get a different insight on it, rather than from Ms Bitter over here?"

"Maybe." I reached out to stroke Wick's ginger fur before my mind went again to my vandalized copy of *To Kill A Mockingbird*.

"Polly?" I asked.

"Yup?"

"Do you know what you're doing?"

She grinned over the rim of her drink. "What do you mean?"

"Like in general? In life? You're an adult. Do you have any idea what the hell you're doing?"

She burst out into her trademark cackle. "Oh my God, what a question."

"Well, do you?" I stopped stroking Wick and he pushed his head into my hand.

"Of course I don't. No one does. Not really. I manage though. I've got my charity, haven't I? My mates. My holidays. My cats." Her eyebrows drew downwards. "Your parents? Your dad. Is he..."

"Oh, no no. He's fine," I said frantically. "They're both fine. It was just something somebody said at school, that's all."

"What did they say?"

"That the end of childhood is when you realize adults don't really know what they're doing."

The glass conservatory wobbled in its panes as she let out another huge cackle. "That's very profound from a teenager. Who said that?"

"Umm...someone from my English class."

"Well I'm glad you've found someone at school you click with. I know it's been hard after Ruby..." She sensed me clam up. "But, yes, I guess there is something in that. Growing up is great too, though. Painful sometimes, but generally better."

We slurped at our tea in companionable silence, breaking it only to make inane comments on the weather, or to ask who wanted the last biscuit. My heart was still pounding from Polly asking about Dad. One of our unspoken rules was never to talk about my parents' marriage. It hung in the air at all times but we never addressed it. I couldn't tell if she just assumed things were fine, as so many people did, or if she just wanted me to have some time where I didn't have to think about it.

Polly popped a lasagne in the oven and the whole house started smelling of bubbling cheese. We ate it comfortably in front of a movie. *The Matrix* – her choice.

"Look, baby, it's you," she said to Neo, plucking him off

the carpet. She swung him through the air before he yowled and twisted out of her arms, running from the room.

I laughed and my whole body laughed with me.

"You want more lasagne?"

"Please."

She picked up my plate. "Coming right up. Hang on, let me just watch him storm this building."

We ate seconds and then thirds as Keanu blew up multiple things while dressed in black leather.

By the time she drove me home, I felt new again. Like I'd had a gulp of oxygenated air before stepping back into toxic fumes. My bag felt heavy with books filled with red pen, my body with lasagne belly. I leaned my head against the window and, when Polly was concentrating on driving, I wrote an invisible message with my finger in backwards writing.

I exist.

The words would stay dormant until the next time it rained and the windows steamed up. My mark on the world hidden from view, a secret silent scream, but it was better than nothing.

"Polly?"

She turned the radio down. "Yep?"

"Is it possible to feel connected to someone you've never met before?"

"You're too young to be going on dating apps."

I laughed. "No. I'm not doing that. I'm just..." I didn't know how to explain it. "I just...have you ever felt like you're really going to get on with someone you've never met? Like…er…" I reached for an old-fashioned way of explaining it. "…a pen pal?"

"How the hell do you know the term *pen pal?*"

"Mum had one when she was younger. She talks about her sometimes. Some French girl, called Gert."

Polly whacked both hands on the steering wheel. "Oh my God, GERT. I'd totally forgotten about Gert."

"They never met, did they?"

She indicated left to the end of our road. "No, they didn't. Your mum was going to go over the summer after exams, I think. They'd been writing for years. God, I was jealous. I kept trying to make my friends be my pen pals, which makes no sense as we saw each other at Scouts every Friday… But yeah, they wrote for *years* and planned this big meet. But then she got with your dad in Year Eleven…" There was never any need to explain anything else beyond that sentence. "But I've made friends with people I didn't know online. I mean, I met Gillian in a Keanu chat room. Why? Have you got a pen pal?"

I shook my head, smiling. "No. No one writes letters any more."

"God, that's depressing."

We ground to a halt outside my house and stopped talking. If Polly stayed chatting to me too long outside, Dad would notice the car and complain about the noise of the engine, and how rude it was she hadn't come inside to say hello. But, if she did come in, that was rude too, because you can't just drop in on people like that.

"It was lovely to see you as always." Polly pulled up the handbrake so she could lean over and give me a hug. "Sorry, I would come in, but, er, I need an early night. Big breakfast meeting tomorrow and everything. It's very hard being such an important CEO."

I nodded and played along. "Yup. Those cats won't protect themselves."

"Exactly. They need me. And I can't adopt them all."

I hugged her tight, wishing as ever I could tell her what the night meant to me, but never able to reach for the words. Scared that my intensity of need would scare her off, even though she was my aunty and she loved me.

It took for ever to find my house key as I had to dig past all my library books, but I eventually retrieved it, and quietly unlocked the front door. I pushed in, stood on the doormat, paused, and tried to take the temperature.

It felt warm. Calm. Good.

"Is that you, Paige?" Dad called. Warm Dad. Calm Dad. Good Dad.

"It's me."

I stashed my bag at the bottom of the stairs and followed his voice to the living room. My parents were the very picture of couple goals when I found them. Both snuggled up on the sofa, limbs entwined, empty wine glasses on the coffee table, the TV news whispering on low volume. And there was mess. *Mess*. Plates of uncleared things on the dining table behind them. Four dirty place settings.

"Hi, Paige." Mum's head lay nestled in Dad's armpit. "Sorry for the mess. We had the Smiths over. You just missed them." Every inch of her body was relaxed, her smile blasted heat into the room. The good vibes made sense. The Smiths were a couple Dad knew from work, and my parents were therefore always on their most perfect behaviour when they came over. There was usually a warm aftermath while they glowed in their pretence, trying to get it to stick. Of course they hadn't told me they were having anyone over. If Adam was still here, they would've made sure he was in so they could drag him out to sparkle.

"They were bowled over by your mum's pavlova," Dad said, kissing her head. "How was your evening in Spinsterville?" he asked me.

He was asking to get a dig in at Polly, not because he actually wanted to know.

"It was fine, thanks."

It was best to be vague when talking about Polly. Accepted adjectives were as follows: *Fine, okay* and *alright.* You could add in a *good* or *nice* as long as you carefully followed it with a *I suppose.*

Dad had a red wine stain around his mouth. "And how was the crazy cat lady?" he asked, laughing at his overused joke.

"Oh Glynn." Mum swatted him.

"What? It's true though, isn't it? How are the only men in her life? Still coughing up furballs?"

"The cats are all fine too."

"I think she misinterprets her job spec. Her role is to protect the cats, not adopt ALL the cats and use them as substitute husbands."

I'd heard this one a million times too, and yet we all laughed obligingly. I hovered in the doorway, awaiting instructions.

"What are we watching?" I asked.

"The news is about to finish but there's some pathetic romcom starting, isn't there, Jane?" Dad leaned down to kiss Mum's head. "Thought I'd see how long I can make it through."

She giggled like a love-struck teenager. "You like this one! It's got John Cusack in it. You like him."

Dad nodded his approval. "*Say Anything*? I do like this one. They're childhood sweethearts. Just like us."

"Just like us," Mum repeated. She snuggled further in, happiness oozing from her while I stood awkwardly on the threshold, awaiting an invitation to join them that wasn't going to come.

Dad and Mum's love story was pretty similar to a lot of films. He was the most popular boy in school. Great at football, good-looking, rich from his job at the video shop. He was the first person in school to get a mobile phone. He could've had anyone he wanted. Mum was the pretty-but-shy girl. Too shy to even notice Dad at first. They inevitably fell in love and Mum soared up the popularity ranks, becoming an unelected queen. Dad made it "cool" to have a girlfriend and all the other boys got one. My parents were the most golden, however. They were voted *Most likely to get married* in their yearbook and married they got. Right after Dad graduated from uni, while Mum waited patiently at her parents' house, pretending to be a secretary.

My parents were getting a bit much on the sofa. I faked a loud yawn to remind them I was there.

"Tired," I said. "I'm going to bed."

"Night, poppet." Mum hardly looked away from Dad's gaze.

I left them to it. Feeling a bit ick about what *it* was, but also relieved they were getting on; but also abandoned, and lonely, and humiliated that I wasn't wanted and wasn't invited. This is what it always felt like in my house. I could never experience one emotion singularly – there were always multiple conflicting ones. Like ordering emotional tapas.

It was almost ten, according to the glow of my hand-me-down alarm clock. I rushed through putting on pyjamas and getting ready for bed.

"Alexa? Did you have a nice day?"

"Today was sunny, with highs of twenty-one."

"Wicked. So you got a tan?"

Silence.

"No sense of humour, robots."

Another sharp tug of loneliness, but there was a jumble of books in my bag to take the edge off. I could not be arsed with Shakespeare so I plucked out *Jane Eyre* and took it into bed. I started reading, but it quickly became scanning.

I knew *Jane Eyre* was supposed to be a romance about a nanny falling in love with her master or something, but it took for ever to get there. My clock read eleven, then half past eleven. Just before midnight, Mum and Dad's laughter came up the stairs and I turned my light off and sat silently in the dark till they were safely in their bedroom. By twelve thirty, Jane was *still* in bloody school, and I hadn't come across one red message. My fingers twitched with impatience, my eyes flickering from tiredness. I started rifling through the book, looking for them, looking for them, looking for them…

BAM.

There. In the margins. Next to a passage from Jane saying she never intended to fall in love with Mr Rochester.

Love is a trap.

Four words.

All only one syllable long.

But my, the power of those four syllables.

Maybe it was the tiredness, but I started crying. The words set a part of me free and I let them unleash and unlock. I stepped into the wonderful, weightless feeling of being understood.

Love was *such* a trap, they were right.

I'd never been in love, of course. Not for a lack of wanting it. Wanting it was part of the trap. But the undeniable truth was that I was invisible as well as unloveable. Nobody could see me at all, let alone look at me and see the potential to store their heart there. People don't fall in love with wallpaper. Or silence. Or the colour beige. You need at least a fraction of glitter, something to say, a reason for existing in order to be someone else's. I had none of those things, so no one would love me, and that hurt...but it also stopped me from getting hurt, so I guess it wasn't all bad.

No, I thought, as the tears made my duvet damp. I had not known romantic love, and yet I still knew it was a trap.

Why?

Because I saw Mum in one. Every single day.

Tonight had been a trap. The lovely dinner with lovely friends, the sofa, the gold, the cuddles, the kisses, the relief, the unspooling of joy from being so very loved so very hard. When Dad was like that he was a lump of cheese on a mousetrap. A carrot luring a donkey up a mountain. A fake recording of someone crying for help so you'd run into the booby trap to rescue them. Because Dad like that never lasted. What made it so ridiculous was that I KNEW it was a trap. I had spent my whole life watching the trap snap shut, the carrot never reaching the mouth, the bomb going off and the building exploding with you still inside. Yet Mum stayed. Bound and broken and sucked dry of life, she chose to stay.

And, despite all this, I, too, longed for the trap of my dad's love. Yet he didn't even bother leaving out any bait to tempt me. All he cared about was Adam. I'd hoped that maybe when my brother went away they might show me the slightest bit of interest... That very evening, all I'd wanted was to ensconce myself in their glow, to maybe take up a bit of space in their hearts. But no.

I turned into my pillow and let it soak up my tears. I wept with rehearsed volume control. Then I lurched up and started flicking through the rest of the book. I needed to know who this person was. It wasn't fair for them to get into my head and not let me know who they were. Authors put their names on their book spines so, if their story wriggled in, we at least knew who was responsible. Who was this DICK who thought it okay to get into my head but leave no trail? How dare they? I flicked page after page, feeling like I'd explode if I didn't find something. *Flick flick* through *Jane Eyre*, then I chucked it to the end of my bed. *Flick flick wallop* through Shakespeare. *Flick flick flick flick* through the poetry anthology where I could see Red Pen had had a freakin' FIELD DAY making annotations. I didn't read the graffiti, just flicked and flicked, and oh, there MUST be something. I wouldn't be able to handle it if there wasn't. Then...

No, it couldn't be.

No way.

There.

In tiny red letters. Right at the end of the anthology. So small you might not notice them.

It read:

I exist

My words. They'd written *my* words. Not only that. They'd written the date.

A date of only a year ago.

The red pen person.

That meant…

…They likely still went to our school.

Year Seven

Do you remember when...

...**Freddy** the magician **sawed** Mrs Collins in half in the talent show?

...**Sophie** and **Aaron** sang a **Disney** duet?

...**Ethan** accidentally hit **Sadik** in the face with his football doing his **keepy-uppy** challenge?

...**Grace** and **Sam** were the first couple to **kiss** at the disco?

I mean, how CUTE were we all back then???!!!!!!!!!! We were all so little and innocent and CUTE. Excited about what this new adventure would bring us. Did we mention we were cute?!!!!!???????!? !!!!???!?!?!?!?!?!?!

WHAT REALLY HAPPENED...

There wasn't a lot of cruelty in Year Seven. We were too young. Just children really – spat out into the big bad world of secondary school, clutching our rucksack straps to our chests, staring wide-eyed at all sixth formers like they were celebrities. It's a shock. Going from being kings of primary school to the youngest again. You're a diddly fish in a big pond, and all you've got to offer the pond is your dedication to wrapping your exercise books in sticky-back plastic.

So, no, there's not a huge amount of cruelty. No time. You're all too busy trying to work out where the English block is, figuring out who to make friends with, and worrying what maths set they'll put you in.

But this is where it begins.

The popular people are the ones who adjust to this new world the quickest. Year Seven is a feeding frenzy. The power's there, just waiting to be hoovered up and popular people realize that and turn their goddamn Dysons on.

When the rest of you are just kids, wondering if

you're too old to still secretly be playing Barbies, they log it all, and then they never let you live it down. They won't let you live your own childhood down.

And now, here, in the *yearbook*, they are still not letting you live it down. They are committing it to foreverness under the guise of nostalgia, reminding you of this important message for ever.

The message is…

We control your story.

We control your identity.

We decide who you are.

We do.

We do.

We do.

And all because you were too busy being an innocent kid in a gold bow tie, or in a Disney costume, and trying to enjoy the last dregs of your childhood before puberty hit.

How stupid you were, to try and do that.

CHAPTER 8

They're here. They go to this school. I've probably passed them in the corridor multiple times. They wrote what I wrote. I exist.

I was in such a daze that I could hardly concentrate in the lunchtime newspaper meeting.

They're here. They go to this school. I've probably passed them in the corridor multiple times. This is too much, too much, too much…

I was doodling stars, my head resting on one hand, hardly listening to Ms Gordon.

"So, Daisy, I have you down to cover the petition the Year Sevens have started about being last to get into the canteen. How's that going?"

Daisy looked up from her notebook with her eye-linered eyes. "Yeah, fine. I interviewed them yesterday. Their major concern is that all the potato smiley faces have sold out by the time they're allowed in."

Ms Gordon laughed from her perch on her editor's desk. Today she was wearing a denim jumpsuit with neon orange heels and matching hairband.

"It could be the splash." She smiled at Daisy with her purple lipstick. "Flesh it out as much as you can. Have you spoken to the head yet for a quote?"

"I asked reception and they said they'll set something up, but I haven't heard back."

"Hmm. I'll have an ask around the staffroom, see if I can hurry it along..."

The door opened and I swear the air got colder. I sat up, stunned out of my daydream as there on the threshold... There they were. The terrible trio of twats – a clusterfuck of populars.

"Girls! You're early! The yearbook part of the meeting isn't for another ten minutes."

"Whoops, sorry." Grace led them in, not sounding sorry at all. "We'll wait."

Their scent overpowered the room. For the rest of my life, I swear I'll be triggered whenever I smell vanilla. Everyone's head turned down towards their notebooks.

Ms Gordon, unaware, picked up her tablet and scanned her notes, while I prayed she didn't call my name.

"And, finally, Paige." She looked up. "How's it going with the Year Eight girls who want to start a cheerleading club?"

All eyes on me. I didn't want all eyes on me. Not their eyes. I felt a trap snap across my leg, ripping through my flesh.

"Cheerleading club?" Amelia raised an eyebrow. "That's cool."

"Yeah," Laura agreed. "Why weren't we allowed one of them?"

"Well, that's the story," Ms Gordon explained, recrossing her denim legs. "Why don't you explain it to them, Paige?"

I could've killed her. I went red, my hands instantly sweating. "Erm." I cleared my throat. "There's just some resistance from some teachers about whether or not cheerleading is, erm, sexist or not."

Grace's nose shrivelled up. "Sexist?"

"Yup."

"What's sexist about cheerleading?"

I was careful to only report what others had said. "Well, Mrs Collins has told the paper that the team would only be made up of girls, and their current plan is only to cheer for the boys' football team. They're not, like, professionally competing as cheerleaders so…umm…her issue is that it's not very…er…modern."

"Well that's just stupid."

I was saved by Ms Gordon, which was the least she could do considering she was the one who'd endangered me. "Our job as reporters is never to take sides," she explained. "We have to be objective. Tell both parts of the story."

"Oh, okay," Grace said, playing with her ponytail. "Cool. Anyway, we've written something for the yearbook and we want you all to look at it."

"I'm not sure if we'd planned…"

But they were already standing, handing out some printouts proudly, like children showing off a painting.

"So, yeah, we've started with Year Seven, thinking of all the funny things that happened and I wrote some 'copy'? Is that what you call it?"

Ms Gordon let the meeting get totally overrun. In fact, she was smiling, like she was proud of them. "That *is* what you call it, well done."

The rest of us robotically passed round the papers. I practised my best neutral face as I read their atrocious "copy". They'd used caps lock and exclamation marks all over the place.

Grace pretended to blush. "I mean, I can't BELIEVE Amelia put that in about me and Sam. So embarrassing."

They all giggled while Ms Gordon scanned it and burst into yet another smile. "This is a promising start, girls. I'm proud you've done this all in your own time. Let's pad out these memories even more. Shall we assign some people to do interviews?"

Amelia put her hand up. "I can interview Grace about the disco."

Grace squealed with faux humiliation. "Oh my God, Amelia. No way, that is too hilarious."

Amelia held out an imaginary mic. "So, Grace, when did you realize that Sam kissed like a washing machine?"

"OMG, Amelia, YOU HAVE TO STOP, YOU'RE ACTUALLY KILLING ME."

They descended into hysterics while the rest of us wondered what the rules were regarding joining in.

"Well, that's one sorted," Ms Gordon said. "Anyone fancy

a crack at any of the others?" We all looked down but today was not my day. "Paige!" I closed my eyes. "You're a stellar interviewer. Want to chat to Freddy about his magic show?"

No, I wanted to scream. *I don't want to talk to Freddy about his magic show. And Freddy doesn't want to talk to me about his magic show. Because he finds it hugely embarrassing, especially now he's all cool and artistic. This was YEARS ago. Why can't people be allowed to live things down?*

Luckily, I was well-rehearsed in placation. I got out the voice I use for Dad. "Yep. Sounds great. I'll track Freddy down."

I avoided eye contact as Ms Gordon allocated the rest of the memories.

"How are the photos going?" she asked them at the end. "Has anyone sent any good ones in?"

Amelia shook her head. "Not yet but we only put the posters up yesterday."

"Plus," Laura added, "we can always raid people's social media if we don't get enough."

"Hmm, I'm not sure that's legal, Laura."

"Oh yeah, of course. No worries, miss."

(They did go on to lift photos from social media anyway and never told Ms Gordon where the photos came from.)

Eventually our meeting was dismissed. The Awfuls left first while I hung around, waiting for the room to completely empty. I watched Ms Gordon pack away her things, humming a tune. I had an exciting idea hatching and had been waiting to get her alone.

"Er, miss?"

"Paige! Sorry, I was in my own little world there. Excited about the yearbook? It's all taking off very quickly, isn't it?"

"Hmm. Yeah. Can I ask you something?"

"Of course." She leaned back against the desk and all her gold bangles clanked down her wrists.

"I was just wondering, off the top of your head, if you knew what the set texts are for Lower Sixth English?"

"Don't tell me you've read all the others already?"

I smiled. "I've just flicked through. But, I, er, am really thinking of taking English onto A level, but don't want to if the books are really boring."

She laughed. "Books? Boring? I'm glad you didn't say that in the library where they could've heard you and had their feelings hurt."

I laughed politely at her teacher joke.

"Umm, well, it depends if you do English Lit or Lang, or both, but, er…off the top of my head, umm…*Atonement*? And *Bird Song*? They're both about war. Jolly stuff. Then there's *The Handmaid's Tale* in the first term. Umm, more Shakespeare. *King Lear* maybe? And poetry. Maybe Sylvia Plath if you're lucky what teacher you get."

I punched them into my phone. "Brilliant, cheers."

"Are you going to stay on here at sixth form?" she asked. "Or go to the college? I'd miss you if you went."

"I…"

Nobody had asked me that question yet. My future was so uninteresting to my family that sometimes I doubted they even knew what subjects I was taking – reminded only when they had to attend parents' meetings to keep up appearances.

"English is a great choice if you want to get into journalism. This is exciting."

I obviously showed my shock at anyone being interested in my future, because she tilted her head. "Everything okay? You've got loads of time to decide. And you're enjoying your yearbook assignment, aren't you? It's nice to get a bit out of your comfort zone, isn't it?"

I paused on the cusp of honesty. But what can you ever say to a teacher to get them to understand? I always wondered how they'd forgotten how school worked. I mean, they were once teenagers themselves, and still spent five days a week in secondary school. Yet they really did seem to inhabit a totally different universe from the students they taught. Oblivious to the pain and torment, bullies and rumours.

I just picked up my bag and played along.

"Yes," I replied. "I'm loving yearbook."

CHAPTER 9

The second I left the meeting I felt drama fizzing in the air. The corridors were dancing with excitement. Something had gone down over lunch. The crackle of gossip invaded lessons. Mr Sanders told us all to calm down. His face was wrinkled like his badly-ironed shirt. Eyebrows ruffled. The gossip, whatever it was, had hit him too.

"*They're saying he'll be expelled.*"

"*Who dared who?*"

"*Is he going to die?*"

"I SAID BE QUIET."

By the end of the day, the school was ablaze. The official line was: Joe had thrown a Brazil nut at Charlie over lunch to punish him for the group detention. Charlie was allergic to nuts – everyone knew this as we got a letter about it at the start of every school year. Charlie was, miraculously, fine, but Joe was suspended. Maybe even going to be expelled…*and it's not fair because Charlie wasn't hurt at all and it was only a joke anyway and Charlie is clearly a dick and poor Joe because suspension goes on your permanent record.*

Grace and co had emerged from the meeting and set the agenda immediately. There was a petition against Joe's suspension. Nobody was allowed to talk to Charlie. All this was his fault. The chaos of it bred more chaos. By the end of the day, the whole school was infected with random drama. I walked past multiple arguments across multiple year groups on my way out of my last lesson.

"Admit it, you copied Jenny's pencil case," a group of Year Sevens told a tearful former friend. "We all know you copied it."

I walked past a group of Year Nines, one of them crying.

"Oh my God, you need to stop being so sensitive. It was only a JOKE. Can't you take a joke?"

Outside, on the concourse, two Year Ten boys were fighting each other on the grass for no discernible reason. Grappling in the dust, while everyone gathered and cheered and Mrs Collins ran over to try and break it up.

I wanted to press my hands over my ears. I wanted to scream.

"So then I told Jessica that I didn't want to be her friend any more and I can't believe she just cried. It was so pathetic."

"Nick, MATE, wait up, you VIRGIN."

"Mrs Collins is such a bitch. I swear she, like, goes to sleep in an actual dog bed."

"Did you see Georgina's haircut? Yeah. I know. I know."

The air was choking me. I couldn't even bring myself to

walk to the school gates. Not now, not when everyone was there.

I wove my way through the chaos and back into the school building. I stared at my shoes making their way along the blue industrial carpet. A few more steps. Just one more corridor. I pushed through the door, with that stupid ugly photo of Lisa on it, and...

It was basically empty in the library. Even Ms Gordon wasn't there – just her assistant. Perfect.

I headed to the fiction section with one thing only in mind. Hope. I needed something to believe in. I needed to hope this crazy idea of mine could work. I needed to hope we could find one another. That there was a reason to come to school every day...

I found *The Handmaid's Tale* and yanked one off the shelf at random. There were seven copies. They clearly hadn't started studying it just yet. There were a million reasons why this wouldn't work. Red Pen may not pick this copy. They may not take library books out any more. They may not've taken English onto A level. They may not have stayed on at sixth form at all. But the urge to reach out was so overwhelming. It was like when I met Ruby for the first time and just felt, instantly, that we were going to be friends. Like my gut yawned open and said, *Yes, this person. Well done for finding them.* So many reasons why it could fail but I was going to sail a ship of hope out into the universe and wave my hanky at it and believe it would return safely with a treasure chest inside.

I checked over my shoulder, opened my one chosen copy to the first chapter, and, without thinking too much about it, I got out a pen and I wrote.

Dear I exist,

I exist too. I found your red pen messages and think we might get along. I leave messages in books too.

Meet you in the pages of The Perks of Being a Wallflower? We can exist together?

From,

Someone who gets it

xxx

CHAPTER 10

The house smelled of cigarette smoke when I got home. A warning sign. It didn't just smell of smoke. It smelled of smoke and open window to let out the smoke and air freshener and perfume all over Mum's clothes.

I was too consumed with hope to notice it at first. I'd walked home in a daze of optimistic fantasy. Picturing Red Pen finding my note, getting in touch. I calculated the amount of time it would likely take for them to find it, and then to reply. It could be the whole term. I played "Guess Who?" – wondering who they were. How many times I'd passed them in the corridor without knowing it. What they looked like. I hadn't tried to connect with anyone since Ruby and my heart thudded like crazy at the thought.

"Paige?" Mum called, as I closed the front door.

"Yep?" I inhaled the warning smell cautiously.

"Can you come into the kitchen?"

I dumped my bag on the bottom of the stairs, ready to take up to my room, and went to meet her.

"Everything alright?"

The window was still wide open, the air cold. She wasn't wearing a cardigan. She sat at the counter, hands clasped, looking at an envelope.

"What's this?" she asked.

I stared dumbly at the brown envelope. "I don't know."

"It's from your school."

"Addressed to you?"

She sighed. "Paige, I don't have time for your nonsense today."

I pulled a face. My *nonsense*?

"I was genuinely asking."

"Well, yes, of course it's addressed to me. To both of us. Your father and I."

"Why don't you open it then?"

"What is it?"

"I don't know!"

"Don't raise your voice at me."

My hope started vaporizing into the air and out the open window. Every time I tried to believe life could be better, it threw me down the stairs again. This was so typical. I only got noticed by my parents when there was a problem. Never a *how was your day, what would you like for dinner, what's your life like, I'm asking because I love you and I care.*

I was just as baffled as Mum but then remembered the Brazil nut incident, and the pieces arranged themselves into place.

"It might be about this year group detention," I guessed.

"I thought they would email, but maybe they've sent letters."

"Detention?"

The word was foreign on her tongue. That was not a word for our family. Adam had an unblemished academic record.

"It's just this stupid thing they gave our whole year group."

"And you think that's what this letter is about?"

"Probably."

Mum stared at the envelope like it was filled with anthrax while I got myself a glass of water.

"Your dad will probably want me to wait before opening it."

I closed my eyes. "You don't have to tell him. Honestly, it's nothing."

"Since when are you getting detentions?"

I gulped at my drink. "I don't! The whole year group got one."

"Well you must've been part of it."

"It happened during the year group photo and I was just standing there."

"Well, they can't just make you all go into a detention if you're innocent."

"They can and they do."

God, she really stank of smoke. I wondered where she hid her cigarettes in the house. Probably the cleaning cupboard where he'd never find them.

Mum's voice softened at random, and she smiled at me.

"Let's open it to check, shall we? Your dad won't want to be bothered with something like this."

"He won't care."

She inserted one painted fingernail into the envelope and ripped the top off, before sliding out the headed paper. She reached around for her reading glasses. She only wore them for the shortest amount of time as Dad teased her – calling her *Professor Trelawney*, even though they were small, designer frames.

"Okay, so, yes, it's about this detention. Hmm…hmm." She glanced over the rest of the letter. "Well I'll sign it. So you're not home till at least five tomorr—"

The key went in the door and we both jumped like frightened children. It opened quickly. It slammed back on itself. Mum's wide eyes met mine, and for a moment we connected. We were both on the same side, we both heard the slam and knew what it meant.

"Your dad's home," she whispered.

"Who the fucking fuck left their fucking bag on the fucking steps?"

My insides shrank. My hope died. All that mattered right then was surviving the next few hours.

"Sorry," I called brightly, like he hadn't sworn four times. "I'm about to take it up."

He was at the kitchen door. It was his eyes that scared me the most when he got like this. They were so cold, glazed, almost like he was being programmed remotely by some evil robot. "Well it's too late for that now, isn't it?

I've already almost tripped over it." His shirt was wrinkled, tie loosened, hair mussed.

"But you didn't." Mum walked over bravely and kissed him on the cheek. He flinched. "You're home early, dear." Her voice was so faux chirpy I'm surprised she didn't grow feathers.

"Do I need to tell you my every movement?"

"No, of course not. It's just I've not started cooking dinner yet."

"I'm not hungry anyway. Don't worry about cooking."

"Well, we can order takeaway?"

"I told you, I'm not hungry."

Dad stormed past to get himself a pint glass, before opening the fridge and withdrawing a beer. We watched him like you'd watch an angry hippo with a splinter in its hoof...aware, waiting for the charge. I wanted to just tiptoe backwards out of the kitchen.

"Well, I'm not hungry yet either." Mum pretended nothing was wrong. "But we might be later."

Dad snapped the cap off his beer using the countertop.

"How was your day?" I asked, knowing the response would be horrible, but also knowing I'd get in trouble for not asking.

"How do you *think* it was? I'm home at four!"

"Oh honey, what happened?" Mum asked him.

"Nothing. Just lost a stupid client is all." Dad tipped the beer into the glass so roughly it almost foamed over. "It's all bullshit. They'd made the decision to leave before I even got a chance to try and make them stay. But I'll get the blame, because everyone is keen to pass the screw-up to someone, and why not stick the knife into the one person who's actually good at their job?" He gulped his beer, wiped his mouth, poured more in. "I mean, if THEY had been good at THEIR jobs, then the client wouldn't want to leave EVER, would they? There's only so much I can polish a turd. Idiots. All of them. Utter idiots."

This was a Code Red situation. Dad was enduring his most feared emotion – humiliation. I feared Dad's humiliation more than I feared my own.

Mum and I made eyes again.

"Oh, darling. I'm sorry. They really do sound like idiots."

"What do you know about it? Nothing. Literally nothing."

He slammed the glass down, sloshing beer over the rim. We knew not to jerk away.

"All you do is sit around here, spending my money. You have no idea what it's like."

"No...I'm sorry... Sorry..."

The whites of Dad's eyes were almost all red. "Just forget it. I don't want to talk about it. Why do you always make me talk about everything?"

Silence slid down from the ceiling and encompassed us all. I was too scared to move, but also knew he'd flip if I watched him for too long. He started circling the kitchen, looking for bait. Mum and I glanced at one another and then down at the brown envelope and, like a highly attuned bat, Dad noticed, grabbing it off the table.

"What's this then?"

"I...er...it's just this stupid thing that happened at school."

"Detention? You've got yourself a detention?"

"It's not just me, it's the whole year." Panic was making me throw up words without thinking them through properly. "I was explaining to Mum..."

His lighthouse beam swung violently in her direction. "You knew about this?"

"I only just opened the letter a minute ago."

"Without me?"

"I didn't know what it was."

He flicked the paper. "It has both our names on it."

"I didn't think it was important."

I tried to take the heat off her. "It *isn't* important," I said, waving my hands like I was trying to distract a charging bull. "It's just this stupid year group detention. I didn't do anything, I promise."

Dad's glare swung back to me. "If you didn't do anything then why do you have to go?"

"That's exactly what I said." Mum stepped behind him, arms crossed. They visibly joined ranks on the kitchen tiles.

"Adam's never got one detention."

"I've not got a detention. The whole year has. Even, like, the super geeky people at school. It had nothing to do with me." My voice came out as a hoarse whisper. I blinked as my heart tapped out urgent SOS signals against my ribcage.

"That doesn't make sense." Dad picked up the form

again. “What am I supposed to do, huh? Sign this piece of paper that tells me my only daughter is being punished for not doing anything wrong?”

I nodded, eyes wide, wanting it to be over.

“That’s ridiculous.”

And, before I knew it, he was on his mobile, googling the school’s phone number.

“Dad? Dad? What are you doing?”

He paced around the kitchen, chest puffed out, ignoring me. “Of course they’re closed,” he said. “Right then, I’ll leave a message.”

“Dad, no. Come on.”

I wanted to grab the phone off him but honestly, truly, I was worried he would hit me if I did. All I could do was stand and watch as he yelled into his mobile.

“Hello, yes, this is Glynn Vickers, I’m leaving a message for the headmaster as it’s come to my attention that my daughter, Paige, has to attend an after-school detention tomorrow for something she didn’t do…or so she claims…”

No. No no no no. I soaked myself in humiliation, picturing the secretary listening to this the next morning. “…this doesn’t make much sense to me as a parent, so I’d appreciate it if you’d get someone to ring me back to explain it. Meanwhile, I will not be signing any piece of paper agreeing to something like this.”

I closed my eyes, counted to one, two, three, four…

He hung up, eyes still red, searching for more meat. “Well, hopefully we can clear this up. Jane? Next time, can you please not hide important things from me? Especially about our children?"

She opened her mouth for a millisecond before the training kicked in. "I'm so sorry." She nodded meekly. "I honestly only opened it a moment ago. I didn't know."

"I don't know why I put up with it. Honestly, some days, I don't know why I put up with it. It's pathetic. My life, you...it's all pathetic."

Mum kept nodding. She didn't know why he put up with it either.

Now we were both quaking with fear, Dad softened. He surveyed the kitchen with satisfaction. His chest deflated. He actually even smiled.

"So?" he asked. "What's for dinner?"

30th October

Amelia fished a used sanitary towel out of the bin and stuck it to Sophia's back.

7th November

Ethan asked out Laney who turned him down. So now Ethan's told everyone Laney is secretly a "trannie pervert" and Grace is saying it's not safe for Laney to be in the school toilets.

24th November

Sam has started calling Rahid "curry monster" and it's really caught on.

7th December

Amelia made a fake profile page for Lisa, saying her activities are "being a slut".

11th December

Charlie hasn't come into school for two weeks now... Nobody cares.

Year Eight

Do you remember when...

...**Melissa Nutley** ended up on **NATIONAL TELEVISION**, making our school famous?

...**Lisa Heartly** forgot her glasses and couldn't **see** the **whole** day?

...**Cormac** got **accidentally** locked inside the Canterbury Tales experience for **hours** after it closed and we were all **really late** home from the trip?

...**Amelia** made neon scrunchies **super**

We weren't as cute as we were in Year Seven but we were still SO CUTE!!!??? How lovely was school before we had to do all our exams?!!!!????

WHAT REALLY HAPPENED...

I mean, it's ludicrous really that they've mentioned Melissa at all. Melissa left our school because she was bullied out. THAT'S why she was on national television – she was on a documentary about bullying. In Year Eight, for some reason no one fully understands, everyone woke up one morning and decided to detest Melissa Nutley. The hate campaign spread within a week. She went from being a slightly odd girl, to being called "Dog Face" and tormented relentlessly. Everyone barked when she entered the room. Amelia left dog treats on her chair. Melissa was a reactive victim. She didn't go quiet, or shake, or cry. Instead she fought back – swearing at anyone who barked at her. She threw the dog treats at Amelia's head. For six months, "Dog Face" provided our entertainment. She was our own personal bull and we were the matadors, waving red rags at her, until the day she didn't come in.

And she never came in again.

Nobody knew what to do without her. There was a bullying void. People struggled to pass the time without tormenting her.

Then, months later, Amelia ran into 8D's form room before registration one morning, phone clutched in her hand, announcing, "You'll never guess what? Dog Face was on the TV yesterday!"

The clip travelled around our year group quicker than a superbug. There was our beloved Dog Face, on a documentary, speaking passionately about how school bullying is an epidemic and that's why she's now home-schooled.

"I had to leave," Melissa said, her eyes wet. "I tried to tell the school what was going on but they were useless. They kept saying there was a *'lack of evidence'*."

Amelia shrieked with laughter as she held the clip up. "You hear that, guys? Lack of evidence? She's the one covering up the evidence that she was a crazy psychopath."

There was a moment before the class's laughter joined with Amelia's. Granting her the power she wanted. By Year Eight, the ecosystem was decided upon. You could either accept it, or leave. Melissa Nutley left. Because of us. Someone dropped out of school because of us.

Never let yourselves forget that.

CHAPTER 11

Cormac struggled to stuff his long legs under the desk in the newsroom.

"Does this *really* have to go into the yearbook?" he complained, folding his knee at an awkward angle. He was so tall he must resemble a pretzel by the end of each school day.

I looked up from my notepad, which, so far, only had his name and the date on it. It was December 11th, with just under two weeks of school left before the Christmas break. A whole term had passed somehow. A third of Year Eleven was safely under my belt.

I left a silence for him to fill in with consent – one of my favourite journalistic tricks. The quieter you are, the more the other person talks.

"I mean, it was years ago… I guess it was sort of funny… I was bloody terrified at the time though."

That was a good quote. I noted it down.

"So, what happened?"

Cormac scratched his ear. "Well, I was hanging out with Joe and Ethan and that lot, and we were quite bored. I mean, you were on the Canterbury Tales trip, right? It was just loads of weird cardboard robot things popping out and talking about the olden days." He went through the laborious process of recrossing his legs. "Anyway, we decided to play hide and seek, but I guess I hid too well as I was so small. By the time I realized no one was going to find me under the Miller's Tale, I wriggled out and tried to leave but the door was locked and it was all dark..."

I followed my "What happened?" question with "And then what happened?", letting Cormac tell his own tale in his own words. As yearbook work went, this was certainly the least painful thing I'd had to do. Cormac had always been vaguely popular. This hide and seek story was pretty funny. No one was seriously harmed. And, despite his pretence he was embarrassed, really Cormac couldn't believe his luck that this was going to take up a whole page.

"...and I couldn't even use my phone to ring for help because Mrs Collins had bloody confiscated it..." He leaned back in his chair to give himself more room. "I only had a snack-sized Mars bar with me. I thought I'd starve..."

The central heating pulsed through the overly hot room and rain speckled the window. It was already pitch-black outside. A limp piece of tinsel dangled half-heartedly over the door, reminding me that Adam was coming home soon for the holidays.

"Anyway, as you know, they finally came and rescued me.

A week's suspension was pretty harsh if you ask me. It's not like I chose to pee in that ornamental pot."

I smiled. "Great, thanks, Cormac. I remember you being suspended," I said. "Well, I remember Grace starting a petition against it."

He laughed and rolled his eyes. "Grace is obsessed with petitions, isn't she? Still, it seemed to work for Joe when he threw that stupid Brazil nut."

After the public outcry, Joe unsheepishly returned to school after only two days of suspension. Charlie had been social Chernobyl since. Having finally come back to school after more than two weeks off, he slunk around quietly, ignored.

I was careful to keep my face neutral as I nodded at Cormac.

"Are we done?"

I nodded again and turned off *record* on my phone. "Yup. Thank you. You'll be able to read it in, like, six months' time."

He laughed. "Thank you...er, what's your name again?"

It felt like a stab in the eye and I blinked the hurt away. I'd spent five years growing up with Cormac – three of those in his English set. "Paige."

He'd already turned away, swinging his bag over his long back. "Right. Cheers, Paige."

"Bye."

I took my time reading back my interview notes, putting stars next to any bits I thought would be useful. Mostly I just wanted the halls to empty out. I spent another ten minutes carving out the words *I exist* on the desk using my maths compass. Back to my old pathetic tricks.

It had been two months since I'd left my hopeful scribble in *The Handmaid's Tale* and, for a while, it had transformed my attitude towards school corridors. I'd felt hope and actual thrill walking from lesson to lesson, trying to get a good look at everyone, wondering if they were Red Pen. But now my hope had dwindled to a sputtering spark that failed to ignite. I'd initially checked the stash of *The Perks of Being a Wallflower* every day to see if they'd replied. Sometimes even twice a day. But after a term of disappointment, I only checked once a week.

I sighed and stood up. It was Friday. Another empty weekend loomed. I padded past quiet lockers and let my brain relax. I'd been anxious about interviewing Cormac as he had such dangerous friends but it turned out that even if I'd done something dumb, he didn't even know my name. I decided to go via the library, to check one last time.

"Hey, Paige?" I heard, echoing down the empty English corridor.

I froze, blinking into the full beam of Grace Langdon approaching.

"Oh, hi."

"Wait up a sec."

Fear fastened me to the carpet. It never failed to stun me how miraculously pretty she was. Grace had won every genetic lottery going. It was like her dad was a film star and her mum was a supermodel…which wasn't far off actually. Word was her dad used to be an actor, and her mum used to be an underwear model *(not a glamour model, never a glamour model, no matter what Amelia said about her during their epic three-week friendship war in Year Nine)*.

"How did the thing with Cormac go?"

"Yep, it was fine."

"Great. That's going to be such a good page."

I used the gift of silence again and she stumbled into it.

"I was worried he wouldn't want us to put it in," she explained, eyes wide with drama. "You know? Because it happened back when he was super short? I mean, who else could've hidden under the robes of a robot?" She giggled. "He gets pissed off when we mention how short he used to be, you see."

I kept quiet but smiled politely.

"…anyway, great that he was up for it. It's so nice when people are willing to laugh at themselves, you know? Unlike Lisa freakin' Heartly, if you know what I mean."

At the mention of Lisa's name, the corridor erupted with landmines. Lisa was on the kill list since she'd refused to give an interview about her "glowing up". I'd been the one tasked with trying to get her to talk. She'd ignored all my emails, and, when I'd cornered her with her boyfriend by the Astroturf, she'd just given me a look of complete pity.

"*I want nothing to do with this Trojan Horse of a yearbook Grace is making to tug herself off to,*" she declared, before exploring the inside of her boyfriend's mouth while I was still standing there. The whole thing was so stressful I'd stopped going to the school newspaper meetings, telling Ms Gordon I had too much work to do. I didn't dare drop out of yearbook though…

Grace tilted her head at me and laughed. "You really are quiet, aren't you?"

"Sorry."

"Jeez. No need to apologize, I was just saying. I think I've only heard you say, like, three sentences since we started being on yearbook together."

I hugged my arms and wished I could vanish into the wall entirely.

She tilted her head the other way. "Have you got, like, social anxiety or something?"

I laughed inwardly. Like I would tell HER.

"I'm just quiet. Everyone always says so."

"It kind of makes me nervous."

And I thought, *You have no idea how loud it is in this head of mine. You have no idea of the thoughts I have about you, and how none of them are good. You are nervous because you know I hate you, and you know so many others hate you too, and what makes you nervous is that you know you deserve the hatred.*

"Oh, okay, sorry."

She laughed again. "Right, I better go. There's that party tonight at Joe's, isn't there?" she asked, knowing there was no way in sweet hell I'd ever be invited. "I've only got two hours to get ready and I have no idea what to wear because Amelia bought this jumpsuit that's really similar to mine but she's claiming it's not similar and is insisting on wearing it, even though I bought mine first, but, anyway, I don't care. But, yeah…anyway…have a great weekend, er…Miss *It's Always the Quiet Ones*." She waved as she walked past while I waited for my heart rate to return to normal.

I held my hand to my chest. "We made it," I told my heart. "We made it, we made it, we made it."

I waited until Grace was fully out of sight before continuing to the library. I felt even more drained now, like, if I were a balloon, she'd sucked the last bit of helium out of me.

"Paige! You're here late. We close in ten minutes, you know?" Ms Gordon wore an outfit made entirely from different shades of yellow. Mustard dress. Neon tights. Pale cardigan. Lemon shoes with actual pictures of lemons on them.

"I know, I know. I'll be quick."

She looked up at the clock. "I love your enthusiasm but seriously, ten minutes. I have swing class."

"I'll only be five."

I scuttled upstairs and settled down, cross-legged, next to the copies of *The Perks of Being a Wallflower*. I skimmed through a copy. Then through two more. I wasn't really paying attention at this point. Half distracted by the thrumming drone of rain hitting the dark windows. Then I flipped over one final page and promptly dropped the book. I swore, and picked it up again.

Red pen.

Wow. Hello!

Dear Someone Who Gets It,

I can't believe you found me. And now I've found you. I've seen your messages in other books in the library and always wondered about you. Great book choice by the way, it's one of my favourites. Was it you who underlined that line in this copy? Isn't it perfect? I enjoyed reading it again. Thank you for existing and reminding me of how much I like it.

See you again in the pages of my favourite book? Catcher in the Rye.

Yes, I'm that obvious.

From

I exist x

Everything fell away. The rain on the windows. The jarring yellow of Ms Gordon's outfit. The emotional hangover of the Grace encounter. My face stretched into the most enormous smile. I traced my finger along the words. They'd found my old messages too! Who was this person? I searched for clues in their note. They liked *Perks of Being a Wallflower* – that already made them an excellent person. They liked the same line as me! Then there was the additional insight…their favourite book was *Catcher in the Rye*. That meant, almost definitely, that they were a boy. It was such a boy book. The new knowledge sent a flurry of tingles across my skin, and narrowed down the mystery. They were in Lower Sixth. They were male. They did

English. That made it around one hundred potential candidates…

"Paige?" Ms Gordon called. "I'm a librarian, not a publican. I'll never be cool enough to permit any kind of lock-in."

I dropped the book on the floor again before scrambling to pick it up.

"One sec." I stuffed it unceremoniously under my arm and jogged over to the "S" section. There were only two copies of *Catcher in the Rye* on the shelf. I grabbed the first, pawing through the pages so roughly I almost ripped one.

"Paige. Please. I need to learn the Charleston otherwise the hipsters won't let me live in Hackney when I grow up."

"Coming!" I shoved the empty one back, yanked out the other and flicked. A blast of red pen. My heart combusted. I shoved it into my armpit and flung myself down the library steps.

Ms Gordon's face fell as she clocked my books, contrasting with her happy yellow outfit. "Paige. You're taking those out? I've closed down the computers." She checked her watch, which had a yellow strap. God only knows how she'd managed that. Then she saw the frenzy on my face. "Okay, okay…if you're that desperate for Holden Caulfield and friends, I can write them down and input it later."

"Thank you," I sighed. "Have a good weekend, miss," I fired over my shoulder and I practically ran out, the doors clanging shut behind me.

CHAPTER 12

Adam is coming home for Christmas. Did you know that Adam, yes Adam, is coming home for Christmas? Yes. Adam. Christmas. He's coming home for it. First term of uni over. Yes. So proud. So grown up. Can't wait to see him. He's coming home for Christmas.

It was like the Dalai Lama was popping over to stay for a month.

Adam's impending return was all my parents could talk about. Mum upped her homemaking so intensely she would've made a 1950s housewife look like a lazy sloth. The house sparkled and shone. Weird chores were discussed that I didn't even know needed doing.

"Phew, I'm knackered," she'd say, leaning back in the polished kitchen chair and mopping her brow theatrically. "But I'm glad I got the inside of the washing machine cleaned ready for Adam coming home." I hadn't known the insides of washing machines were particularly dirty… I'd always assumed they were kind of…self-cleaning, but only the best for Adam.

“Have you got the ham shaped like a bear?” Dad asked, when Mum returned from the supermarket the day before my brother’s arrival, laden with bags of all his favourites.

Her hand froze in the bag-for-life from which she’d been unpacking three tubes of sour cream and onion Pringles. Adam’s best flavour.

“He’s not eaten that since he was a boy.”

“For Christ’s sake, Jane, it’s his favourite.”

“I’m sorry. I’ll go back right away.”

The air crackled. Over the last few days of school, when teachers were too exhausted to do anything other than shove us in front of a movie, I’d return home to daily fights, tears and Dad slamming doors.

“What do you mean he’s not coming back until the fifteenth? But he broke up on the twelfth.”

“I don’t know. That’s what he said on the phone.”

“Why was he calling you anyway?”

“You were at work.”

“What did you say to him to put him off coming home?”

“I didn’t say anything!”

“It’s your stress levels. You’re always so stressed. No wonder he doesn’t want to come home.”

Usually I’d be absorbing all the unpleasant emotions but, this time, the drama of Adam’s homecoming was on low-volume, eclipsed by the boy who wrote to me in books.

* * *

I'd run home the night I found his first message, and laughed into the winter's air. I stopped at the end of my road, my body both freezing and sweaty. I slumped onto the bus stop bench and my hands shook as I whipped out *Catcher in the Rye*. I'd read the book last summer so I reckoned it was okay to skim through. He'd desecrated it with red ink and underlined more than he'd left. It really must've been his favourite. This person. This person I did not know who had left me a message in his favourite ever book. I knew I'd reread the book once I'd found his message. The fact he clearly loved it so much was contagious. I wanted to see the story through his red-pen eyes. But there wasn't time for that now. My freezing fingers flicked till the text became a blur, my eyes trained to spot the red pen, glancing over it all, looking, looking…

There.

The red ink was slightly brighter. Only noticeable to my trained eyeball. A brand-new scribbling, right next to a paragraph about how Holden hates everyone at his old school for being "*phonies*".

> *His school is full of phonies, and so is ours. Don't you think? Are you a phoney? I feel like you're definitely not. Shall we meet up and find out, Someone Who Gets It? Tell me which book to meet you in Xx*

I must've read that page a million times. I could hardly think of anything else in the coming days, as I stayed up rereading *Catcher in the Rye*, just so I could feel close to him by seeing what bits of the book he liked. I spent the weekend hiding from my parents, agonizing over how to reply and in which book.

The last Monday before term ended, I sneaked past Ms Gordon, who was comforting Candise as she freaked out about her mocks, and ran over to the "S" section and returned my copy of *Catcher in the Rye*, with the added message:

To meet me in real life, meet me in STARGIRL.

I padded over to the location of my chosen book. I'd been tempted to choose an important literary novel to impress him, but after all his underlined passages about "phonies" I knew I couldn't. I'd never been into stuff like that. So I went over to the YA section and hunted down the neon pink cover of one of my favourite books. I'd read it in Year Eight, during a particularly painful patch, the loss of Ruby a fresh scar. I must've read it at least twelve times. I pulled out a copy and flipped through the pages, and blushed when I came across a message I'd forgotten I'd left there.

I exist, my old handwriting read. It must've been Year Eight because I'd dotted the "i"s with hearts. I felt a pang of tenderness for past me, thinking hearts over her "i"s would make her stand out in some way, any way, trying anything to make anyone notice her. I turned the pages quickly, looking for the sentence I remembered loving when I first read it. Worried I'd miss it. But no. I skidded to a halt as I saw a star in the margin.

I had never realized how much I needed the attention of others to confirm my own presence.

I smiled and each word carved themselves into my heart. The trueness of them. I clicked my biro and wrote next to it.

> Not a phoney, I promise. Let's meet. Caffè Nero? First day of holidays? 10?

I read back what I'd written, closed my eyes and said a quick prayer. *Please,* I sent out to every omnipotent being. *Please let this happen. Please let it be good. I need this.*

I needed it so much.

The hope I'd dared hope was re-blooming. It was stretching out its sleepy limbs, yawning, and apologizing for getting up so late. What I was doing was crazy. So, so unlike me. I felt sick, but in a good way. Terrified, but too excited to let the fear win. I shoved the book back onto its shelf and left the library. My heart going berserk like I'd just got away with a crazy crime. Hoping it wasn't self-harm to still have hope.

The last day of term felt long and heavy, like sodden laundry that would smell damp before it dried. Adam would be home when I got in. Or so he claimed. He wouldn't give the family group chat the exact time of his train, though Mum and Dad had asked for it twice.

Adam: In the afternoon I think.

Dad: What time? I can come pick
you up from the station.

Adam: No worries. I can walk.

He'd randomly sent me a private message too.

Adam: Hey Paige, looking forward to
catching up x

I actually said, "Huh" out loud when I saw it. He never messaged me usually. We weren't exactly close. I had too much resentment of his elevated status, he had too much guilt. I wished he'd send friendly messages to Dad instead. My guts started their awful jig of anxiety. The stress Adam's complacency would cause. How somehow it would be Mum's fault. Or mine.

With only two hours left before the holidays, the school frothed with festive energy. Grace and co tied tinsel in their hair like ribbons, and every other girl cursed themselves for not thinking to do the same. Joe ran riot with a bunch of plastic mistletoe, grabbing girls at random in the corridor and planting sloppy, non-consensual kisses on their cheeks.

We stood for way too long waiting to get into the hall for the mass Christmas assembly. Despite the central heating being on full blast, my skin erupted in goosebumps whenever I saw a sixth former in their home clothes. Was it them? Was it them? Was it them?

"Year Eleven, file in, please," Mrs Collins barked, and we smooshed our way into the hall with the rest of the school.

Was he here? Was he here? He must be.

The sixth formers sat on benches at the back – wearing their usual air of boredom and superiority. One of the guys was dressed as a full-on Santa Claus and was bloody pleased with himself, yelling, "*Hoe-hoe-hoe,*" at some girl with long hair sitting to his side.

Please don't be him. Please don't be him. Please.

I scanned the benches, looking for any sign in any of them that they could be Red Pen. But, before I had time to properly analyse them, our head, Mr Steele, turned off the Mariah Carey entrance music and clapped for attention.

"Merry Christmas," he said, his suit offset with a novelty, festive elf tie. "I hope you all have a wonderful holiday and rest but also get lots of important coursework done." No one laughed. "But, before we set you all on your way, we thought it would be nice to get you together as a school to remind you what Christmas is really about." He beckoned our school's chaplain up from the side. "Reverend John? Over to you."

It was at times like this I wished I had a friend to roll my eyes with. We had to sit through this speech every Christmas.

"Welcome everyone, welcome." Reverend John clasped

his hands together earnestly, like he was trying to milk them for more religious juices. "Now, sometimes, not all of you, but some of you, may forget what this holiday is really about. And that's fine." He waved his arms up from under his white showy-sleeved dress. "But, remember none of this would be going on if it wasn't for a very special someone. So, let's just take this assembly to remember this remarkable man. Let's take a moment to..." I spoke silently along with his famous line. "...put the *Christ* back into Christmas."

What followed was the same assembly I'd sat through every last day of Christmas term from Year Seven. Reverend John didn't let something like the teenage need for novelty vex him. Not when he had such a captive audience. The assembly blurred into a smudge of religious repetition, broken up by a few cute Year Sevens reading Bible passages out loud. When it was time for the singalong of Cliff Richard's version of the Lord's Prayer, we were all forced to stand and everything went a little bit berserk. The choir got out some giant flags and waved them about, and Year Sevens reached into some buckets and started chucking ripped-up bits of paper over everyone, in what I guessed was supposed to be a fake snowstorm. I kept my singing voice to a low hum and used the hubbub to stretch my neck around again to scan the back, wondering who from the bench would come to Caffè Nero. If they came at all.

The bell went and we were free. The doors of the main hall were flung open and cold air rushed in to greet the sweaty suffocating oxygen we'd been group-inhaling for the last hour. I weaved around all the groups of friends hugging and saying, "Merry Christmas" and left as quickly as I could.

It was dark out, the orange of the street lights fuzzy in the thin veil of drizzle. I wrapped my arms around my chest and made my way back to home and to Adam. Thinking how much better things would be with him in the house. I mean, we weren't close, but his presence made my parents happy.

Something was wrong when I opened the front door.

"Hello?" I called, expecting warm reunion faces and hugs we didn't quite mean. "Hello?"

Mum careered into the entrance hall in her socks. "Don't wake Adam."

I raised both eyebrows. "Adam's asleep?"

"Shh! Yes. He went down just over an hour ago," she whispered, like she was describing a napping baby.

"Tell her to be quiet otherwise she'll wake Adam," Dad barked from the living room, much louder than my hello.

"We're waiting for him in here." Mum didn't ask me how my last day of school had been because why would she? "It's furthest away from his bedroom."

I hung my bag on the hook. "Okay, I'll just go upstairs and change and then I'll come—"

"No. You might disturb him. Change later." She held out her arms to herd me in.

I would've theatre tiptoed if I wasn't so on edge. A zing of hatred lightninged through me. Why would Adam do this? He knew them. He got it. Why would he go to bed?

Dad sat tensely in his armchair, pretending to watch some Christmas-themed talk show.

"Hi."

"Shhh. He's sleeping. Sit down."

Another flash of rage. I had no choice but to sit as far away as I could and become as invisible as possible. Mum perched on the sofa's edge but got up a dozen times to go into the kitchen to stare at it. Dad flinched whenever she stood, making a little clucking noise of annoyance.

"Sorry," she said, sitting down.

"Sorry," she said again, standing up.

"Sorry, she said, sitting again.

"For Christ's sake, Jane. What the hell are you doing?"

She'd made even more effort with her looks. Hair freshly washed and blow-dried. A light pink blouse tucked into her skinny jeans with just the right amount of tuck. She quivered like unset jelly. "Sorry," she said. "I just don't know what to do about dinner."

"What about dinner?"

"Well, when to put it on. It will take a while. But I don't know when he'll get up...I don't want it to burn."

"Stop being so stressed."

"I..."

"You'll wake him with your bloody stress."

"Sorry, I know, I..."

"Don't blame the boy. Walks in the door and right away gets this powerful urge to nap."

Mum's eyes filled with unspilled tears.

The door swung open, in the nickiest of times, with Adam standing on the threshold.

"I only needed a nap because I was up till four this morning." Adam stepped into the living room with ruffled hair, wearing an open dressing gown over his clothes. "Mum, dinner would be amazing, thank you." He noticed me wallpapering in the corner. "Hey, Paige. You're home!" I got up and we met in the middle for an awkward hug. When he withdrew, he looked at me with genuine affection. "You look older," he commented. "Your hair's grown."

It was because I'd been too scared to ask for money to get it cut. But I smiled, like it was deliberate. Adam looked pretty different too. He was semi-successfully growing himself a beard, it seemed. He'd not cut his hair either, letting it flop into his eyes. He smelled different. Staler.

"Yours too. How's uni?"

His whole face brightened "Yeah," he said. "Amazing. Totally amazing. I've had the best first term."

Dad stood up and clapped him on the back, grinning wildly. "Best days of your life, eh? Mine too. The same. The same."

It was a miracle Dad didn't say *Chip off the old block*...

"Chip off the old block," he added.

Adam flinched as Dad touched him. "Yes," he deadpanned. "It's totally unique to enjoy your first term away at university."

I stiffened until I watched Dad smile and wipe the dig away.

"You still all drinking pints of snakebite?" he asked his son.

"Occasionally."

"Those were the days. Oh my. Even you talking about it brings it all back."

Adam took Dad's spot in the armchair while Mum took her nervous energy into the kitchen. The TV was turned off, so we could give him our undivided attention.

"So you finished school today?" Adam chose to speak to me. He stretched out his legs.

"Just over an hour ago."

"Did Reverend John put the Christ back into Christmas?"

I giggled. "He did."

Dad put his hand up to interrupt us. "We went to church for six years, SIX years, to get you into that school. Best state school in the area."

Adam got out his deadpan again. "Thank you for the sacrifice."

Dad either deliberately ignored him or just didn't notice it. "Every Sunday morning, six years. Your mum even had to volunteer at the church crèche, just to make sure the vicar really knew who we were."

Adam stretched his legs further across the carpet. "Did you have to sing the Lord's Prayer?" he asked, turning to me again. "The Cliff Richard version?"

"It's not Christmas without it."

He shook his head. "God, I do not miss that place. Not one bit."

Dad held up his hands again. "Well, if it wasn't for that place then you wouldn't be at uni now, would you?" I could feel the panic flooding off him that he wasn't getting his full allocation of attention.

Adam looked at Dad with the same amount of interest Dad had for me, and Dad was squirming with discomfort because of it. Nobody tells you that showing disinterest towards someone is one of the most powerful ways to hurt them. It hurts all the more because it's subconsciously done. If you despise someone, you still care about them. If someone is choosing to hurt you, at the very least you matter enough for them to notice you and torment you. But disinterest...sometimes invisibility hurts most.

"Yeah, I guess," Adam replied, hardly registering Dad's point. He looked around the room adorned in all its festive glory. "Mum's done a nice job on the decorating," he commented. He stood up and wandered over to the tree, plucking a bauble at random. "This one's my favourite."

We knew this. That was why it was right at the front.

Mum arrived with a bowl of olives and a side order of frantic. "Olives," she said needlessly, plonking them on the table. "To keep us going. Though it won't be long, I promise."

"Relax, Mum."

"Yeah, relax, Jane. The boy's only just woken up."

"Sorry, I...well...olives."

She cooked quickly and efficiently and quietly and all

the "ly"s that Dad required while we ate the olives and Adam and I feigned interest in Dad's latest celebrity spotting at work.

"John Cleese," he announced proudly.

"Who?" Adam asked.

"How do you not know John Cleese? He was there. In the lobby."

"Maybe because I'm not old like you."

Dad roared with forced laughter, his eyes glinting with darkness, giving him away.

Soon enough, we were sitting at the table, using the good plates, and uncorking a nice bottle of red.

"You shouldn't have made all this fuss for me." Adam sliced into the best cut of beef, perfectly grilled to medium rare.

"Nonsense," Mum shrilled. "We're happy to have you back. So, you're having a good time in Bristol I take it?"

"Hmmphh, yeah, hang on, chewing...Yeah, it's amazing. Actually amazing. My corridor are all really nice. I told you. Lectures are interesting." Adam's face got more animated, more relaxed at being the centre of attention. His initial discomfort thawed and dripped onto the ironed tablecloth. Oh, yeah, this was the Adam I knew and remembered. Basking in the limelight. "...and the funniest thing happened with the corridor downstairs. It's all girls. We're taking it in turns to play practical jokes on each other... hilarious...they put oranges on our door handles. Poor effort. We responded by putting Weetabix down their loos.

Blocked them by mistake… And don't worry. I am still taking it all seriously…got a seventy-one in my first essay…"

I tuned out and thought about Red Pen, while Mum and Dad hung so determinedly on Adam's every word that I'm surprised they didn't suffocate. Dad had already drained two glasses of wine, staring misty-eyed at Adam, like he'd just returned from a war. Mum's gaze swayed between the two of them.

My boys, I imagined her thinking to herself.

"My boys," she said, out loud. I stifled a laugh into my napkin.

Over steak, we listened to how much better it was to go to the union on a Wednesday rather than a Thursday. And over dauphinoise potatoes we listened to how Bristol is actually a much better city than London. And then, over home-baked apple pie – Adam's favourite – with real vanilla ice cream, we listened to – *Oh my God, so the medic bar crawl was so funny and you wouldn't believe the fancy dress, people went so far out, hang on, let me show you the two hundred photos on my phone.*

I chewed my slightly overdone beef, and slurped at my ice-cream soup, and figured a very long monologue was a small price to pay for Dad being in a good mood. I'd forgotten what a soothing impact Adam's presence had on him. Like seeing his DNA go forth and exist calmed his insatiable need to matter and be the most important. University sounded brilliant too. Not that I was sure I'd go. My future wasn't something the family ever really discussed. I guess I was supposed to just figure that out for myself, apply for a loan myself, take myself on open days. Then maybe mention my life-changing decision one night when there wasn't anything too good on the television.

The plan for the rest of the Adam Evening was set in stone and sealed with wax and then locked away in a Swiss bank account. After dinner, we would pour more wine, and put the family's favourite Christmas album on. We'd let Adam put the star at the top of the tree to mark Christmas starting and maybe watch a film. I hadn't dared put my bag up in my room in case that wasn't built into the agenda. I hadn't even dared pee. I'd just sat quietly on the chair with the botched cushion and let my parents enjoy the Adam show, staying out of the attention, and planning what to wear the next day for meeting Red Pen. In less than twenty-four hours I would meet them. I would actually be meeting a human I'd planned to meet. I hadn't done that in years. It felt almost insurmountable.

So when Adam stood up, his glass of wine only half-finished, and said, "Anyway, thanks, guys. That was lovely. I better get ready to go out," he set off an earthquake.

"What?" Dad's red eyes widened.

"Sorry, did I not say? I'm meeting Ross and Abdul and a bunch of the others. First night back and all that. Don't worry, I'll be quiet coming in."

He stretched both arms up and let out a small, contented sigh before he strode out of the room. We sat in silence as we heard his footsteps echo above us, heard the faint hiss of him applying deodorant, before it was drowned out by muffled music I'd never heard him play before. Some kind of sad, indie type stuff. I considered sliding against the wall and side-stepping out.

"I didn't know he was going out," Mum said, like she may be accused of deliberately withholding the information.

Dad's eyes were rimmed with red. His wine glass quivered in his bunched fist. "Of course he's going out," he said eventually. "It's his first night back." He turned to Mum and I saw the red target float to her forehead. "Honestly, woman. You can't keep him a mummy's boy for ever."

Mum's lips sewed themselves shut while Robbie Williams crooned about a *White Christmas.* With no reaction to feed off, Dad's eyes blearily found me. I looked back, a stoat caught in his headlights, waiting for him to step down on the ignition and run me flat.

He laughed. "I mean, it's not like he's going to get much entertainment in this house to tempt him to stay in, is he? Not with *Little Miss Nobody* over here."

I knew it was going to hurt but it always surprised me how much. I kept my face blank, tried to play dead, to stop him reversing back over me and finishing the job.

Dad sensed my pain, even though I'd not moved a muscle. As if he could see internal bleeding.

"I honestly don't understand how we made you sometimes… And then how we made Adam. You never speak. Never! You just sit around like a…a…slug." He turned to Mum, smiling. "Jane? You gave birth to a slug."

He twisted back. "See! You're still not talking, are you, little slug? Why don't you ever say anything?"

Because you don't want to hear it, I think.

Because I annoy you whenever I speak, I think.

Because anything I do say will be used against me, I think.

Because I don't matter, I think.

Though my face was on pause, my eyes filled with inevitable tears.

A *slug.*

In that moment, I truly felt like one. Slimy and nondescript and grotesque and slow and leaving nothing behind but a trail of snot that washes away in the rain.

He noticed my tears and disgust erupted through his face.

"Oh my God, love, I was only joking," he said, pouring salt on me and watching me turn to goo, then claiming there was never any salt. "Why are you so sensitive?"

I blinked. There was nothing right to say, only wrong.

"I can't believe I've raised a daughter who can't take a joke. You don't get it from me, that's for sure."

If it didn't hurt so much, I would've found that funny. Dad's ego was the most fragile I'd ever known. One bad appraisal at work and he was in a foul mood for six months, and we'd had to hear all his elaborate schemes to get revenge on his manager. He only actually recovered from that appraisal when his manager left, and then Dad delighted in telling us that he stole money out of his leaving collection so the man thought no one liked him.

Bored, Dad turned on the TV and the news clashed with the Christmas music playing.

"Turn off that cheesy crap. God," he snapped.

Mum reanimated and did as he said, then, sensing the danger, muttered very quietly, "I'm just going to make a start on the washing-up," and exited stage left.

I knew I had to stay there for a while to show I wasn't too sensitive.

I couldn't sniff, even though my nose was desperate to. And I couldn't wipe away the snot, because that would annoy him too. So I just slid further down my chair, like the disgusting slug I was, and pretended to watch the television.

I felt stupid for being excited about meeting Red Pen. Shamefully stupid.

Why would anyone want to meet me?

Should I even bother going? They'll only be disappointed once they know who I am.

Because I'm a boring, nothing slug with a boring, nothing life.

Adam thudded down the stairs.

"Right, everyone, I'm off." He arrived on the threshold, lit up by the Christmas tree. There was a lot of black involved in his outfit. He'd gelled his hair differently too – swept down over one eye. "Mum, where did you put my coat?"

Her head popped around the kitchen door. "Oh sorry, love. It's in the cupboard under the stairs."

He smiled. "Of course. Couldn't leave it hanging usefully near the door where I left it now, could we?"

She put her dishcloth down. "I'm sorry, I'll go get it…"

"Oh my God, chill! I was joking. You guys are so…" He glanced around the room and, even though I looked away, he saw the state I was in and instantly knew everything that had gone down. I saw the question cross his forehead – a millisecond to make a choice. He could stay in and the evening would be saved. He could allow us to need him as desperately as we all did.

He turned his gaze away from me. "Yeah, so, as I said, we're going out for a few. Big catch-up. Don't wait up." He retrieved his coat, and jumped around on each leg as he tried to pull his black trainers on without undoing the laces. He shoved a black beanie hat over his new hair, then waved goodbye.

I felt the house gulp as he left.

I couldn't blame him. Why would he stay and be our performing monkey when he could go out? It hadn't gone unnoticed that he hadn't once been home the whole term.

I waited for further attack. Breath held. Heart berserking. Tears blinked back.

I'm a slug I'm a slug. I'm a pointless disgusting slug.

But Dad was bored now. There was nothing in the house that interested him, except maybe the television. Without speaking, he picked up the remote and turned the volume back up. And, when the next advert started, I took the opportunity to go upstairs to my room – glad he was blasting it so loud that nobody could overhear me cry.

CHAPTER 13

The next morning, for the first time in a long time, I worried about my appearance. I felt a novel urge to stand out. To be pick-out-able from a crowd.

I yawned as I stared at my wardrobe's interior, hoping the act of staring at it long enough would magic a suitable outfit into existence. I had nothing "nice". Just jeans and tops. Otherwise there was one pair of shorts, for obscenely hot days, and an old dress I wore to my cousin's wedding three years ago. I stared at the dress, wondering if it was too much if I dressed it down with tights. I pulled it on to find it sort of worked. I yawned again as I applied a bit of make-up. Adam had crashed in at gone two, giggling like a maniac, and then stank out the whole house by frying bacon, leaving the kitchen in a state. Not that anyone had woken up to it yet except me. It was seven thirty and I was getting ready, no matter how tired I was, and planned to be out the door by nine. Hoping against hope that at ten thirty, Red Pen – whoever he was – would be where I'd asked him to be.

* * *

It was freezing out, and I wasn't the only one having an early start. Pre-Christmas panic laced the streets. Wild-eyed parents pushed buggies around, frantically grabbing gift sets off shelves without even checking the prices. All the till-workers were the unproud owners of a thousand-yard stare. I got to Nero an hour before Red Pen was due, keen to get a good table. I ordered a latte but the caffeine was a mistake. I was already so nervous and, after downing my drink, I felt like a wind-up toy that had been wound to the brink and then thrown out a window.

I sat and slurped and vibrated as an endless cycle of coffee-drinkers came and went like waves crashing upon the sand. A wave of mums rode in, ordering babyccinos and whining loudly about how little their husbands did in the build-up to Christmas. They were promptly replaced by an eager group of what must've been Year Sixes, all on a "grown-up" trip. They bulk-ordered drinks that came served in tall glasses, topped with foam and syrups, and took a bazillion group selfies. Then their wave spilled and was gone – replaced by two old men sipping builder's tea and grumbling about how busy everything was and how stupid drinks were now. I watched and drank, and worried and waited, and checked the time on my phone every two seconds to see that only two seconds had passed. I kept an eye out for anyone from school, but had chosen Nero as it was not the place to go. Everyone went to Costa for the upstairs bit with squishy sofas. Sweat poured under the armpits of my dress. And the voice in my head kept asking me, *What are you doing? Nobody's going to come. If they do, they'll think you're a slug anyway, and—*

Then a boy was walking towards me.

Elijah Jones was walking towards me.

Scanning the tables. A tiny espresso cup in his hand.

Elijah Jones from Lower Sixth spotted me, smiled, and headed right for me and I almost laughed because *of course* it was Elijah Jones. Of course, of course, of course.

Here is what I knew about Elijah Jones through the osmosis of school gossip. Elijah Jones didn't dress how everyone else dressed. He came into school every morning wearing a long red chequered coat over a different daily assortment of "wacky" shirts. Hawaiian, paisley, neon green, pink and stripy. Nobody knew where anyone could buy one shirt that weird, let alone what seemed to be a never-ending carousel of them. He always teamed them with tight dark jeans, posh-ish leather shoes, hair gelled like he was an inventor who'd just blown himself up, and a necklace of noise-cancelling headphones. The official diagnosis, from St Benedict's point of view, was Elijah was eccentric at best, very weird at worst. He hung out by himself in a stand-offish alluring way, rather than a loser way. His good looks meant he dodged a lot of judgement. And he was always reading – which should've given me a clue, though he wasn't often in the library.

He had the neon pink copy of *Stargirl* in his other hand. His smile got wider as he reached my table, pulled out a chair and didn't even say hello, just:

"Oh my God, this book was SO good. Thank you for introducing it to me."

I spluttered my response. "You're...umm...welcome."

He widened his legs, plopped the book down between us, and then threw his head back to down most of his coffee like a sambuca shot.

"Ms Gordon looked highly impressed when I borrowed it. Surprised too, I guess. Although who is she to think it's wrong for a seventeen-year-old boy to read a bright pink book with the word 'girl' in the title?"

"Er... Yeah."

He bashed his cup down, grinning, then picked the book up again and flicked through it to where my note was. "And this quote! Congratulations. You sifted it for the best paragraph. You're an amazing book sifter."

"*Sifter?*"

"That's what I call it. Essentially, the way I see it, the whole of any story can be condensed into its very best sentence. It's my hobby to try and find them. I've got good at it...you have the gift too I see."

"I...I..."

Of course it was Elijah Jones. Of course, of course. It was like I'd always known it. Now he was sitting in front of me, hyper and open, weird and wired, it made the most perfect of all sense.

He seemed to remember that complete strangers usually greet one another before rushing into deep conversation.

"Sorry, I'm Elijah," he said. "I would shake hands but we're not adults so that would be a bit weird."

I laughed, still coming to terms with the shock of him, and half waved back.

"Yeah, a wave. That works. I'll wave too." We sort of just waved at one another over the cluttered coffee table. He smiled an even warmer smile.

"So, you're Paige, right? I wondered if it could be you. You were on my shortlist."

I almost spat out my cold sip of coffee. "You...know who I am?"

"Yeah, of course. You write for the paper, right?"

"Umm, yeah."

"Well I read your stories. You get the front page a lot. Very impressive. I sometimes toy with the idea of doing the paper but then I remember I'd have to talk to a lot of people I don't like and pretend I find their lives interesting when I really, really don't."

It was unimaginable to me that anyone, *anyone*, would know who I was. Especially from the Year Above. Especially Elijah Jones.

Elijah's eyes registered my surprise. "I hope I didn't insult the paper," he said. "What you write is really good. I'm just not sure I could do it."

I nodded. "Oh, yeah. I'm not mad. I guess I'm just...well, this is all a bit weird, isn't it?" I was so unused to making conversation that I felt like a toddler taking their first wobbly steps.

Whereas Elijah was clearly relaxed. He leaned back and crossed a leg, balancing one foot on his knee. "Is it? Yeah, I guess maybe it is. Doesn't feel weird though, does it?"

And, despite my nerves, he was right. There were a hundred and ten reasons why this should be weird and yet it wasn't.

"But I still can't believe it's you. Finally! I found my first of your *I exists* last year, in *I Know Why the Caged Bird Sings*. And I was like, *Oh my God! Someone else who writes in books.* But I had no idea if you were still in school, or alive, or where else to find your messages."

"What?" I couldn't believe it. The odds seemed so small, and yet here we were. I'd written out all those messages in multiple margins of multiple books, but I guess I'd never thought what would happen if anyone read them.

Elijah, way less cosmically flustered than me, tapped the book. "Anyway, this book. THIS book. I loved it. Where did you find it? I don't normally read teen fiction but woah am I stupid."

I laughed openly. "You are. It's one of my favourites. It sums up school so well! Anyway, don't you get scared Ms Gordon will kill you if she sees what you do to her library books? Like, you REALLY annotate them." I swirled the leftover remnants of my coffee around my cup, watching loose grains climb up the side of my mug.

He laughed. "She probably would. But then I'd explain

it to her and hopefully she'd get it."

"Explain what?"

"How this is the only way to do it."

"Do what?"

"Read." He paused. "Live," he added.

A smile had been quietly sneaking up on my face and, at this, it crept up further. "What? Scribble all over it?"

He nodded. "To some degree, yes. Life's a blank page to be filled and all that." He tipped the dregs of his tiny coffee right to the back of his throat. "But, the way I see it, a book is someone out there in the world telling you a story – their story, right? And that's great. Everyone has a right to tell their story, but it's theirs, not yours. They can tell you a story, but you don't have to agree with it." He leaned back in his chair and ran his hands through the dark curls of his hair. "So my scribbles in the margin are just me disagreeing with it. I don't have to fully accept someone else's story, I'm entitled to put my own take on it."

"I'm sure Ms Gordon would argue you could disagree with it quietly in your head…or in pencil," I added.

He laughed so widely he fell further back in his chair. "Ha! True. The red pen is probably just me being dramatic. Attention-seeking. But then aren't we all attention-seeking all the time?"

"I'm not," I found myself replying to my empty cup.

"What was that?"

I put my drink down and made myself look at Elijah Jones.

"I said, I'm not."

"Sure you are," he said, nonplussed. "Everyone is."

"I don't know. I don't think I am." Even talking about it made my arms retreat up their sleeves. "I try to keep myself to myself."

"True." Then he pointed at me. "But then you're also doing the school paper. Getting the front page loads." I had literally never had anyone smile at me the way Elijah Jones smiled at me. So warm you needed SPF applied. "Don't be upset. It's not a bad thing – it's human. All of us need to be noticed. Even when we pretend we don't, it leaks out in other ways."

Just like his red pen, the words coming out of his mouth felt like medicine – like swallowing two paracetamol specially created for the headache of life. I shook my head to try and dislodge my overwhelm. Nothing about this coffee shop seemed real. The world seemed fuzzy around the edges.

"You say scribbling in books is the only way to read," I started. "And I get that. Well, I think I do...but how does that relate to *life* too?"

He shrugged. "Easy. Alongside people being obsessed with telling you THEIR story about who they are, everyone's also obsessed with telling you the story about who YOU are." He stretched his hands above his head, fingers interlocked. "And you're totally entitled to disagree with it. In fact, the only way to stay sane is to always argue with somebody else's story about who they think you are.

Oh my God. Sorry. I didn't mean to make you cry. Are you okay?"

He leaned over and put his hands on top of mine. It was the first time anyone other than Aunty Polly had physically touched me in years and I flinched and ripped them away.

"Sorry," I managed to get out. Wiping under my eyes, dying of embarrassment. "Sorry. I don't know why I'm crying. Sorry."

"No, I'm sorry. I didn't mean to upset you. Ignore what I said. I say a lot of things. My mum's always telling me to just shut the hell up, but I'm incapable."

I wiped and gasped and tried to get myself under control, utterly hating myself. The first chance I'd had to make a friend and, within minutes, I'd ruined it by blubbering like a whale.

"I'm fine. Not sure what's happening. Bear with me."

"If I just stare at you intensely until you stop crying, will that help?"

A laugh pushed its way out alongside my sob.

"Ahh, see it did help."

He continued to hold direct eye contact, grinning away, and I was giggling within seconds.

"Stop staring at me."

"But it's working so well."

"Literally, you've not blinked."

"It's my sacrifice for you."

My gurgles of grief morphed into gurgles of laughter and, within moments, we were laughing together, shaking our cups with hysteria. I wiped away the last of my tears.

"Sorry again," I said. "I…umm…I'll understand if you suddenly receive a fake phone call telling you your house is burning down and you need to leave immediately to rescue the dog."

Elijah raised both eyebrows. "Why would I want to do that?"

"Because I just started crying like a train wreck…"

He waved a hand. "So?"

"Well…okay then…umm…?"

The mental muscles required to ask questions and respond to them were weak, and had wasted away from my aloneness. Not being able to hide behind my detached reporter mode was pretty tricky too. It was especially difficult because this was Elijah Jones I was making small talk with. *Elijah Jones.* The sort of person in school who always got referred to by his full name.

"Do you want another coffee?" Elijah asked. "Or we could go somewhere else?"

The shocks kept arriving. The fact he'd come at all. The fact he was Elijah actual Jones. The fact I'd showcased such a staggering display of emotions and it hadn't fazed him. The fact that he still wanted to spend time with me.

"Where can we go around here? Everywhere is crammed."

"Well, sifter extraordinaire, why don't we go to Leaker's bookshop, and see what you're made of?"

"Leaker's?"

“Don’t tell me you don’t know it?”

I shook my head.

“Sacrilege! Oh my God, it’s going to rock your universe. Right, that’s it. It’s decided. We’re taking you there immediately.”

CHAPTER 14

I shrugged my coat on and followed Elijah Jones outside, the cold air hitting me like a smack.

"Woah, it's freezing," he said, mirroring my thoughts and wrapping his long coat around him. "Don't worry. It's not too long a walk."

We set off through the now-manic high street. I was still trying to figure out how there was a place in town I hadn't heard of. I mean, it's not the biggest place...but then again, I spent most of my time holed up in my room. The town was cupped gently in a dark grey mist and the Christmas lights blurred in it, as frantic people panic-bought last-minute presents.

"Do you like Christmas?" I asked as he led me through the dankness.

"I like the Christmas story," he said. "Totally crazy when you think about it. That every kid in this country knows it, gets taught it, has to act it out. I mean, every kid in this country knows the words 'frankincense' and 'myrrh' before they can even spell their own names. How weird is that?"

"I still don't really know what frankincense and myrrh actually are." I reflected on my own nativity play as we dodged passing shoppers. I'd played what every indistinguishable child plays – a sheep. Ruby managed to scrape the part of angel number three. Guess who Adam played…

"Neither do I," Elijah admitted. "Okay, so we're never, ever allowed to google it. Promise me? We're only allowed to discover naturally. Deal?"

He was using the word "we" like we knew each other. It was so very bizarre and yet felt so brilliant. No one had referred to me as part of a "we" for years.

"Deal." I smiled. "For what it's worth, I think frankincense is some kind of burny thing that smells," I said. "And myrrh is a type of oil that also smells."

"Nope. Not allowed. We can't be having unsolicited, undescriptive guesses like that. It doesn't count. Right, there's a cut-through here."

He led us down a quieter side road where all the independent shops lived. Their windows gleamed with tasteful decorations to lure people in – all silvers and sophisticated golds, compared to the garish reds and greens of the high street.

"But, if you think about it," Elijah Jones continued, "it really is quite a story. It's got everything. Angels, prophecies, a virgin birth, one hell of a bad guy in Herod. I mean, what was with his obsession with counting things? That heroic donkey." He rambled on as I scuttled after him. I wasn't sure what I'd been expecting but I had assumed the first encounter with Red Pen would be slightly awkward, with small, *getting-to-know-you* questions. Maybe a second cup of coffee and moving onto discussing which teachers we did and didn't like if things went really well?

But no.

Elijah had just launched into some gloriously profound musings about life, made me cry, thought nothing of it, and was now discussing what the Christmas story would look like from the innkeeper's point of view.

"I mean, think about it. If that happened now, it would be all over the papers. Wanna stay where the Son of God was literally born? You have to pay extra for the 'Stable Room'. How unfair that I keep getting one-star reviews on Tripadvisor because the Star of Bethlehem is no longer hovering right above the place. I TOLD them that was a ONE-OFF. Oh, here we are, Sifter."

We drew up outside a ramshackle door with a ramshackle sign spelling *Leaker's* with *Second-hand and antique books* underneath. I could see now why I'd never noticed it. It was down two alleys and basically looked shut.

Elijah turned to me, grinning, the latch of the door half-opened. "Are you ready for old-book smell? One, two, three, BREATHE," he said, pushing the door open and me through it.

There was a smell, a musty one that made you feel smarter and the need to talk quietly. There were piles of old books everywhere, in shelves up to the ceiling, and, when they'd run out of space, in piles just on the floor. I don't think the place had been vacuumed since before I was born. An old man sat reading behind a desk, hardly visible behind a giant pile of more books. He was wearing a very bright purple cardigan and I wondered briefly if he was Ms Gordon's granddad.

"Alright, Brian?"

"Elijah." The man didn't look up from his book.

"Oooh, he's talkative today," Elijah whispered.

Old wartime music echoed from hidden speakers and Elijah beckoned me to a little iron staircase. "The fiction section is up here. Come on."

I followed the cool air clinging to his coat up the rickety stairs and we stepped out into this little alcove. An old sofa burped up padding through worn leather holes, and more paperbacks rose to the ceiling in dilapidated shelves. *How did I have no idea this place existed?* It was such a heavenly, musty-smelling escape. I trailed my hand over the spines of one shelf – lots of the books faded to only a hint of their original colours, the spines crinkled from historical read-throughs.

Elijah watched me stroke the books like they were Polly's cats. "Those are the best ones," he said. "The ones with the spines all gone like that. Just imagine how many people have read them for it to be like that." He leaned over and plucked out a yellowing book and I got a smack of his scent. He flicked through it before coming to a stop. "See." He pointed to a corner crease at the top of one page. "Don't you ever see corner creases and wonder what led to them? Like, there was a person who read this book once, God knows when, and this page is the precise moment they stopped reading for the day. That tiny moment in history, about a rather inconsequential decision, is marked for ever. A clue for us to find. How cool is that?"

I got another smack of his smell as I leaned in. "I wonder who they were," I replied, letting my imagination unfurl. "I wonder why they were reading this book. How they got it, why they chose it. I wonder what was happening that made them put it down. Like, was dinner ready? Or were they sleepy? Or did the phone ring, and, on the other side of the line there was life-changing news?"

I looked up to find Elijah Jones smiling at me. "Exactly. They've left a mystery behind without even realizing it."

He snapped the book shut and I jumped and he laughed, before returning it to the shelf. "Of course, the BEST things to find are letters and postcards and ticket stubs people used as bookmarks and forgot to remove. Ultimate jackpot!" He spun around and started rifling through the rows of battered paperbacks. "Right, so our mission, if we choose to accept it, is to test our sifting skills over Christmas." He spun around again, pointing. "Are you dreading loads of family time over the holidays?"

"I...er...well, yes."

"Brilliant! Me too. So let's set ourselves a challenge to make the time go quicker. Let's find two copies of the same book, read it, and see if we sift out the same paragraph."

He spun back to the shelves and I imagined him in a cartoon tornado. "Ready? You start with Z backwards, and I'll start with A onwards, and we'll see who can find two copies first. Ready, steady, GO."

I had only known Elijah Jones an hour, yet I'd already learned it was best just to go along with it. So I squatted at the Zs and started scanning. I hadn't even got as far as "W" before a hoot of triumph pierced the air.

"Look," he said. "Oh my God, it's so perfect. So festive! What are the odds, Paige? Look. Look!"

He was cradling two copies of *A Christmas Carol* by Charles Dickens. One was a very old hardback. The other looked like a rather modern reprinting, with some "edgy" graphic cover. It looked pristine and unread, likely an unused Christmas gift from the year before.

"We're going to read *A Christmas Carol*?" I asked for clarity. "Together?"

"Yes. Well, together, but apart. Then we'll see if we sift the same bit. Can I take the old one? I love old books. Smell it, just smell it." He practically shoved the book in my face, engulfing me with the aroma of slowly decomposing pages, and I laughed and shoved it back.

"Sure, take it, take it. God though. Reading Dickens. For fun. Over the holidays…"

"The book chose us, Paige. We cannot argue with fate."

Another cartoon tornado spin and he was sprinting down the stairs, coat flowing behind him, handing the books over to Brian.

"Very festive," he said, ringing them up.

I reached for my purse but Elijah waved my money away. "Don't worry about it, it's only a quid." He beamed at Brian. "So, shall we get another hot beverage somewhere? I feel like we've not had a normal conversation yet."

It took a moment for me to digest the wonderful significance of Elijah not wanting to run away from my company. "I think that's very much been steered by you."

Brian snorted behind him and Elijah laughed again. "Fair, fair. Right, coffee? Somewhere idiots from school are unlikely to be?" He spun again. "Where would that be, Brian?"

Brian shrugged. "I dunno. The church cafe?"

"Perfect."

"I was joking."

"But it's perfect. Right, to the church cafe." He pointed to the air with such vigour that, for a second, I thought he'd fly there like a superhero. He grabbed my hand, like that was a normal thing to do to someone you'd just met, and tugged me out of the ramshackle shop and into the cold air again. My body fizzed from the physical contact and I just about managed to keep up with his pace as we threaded through the chaos of the shopping precinct, drizzle decorating the hair of everyone pushing past each other. I spotted Joe and Ethan leaning against a wall outside McDonald's, sipping milkshakes and perving on girls walking past. Ethan spat on the ground and I turned my face away so they wouldn't see me. Not that they'd recognize me anyway. I must've slowed, because Elijah turned to follow my gaze.

"Who are they?" he asked.

I almost tripped when he said that. The unbelievable fact that there was someone in my school who didn't know who Joe Vividichi and Ethan Chambers were...it would've ruined their Christmas.

I hurried my pace again. "Just some popular guys from my year."

"Are they nice?" Elijah started laughing before he even got the question out.

I giggled too. "Oh, the nicest," I deadpanned. "So nice, in fact, that this guy, Charlie, who they've decided to hate for no reason, stopped coming to school for a while."

Elijah rolled his eyes as we dodged a father trying to get a floppy, tantruming toddler into a stroller. "School refusers are the most sane people in the world, I reckon," he said. "I mean, if you think about it, you've kind of got to have a problem to think the whole set-up isn't totally crazy. Being legally forced to sit in a building five days a week, with people you'd never choose to see otherwise, stomping around like zombies whenever a ringing bell tells us what to do." He sighed and glanced back at Joe and Ethan as we walked. "Anyway, these guys may be gods in your year, but no one in my year knows they exist."

I pondered on this as we dashed through the determined drizzle towards the small church at the end of the high street. I guess it made sense that every year group was its own microcosm. Which, technically, should make everything matter less. Like, I had no idea who was popular in the year above me, not really. There were a few characters I knew of, because they were characters rather than popular. Like Elijah, or that girl, Dolphin (yes, her real name) in Year Thirteen, who always got the main part in the school play. But that was it. What Elijah'd said was a mixture of reassuring, and totally depressing. Reassuring that people like Joe, who believed themselves to be so important, were not very important at all. But depressing that we all still bought into their ridiculous hype.

We arrived at my old church, which I'd not visited since Year Six. It looked just the same. Modern red brick with a concrete cross topping the flat roof and a little cafe on one side, adorned with a mural of Jesus so badly painted I'd seen it scare several children. When Elijah and I pushed through the door, there were only a cluster of old ladies sitting in the corner, nursing strong cups of tea.

"I'll get these," I said, still feeling bad he'd paid for my book.

"I'll grab a seat."

He settled himself away from the curious eyes of the elderly while an equally old man took my order.

"Two teas? I'll bring them over in a jiffy, my dear."

"Thank you."

I felt a gush of nervousness as I sat across from Elijah. "The teas are coming soon."

"Brilliant. Thank you." He put his hands together,

showing me full interest. "So tell me about you," he said. "I'm aware that I've done all the talking, as always. Sorry. I get a bit excited by new things."

I raised an eyebrow. "I'm a *thing*?"

He laughed. "You're right. You're not. You know what I mean, though. So, you don't like those boys from your year then?"

I shook my head. "As I said, they've made someone stop coming to school… There's a lot of people like that in my year."

"Yeah, there's loads in mine too. I thought sixth form would chill everyone out a bit. But, if anything, it's worse. All the decent people went to the college, leaving me stranded with those desperate to make their 'glory days' last as long as possible. I was going to leave, but they don't offer philosophy there so I'm trapped."

"At least sixth formers can go home over lunch."

"Yes, I escape the complex as much as I can. It's bliss."

"That's why I never see you around much…" I blushed the second I said it, as it was like I'd admitted that I looked out for him. Which I didn't. I hadn't thought much about Elijah Jones until the moment he sat down at Caffè Nero. Now I had a feeling I was going to think about him a lot.

"That's funny," he said. "Because I saw a lot of you."

My mouth fell open just as a shaky old man wobbled over with our half-spilled drinks. I stood, to escape my blushes, and reached for a cup.

"Sorry," I told him. "I should have come to help you."

The old man slopped them down, spilling even more. "No, no. Bert still has life in him yet."

"Well, thank you again." I took a gulp which was way too hot. Elijah watched me, smiling, as I pretended I hadn't just burned off my top layer of taste buds.

"I wasn't spying on you or anything," he said. "Don't worry. I just see your byline in the paper a lot. And I notice you in the hallways. You seem above it all somehow."

I started laughing.

"What? What is it?"

"Above it?" I laughed again. "I only keep to myself because I'm totally petrified."

He shook his head and picked up two brown sugar lumps to plop into his drink. "No, you're not." He swilled the whole mug to stir them in. "You wouldn't put yourself out there, writing for the paper and stuff, if you were scared."

"I do that *despite* being scared. And the paper is pointless anyway. We never cover anything important."

"Well, you know what they say." He looked at me with a sudden intensity. "*If you're not scared, then it's not courage.*"

We stared at one another for a second. His eyes were such a dark brown you almost couldn't see his irises.

I looked down at my tea. "You wrote that, in *To Kill a Mockingbird.*"

"I did, and it's true." I glanced up and he was still staring, and it made me start babbling from nerves.

"Sometimes I think popular people like Joe and Ethan, well, I think they find school so easy," I said. "And other times

I think they *must* find it hard. I mean, whoever you are, someone, somewhere, is definitely going to make you feel bad about yourself." I took another too-hot sip. "The popular kids make you feel bad because you're not as cool as them. And the smart kids make you feel bad because you're not as clever as them. And the sporty ones make you feel bad that you can't triple-bloody-jump very far. And the drama group ones make you feel bad that you're not in the school play, even though it always sucks. And the music ones make you feel bad because you don't know who Mogwai are. And the subversive ones make you feel bad because you're not anti-authority and pierced enough. And the geeky ones make you feel bad that you don't know how to code yet. And the quiet ones, well…" I thought about how Grace said I made her nervous.

"Well, the quiet ones probably make you feel bad too. You don't know what they're thinking, so you assume the worst. But I guess the most painful thing to think is that nobody is thinking about you at all. That's school in a nutshell. Everyone feeling scared and irrelevant and terrified they're going to be found out, or even worse, not noticed at all, and somehow we're supposed to learn algebra on top of all that? And not have a nervous breakdown…" I stopped at the sound of Elijah clapping. "Sorry," I said, feeling blood surge into my cheeks. "I didn't mean to go off on one."

He shook his head, still applauding. "No, this is what I hoped would happen. I had an inkling about you," he said. "I thought you were likely to be the type of person who has a hell of a lot to say, even though they don't say a lot."

My hand self-consciously went to my voice box.

"You're not just a sifter of books," Elijah went on. He picked up his mug and took a big slurp. "But you sift through people as well, and get right to the heart of them. It's your superpower almost...you're quiet and that makes you notice everything, everyone. I like that..." He paused. "You say you're scared all the time, but, you're right, people should be scared of you too."

We drank our half-spilled teas until the early sunset surrounded the hut in darkness. We talked about favourite books, favourite reading spots, who we hated most at school, worst teachers, most random thing we'd ever found on the ground. I found myself talking and talking, and using my hands to talk, so excited to have words tumbling from my tongue and another human being's ears wanting to hear them. It's strange how quickly time passes when you're not invisible.

When Bert told us, "Sorry, young guns, but we're closing," we both jolted and registered the dark sky with utter surprise.

"Woah, who knew the church cafeteria was such a time warp?" Elijah hit his head. "I totally forgot! I need to buy Christmas presents today. We should go."

I stood up, almost knocking over my chair. "Sorry. I didn't mean to take up so much of your time. Sorry. I hope you still have time to shop. I didn't mean to go on...I—"

"Chill, Paige. It's been fun. I wasn't complaining."

Even with his reassurance, self-hatred pulsed through my blood. *I shouldn't have spoken so much. I've ruined his day. I've screwed up his shopping. Spoiled his entire Christmas. He will never want to see me again.*

"Let's do this again," Elijah said as we slid down the cafe ramp into the early night. "After Christmas. Before the holidays are over. In the meantime, shall we swap numbers?"

He was already pulling out his phone. Wanting to see me again. Wanting all these impossible things. I truly believed for a moment that it could be a hoax. That hidden cameras surrounded me, everyone laughing at how pathetically gullible I was for thinking this was real.

"Oh yeah…umm…"

"I mean, we don't have to. If I've put you off by talking too much about too many intense things, that's fine. It will not be my first time at that particular rejection rodeo."

"No no. That would be…great." I got my phone out of my coat pocket.

"Woah, relic," Elijah said, taking in my mobile. "I've not seen one of those in a while."

"Oh, it was my brother's." The only way I'd ever got a phone was when Adam didn't want his any more. I punched in Elijah's name – he was only the sixth number on there.

We walked back to the precinct, pointing out our favourite awful festive lights. For the first time in a long time I felt the spirit of Christmas engulf my body. All those warm sensations promised by November adverts became a reality. My smile could be felt in my stomach. We drew to a halt outside a high-street bookshop.

"This is me," Elijah said. "I need to get a popular psychology book that's been widely disproved to troll my mum." Elijah had explained over cup of tea number two that his mum was a clinical psychologist. But not one that really worked with any clients. "She spends all her time in the lab, doing experiments on children," he'd said.

"Sounds like a sensible plan."

"Yep, I may get books for my dad's family too." He saluted. "Christmas, you do not intimidate me."

I wiggled my toes in my boots to try and warm them up. Even though it was freezing, I wanted to stay put.

"Well, have a good one," I said. "Or a merry little one."

Elijah smiled at me in a way that I hadn't been smiled at in years. "You too, Sifter. I look forward to hearing your *Christmas Carol* conclusions."

We danced in the cold a moment or two longer, figuring out how to say goodbye.

"Bye then." I turned and walked off into the fuzz of lights without risking a hug or a kiss.

"Bye, Paige." And then, after a few steps, he called back to me. "See you after Christmas."

I smiled the entire walk home.

CHAPTER 15

The days of Christmas passed without major incident, which was both a rarity and a blessing. We put on our Perfect-Family masks, smiling and happy and basically auditioning to be in a festive commercial where it's always snowing outside and everyone's hugging each other in paper hats. Christmas Eve was spent at Nana's where we really had to up the ante to try and impress her. Adam returned to full Golden Boy form, allowing Nana to fawn over him, feed him up, and ask him endless questions about university. Dad looked on, grinning, so glad to have finally done something to make his mother proud.

"Like father like son," he said several times over the plates of Iceland canapés.

Nana ignored him every time he said it, but Dad pretended she hadn't.

"Like father like son," he'd just repeat, basically to himself, smiling and drinking more red wine.

I sat, ignored, like I always did. Smiling through my

teeth and watching Adam get enough devotion for two with no inclination to share. The highlight of the day was Nana asking me, "So what subjects are you doing again, Paige?" then glazing over before I'd finished telling her for the third time. She looked just like her son when she tuned out like that.

It got to the point where my Mastermind topic could be, *Adam's first term at university*.

Adam's favourite module is Richard the Third. Adam's favourite club night is Motion on a Friday. Adam's favourite place to get coffee is the Boston Tea Party. Adam's already chosen who he's going to live with next year. Four boys. Yes, it really will get messy, won't it? He's not drinking too much, don't worry. Oh, he knows they're proud. It's great. He's great. Adam is so endlessly great.

Christmas Day itself was terse, as usual, once we didn't have to pretend any more. Dad was terse about the fact Nana always spends it at Uncle Jack's. Mum was terse about the fact Aunty Polly was there and Dad hates Aunty Polly. Aunty Polly was terse about all the terseness but hid it with wide smiles, overly extravagant presents, and an incredible ability to Teflon all Dad's endless digs.

"How much did it cost you to buy presents for all your cats?"

"Twenty grand. I remortgaged the house. Would you like some more turkey, Glynn?"

"Must get lonely, you know? Over the holidays? No one to share it with."

"Are you kidding? Getting the whole tin of Celebrations to myself without someone picking out all the good ones? It's bliss. By the way, do you want twenty miniature Bounties?"

Mum was a contagiously anxious scribble the whole day; my heartbeat doubled the moment she walked into the room. Everything had to be perfect, but perfect in a way that looked like it wasn't any effort whatsoever.

"God, you're so stressful," Dad said, multiple times. "Relax, it's Christmas." Then, ten minutes later... "These pigs in blankets are soggy, Jane. Can you put them back in the oven? You know what? Never mind. I don't want them any more anyway."

I watched Polly watch her. I saw her fingers grip the table. "Please, let me help," she uttered countless times to the flap of a dismissive hand. But, despite all this, we made it through the day. I even managed to enjoy segments of it. Like unwrapping the stunning notepad Polly gave me as my present.

"Oh my God, it's gorgeous," I said, stroking the peacock blue silk cover. "It's so pretty I'll be scared to write anything in it."

"Nonsense," she said. "You OWE it to a notebook this beautiful to fill it. Otherwise the notepad will get hugely offended and depressed, as you'll be denying its true purpose."

I turned the thick, empty pages, blank and heavy with possibility. My first thought was to use it as one of my school reporting notebooks, but it was just too gorgeous to besmirch with tales of Grace's bullying antics.

"What do I write in it?" I asked.

Polly laughed and hugged me. "Whatever the hell you like. Your thoughts, your interviews, your journalism, what it means to be you."

Dad eyeballed it suspiciously, like she'd given me a live bomb. "Careful, Polly," he said. "She'll suddenly start thinking she's going to be the next Shakespeare."

"And what's wrong with that?" Polly didn't even look at him. "We are well overdue another Shakespeare if you ask me."

He used his hand to make a chattering sound while her back was turned, and I hated him so potently in that moment, I could've hit him. Then the rage passed, and all I felt was stupid to think I'd have any thoughts worthy of filling a notepad.

Elijah: Christmas is weird, isn't it?
Elijah: Like, so weird.

Paige: Weird how?

Elijah: Just how everyone's doing exactly the same things in the country at exactly the same time. Like a flash mob, but in the privacy of our own homes.

Paige: We might be doing different things!

Elijah: Oh yeah? What are you doing
right now?

I sent a photo of my feet up, surrounded by balls of scrunched-up wrapping paper, the TV in the background playing *Frozen*.

Elijah: SNAP.
Elijah: Told you!

He sent back a practically identical photo apart from the different carpet.

Paige: OK, so it's weird.

Elijah: Are you eating some Roses out a tin
right now?

Paige: How did you know?

Elijah: I'm watching you through the
window.

Paige: You're hilarious.

And, later, when Dad and Adam were on the brandies,

swilling them around with their swollen stomachs puffed out – like they were old gentlemen in the first-class cabin of *Titanic* before it hit an iceberg.

Elijah: You finished the book yet, sifter?

Paige: Almost.
Paige: It's OK, but I get a bit bored of reading books that were written in the olden days.
Paige: Use a full stop or two, Dickens.

Elijah: That's your critique of Dickens? He wrote some of the most timeless pieces of fiction ever, revolutionized what we know as "the novel", and your feedback is... Charlie, use more full stops?

Paige: Yep.
Paige: I love full stops.

Elijah: ...

Paige: That was technically an ellipsis...

Elijah: Wound.
Elijah: .

Elijah: .
Elijah: .

Paige: Best Christmas present ever.

Elijah: Don't you mean...
Elijah: Best. Christmas. Present. Ever.

Paige: I'm. In. Heaven.

It was crazy how easy it was to write messages to him. How much of...*me* just came out. Parts I'd forgotten I had since Ruby went away and parts I'd forgotten I liked. I smiled at my own words as I punched them out, not even overthinking them, and everything landed with him. Like we spoke our own language, even though we hardly knew each other.

Christmas Day drew to an undramatic close. I was the only one to walk Polly to the door after Adam won Monopoly.

"Merry Christmas," I said, hugging her tight. "Thanks again for the amazing notebook."

"Merry Christmas yourself. And, as I said, I want you to fill that thing with your thoughts."

"I'll try."

"Good. And who have you been messaging all day? Has Ruby been in touch or something?" Ruby hadn't been in touch since the last, terrible time I saw her. I got a flash of hearing Ruby's voice on the phone in my hallway, muffled, laughing, cruel. Polly sensed me tense up and glanced over my shoulder. "Want to walk me to my car?"

I nodded. We stepped into the bracing cold. The street was serenely empty with fairy lights blinking in most windows.

"So, who is it?" she asked with the door shut behind us.

I smiled from my stomach. "Just a new friend."

The word *friend* felt tingly on my tongue, like it was a dare to say it aloud.

Polly caught my smile. "Oh yeah? How did you meet?"

"At school. We've only been for one coffee. It might not be anything. They'll probably not want to meet up again."

"Don't be stupid. They're lucky to have you."

I rolled my eyes. "You have to say that because you're my family."

Her eyes darted back to my house and I knew we were both sharing the same thought. That, actually, that wasn't the truth at all, if my own immediate family were anything to go by. She shook her head.

"You're a wonderful person, Paige," she said. "Honestly, I'm not just saying that because we share blood or whatever – though I'll be hitting you up for a transplant if my cancer ever comes back." She laughed, whereas I never could when she joked about getting sick. "You're kind, and real, and see the world for what it is. That's rare, you know? Especially for someone so young." She laughed again at my squirming.

"It's all true," she promised. "This new friend is very lucky to have you."

"We'll see."

"I don't lie. Right, I better go see if the cats have all gone feral after I overdosed them on catnip this morning. Merry Christmas, poppet. I had a great day."

After one last bear hug, I crept back inside. The sounds of some comedy special blasted from the living room. Mum clattered in the kitchen, returning the house to perfect again after the wrapping-paper pile and plates of dried-on gravy had bastardized her show home. I felt happy in that moment, and full, and therefore it was a good idea to avoid everyone and go to bed.

I climbed into the new pyjamas Mum had got me, like she does every year. And, with my smile still smiling, I picked up my copy of *A Christmas Carol*, snuggled down, and promised myself I'd finish it before sleep.

It was Boxing Day by the time I reached the end, and the house was silent. I thumped the book shut, and stared at the front cover, letting the story of Scrooge sink in. Then I skimmed back through it, looking at the passages I'd highlighted along the way, reflecting on how much my book looked like the ones Elijah had got through before me. I found the page I was looking for and nodded to myself. This was it. The diamond of the story. I scrambled out of bed, looking for my new notebook hidden under a Cadbury selection box. I yanked it out, and a pen, and opened it to the first page. There's something so poignant about marking the first page of an empty notepad. And the nicer the stationery, the higher the stakes. I hesitated, wondering if I really wanted to start it this way. Then the pen was bleeding ink onto the page, my handwriting staining the thick paper of this fresh start. My hand moved for me until the line was written. And when I read it back, I was glad I'd started the notepad this way.

> *"No space of regret can make amends for one life's opportunity misused."*

I closed the book with a *thwack*, shuffled down under my heavy tog duvet and stumbled wonderfully into the nicest of sleeps.

CHAPTER 16

Elijah: Happy Boxing Day. Does anyone ANYWHERE know what that means?
Elijah: You're not allowed to google it.

Paige: Morning! Umm, I thought it was because you put all your Christmas presents into boxes?

Elijah: Just after you've received them? Shove them in a box the next day? Oh my God, you're SO ungrateful.
Elijah: Remind me never to get you a Christmas present.

Paige: Does this book not count?
Paige: PS: It loves its new box home.

Elijah: Heathen! I can't believe you put Dickens in a box.

Elijah: He's going to send three spirits to haunt you and make you think about what you've done.

Paige: Jeez. Is that his default way to solve problems? A bit dramatic, don't you think?

Elijah: LOL
Elijah: I wrote that because I did, literally, laugh out loud.

Paige: *bows*

Elijah: What are you doing today anyway? I'm in divorced parents hell. I have to go to my dad's house and have Christmas again and pretend it is actually still Christmas.

Paige: You are gaslighting Christmas.

Elijah: LOL OMFG

Paige: I am hiding in my room away from my hungover parents, and feeling smug about the fact I've finished A CHRISTMAS CAROL already.

Elijah: You have? I'm only up to the ghost

of Christmas present. I blame my mum making me pretend to be all happy families yesterday. Have you sifted yet?

Paige: *bows*

Elijah: I knew you would've. Gah! OK, wait for me to catch up. I'll get lots of reading done tomorrow when the gaslighting of Christmas is done. Want to meet up on New Year's Eve for coffee to compare our findings?

Paige: Sure. That would be great!

The days leading to New Year's Eve dragged so badly I felt like I was crawling along on my stomach using my elbows.

"Alexa, why won't time hurry up?"

"Your computer may be slow for a number of reasons. When did you last update it? How much memory have you used…?"

"That isn't what I meant."

Silence.

"Alexa, what is *A Christmas Carol* about?"

"It's a festive tale of redemption and compassion."

"Alexa, I love you."

The song "Can't Take My Eyes Off You" started playing from the speakers.

"Was that an '*I love you too*'?"

Silence.

A day sludged past. Another day passed even sludgier than the previous day's sludge. I was always too nervous to message Elijah first, and always waited before replying. I convinced myself I was annoying and needy and desperate, and he'd smell it on me and not want to message any more. But he messaged regularly, and our conversations were long and rambling, philosophical and funny. It was such a weird juxtaposition – my phone pinging silently with alerts, while my parents hovered around Adam like flies, and hardly acknowledged me at all. At least Dad was being calm. It was almost worth all the ignoring for that.

Far too slowly, the last day of the year arrived. I woke up super early – a pathetically eager response to a simple coffee meet-up. Elijah hadn't mentioned New Year's Eve night, but I assumed he had great fun plans, like everyone else in the universe who wasn't me. Adam was going into town with who he now referred to as his "hometown friends". Dad and Mum were doing their annual jolly to the local four-star hotel's "Shindig". Yes, that was actually what it was called. None of them had asked me what I was doing.

I started getting ready at twelve, wondering if maybe I was more like my mum than I'd thought. I washed my hair, and found a YouTube tutorial to work out how to blow-dry it in a nice poofy way. It came out only a tenth as good as in the video but, still, a huge improvement. I stole a few pumps of Mum's nice-smelling creams from the bathroom and blinked my old crusty mascara onto my eyelashes. I was even grateful for the mustard hat-and-scarf set Mum had got me for Christmas. I arranged the rest of my outfit around it, after asking Alexa what went with yellow.

By two, I was all ready.

By two-thirty, I took off my hat, scarf and gloves because I was too hot.

At three, I put them all back on again.

At three-fifteen, I went downstairs with my bag.

"Just off out," I told Dad, who was watching the TV in his favourite chair.

He nodded.

"Just off out," I called up the stairs. My reply was the running water of Mum's shower. Adam, at least, called down a disinterested "Bye".

It was dark already, the Christmas lights now taunting everyone rather than cheering them.

I kept checking my phone, for a message from him cancelling. I thought I'd be first to arrive as I was ten minutes early. I looked through the coffee shop window to find it empty compared to the week before. But there, among the non-crowd, was Elijah, sitting at the same table as last time, lost completely in *A Christmas Carol*.

I felt a ridiculously overwhelming urge to break into

tears. He *had* come. Of his own free will.

I took some deep breaths and, when satisfied I'd disguised my patheticness, I put a smile on my face and walked through the door.

CHAPTER 17

The warmth from the central heating was nothing compared to the warmth of Elijah's smile. He even stood up to greet me, arms open for a hug.

"Paige, hi. Oh my God, you have to try the festive orange hot chocolate. I've only just discovered it and it's being discontinued tomorrow and won't be back till the sixteenth of November NEXT YEAR, can you believe it? Life giveth and life taketh away. Anyway, get one, get one. I'm going to get another. I've already had two. Full of sugar, can you tell?"

I laughed, shedding off my layers on the chair opposite him. "Okay, I'll get one. Though maybe you need to take a break?"

"What? Never. I need the sugar otherwise we'll never make it till midnight."

I went up to order, smiling.

We'll.

Did he really just say that? Was our one-hour coffee

window actually an eight-hour one? I glanced back at him as the barista steamed milk for us and he was glued to his book.

Elijah broke into another giant smile when I handed over his drink.

"You sure you should have a third? I'm jittering just looking at you."

He held out a shaking hand and laughed. "Discontinued tomorrow, remember? We must seize the day, Paige. Carpe diem, etc. Anyway, you've not tried it yet. Try it. Try it now."

"Okay." I sat down, blew on my drink and took a hot slurp. He watched my face change. "Oh my actual God."

"I know, right."

"They can't discontinue this," I said. "It would be a crime against milky drinks."

"Now can you see why I'm on my third?"

"I withdraw my initial judgement and humbly apologize."

"Good. Anyway…" He gestured out to me. "How are you? How was Christmas? Doesn't it seem like the longest of times ago?"

I nodded. "Christmas was…fine. Yep. Same old. You?"

"Oh yes. Nothing like the adverts at all, as usual. Though my stepmum managed to buy me one present that vaguely gave me a vague idea she had the slightest inkling of who I am as a person for the first time ever, so that gave me the tiniest hope."

"What was the present?"

"Some socks."

"Oh right. Any particular kind?"

"Navy blue."

"Well."

"This is huge progress, Paige. You see, I have feet. My feet need socks. She gets me, she finally gets me."

I took another syrupy slurp of my drink. "I'll take your socks and raise you a generic knitted hat and scarf set." I pointed to myself, then felt weird that I'd been mean about my mum.

"It's generic but yellow suits you."

I then felt weird that Elijah had complimented me and hid behind my cup again. "So, er, you don't get on with your stepmum then?" I asked.

"Nah, it's nothing as dramatic as that. No, just her and my dad...they have their own family...they don't have time to really know me. Which is fine. Fine. But you know, also not great. But not awful enough to merit whinging about, you know?"

"God, I know," I said. "Your stepmum should meet my dad..."

The second I said it I was seized with guilt. Elijah noticed. He didn't say anything though. He just picked up his book and returned to sunny weather mode. "So then... I think I'm going to win this sifting competition. No biggy. But I'm quite sure I sifted to the sweetest of sweet spots in this bad boy." He flicked the faded front cover.

I raised my eyebrows. "Oh, really?"

"How cute will it be if we sifted the same sentence?"

I dug around in my bag. "I mean, that would be something."

"It would mean we would definitely have to get married. Right away. We'd have to elope to Gretna Green."

I ducked down to put my bag on the floor, using my hair to cover up my instantaneous blush. I knew he was joking, but still. Elijah should know better than to joke about something like that when he was as good-looking as he was. I sat back up, and tried to continue acting totally unflustered. "Right, so how are we going to do this?"

Elijah bit his lip, and grinned. "Well, we can do it two ways. One, two, three, then show…or take it in turns to reveal, with a brief speech citing why this quote is the best quote in the book."

"Elijah, I have not prepared a *speech*."

"Those are the best types of speeches. Ones without prep. Straight from the heart." He started rifling through the pages. "Shall I go first? I love going first. To be honest, if I don't go first, I won't concentrate properly on your speech as I'll be too busy thinking about mine."

I snort-laughed at his total, blunt honesty. "That sounds like an area for personal development."

"I'll add it to the hugely long list. God, this drink is good. Hang on, let me have a bit more." He took three giant slurps, giving himself a tiny chocolate moustache. "Right, okay." He wiped his mouth and did a loud, dramatic cough that echoed around the coffee shop. "Here it is…*A Christmas Carol*'s most significant line is… '*I wear the chain I forged in life,' replied the Ghost. 'I made it link by link, and yard by yard.'"*

He looked up at me over the top of his yellowed page. "Same as you?"

I shook my head. "Nope. A noble effort though."

"Bollocks. Now we can't elope to Gretna Green."

"Alas. And my mum had bought a hat."

Still somewhat uncomfortable with his hint of flirting that couldn't possibly be flirting, I tapped the top of his book. "So, why this quote?"

"Do you like it? I really like it."

I nodded again. "I like it. I'm not sure I picked up on it when I read it, so I'm interested to know what landed with you that didn't land with me."

His grin rose to both of his eyebrows. "Well, I liked the metaphor in it. How our lives are chains that we make, one link at a time. Because that's all life is, right? Just a bunch of tiny decisions, one after the other? And if you make bad decisions and more bad decisions, decisions that hurt people in particular, well, it drags you down over time. You're, like, pinned to your cruelty." He sat back in his chair. "Plus, karmically, I like the idea that if you're a twat, it means, when you die, you have to literally drag the chains around with you in the afterlife."

He beamed at me proudly. "And so, Miss Vickers, FURTHERMORE, and in conclusion, I believe this to be the strongest sentence in *A Christmas Carol*. Thank you for your A star, and your sticker, and your trophy. I will be taking bookings up until the end of the year." He stood up and bowed in all directions, confusing the barista clearing the table next to us.

"Bravo, bravo," I said, clapping quietly.

He sat down. "Tough act to follow, Vickers. I'm worried for you."

"I'm worried for me too."

His speech had already found a comfy warm spot in my heart. I'd read the book twice over Christmas and not noticed that line, but now, with his view on it, it came alive and danced and made me love it.

"Right, missy. Your turn."

"Hang on. I just need some of this sweet chocolate milk from the gods." I composed myself with the cup to my lips. Everything about this social interaction was still too much. Felt too good. Too natural. Too long overdue. Too precious. Like it was going too fast. I was scared to gorge on it, worried it would make me sick.

Fuelled by the sugar, I picked up my book. "Right, here we go… *No space of regret can make amends for one life's opportunity misused.*"

Elijah sat back in the chair, letting out a long whistle, and ran his hands through his hair. "Woah, strong contender."

"Thank you. I thought so."

"And your speech? From the heart, remember?"

I looked down at the underlined text, and traced it with my thumb. "I guess I like how…blunt it is. About regret, and how…pointless an emotion it is. How regret can't bring anything back. Can't transport you in time to redo things. Like, we only get one life. One. One opportunity at every moment we are given, and every moment we are given is totally irreplaceable…these precious gifts. And, if you waste them, then…well, *regret*, what do you do with it? It makes no amends at all. Like you said, if life is just a bunch of decisions that make you who you are, if you don't take advantage of life because you're scared, or you upset people by being an arsehole, regret doesn't make amends. Regret just proves you're a coward, or a dick. Or both."

The page blurred and waves of pointless regret washed over me as I reflected on my own tiny, quiet existence and all the nothingness I'd done with the opportunity of life. I blinked. Gulped.

But I haven't been cruel, I reminded myself.

I may not have done much, but at least I hadn't ever really hurt anyone. At least I didn't have the regret of that. The only harm I'd ever done was to myself.

I made myself look up and Elijah's eyes were waiting for me. He was quiet for the first time since I'd met him. A heaving sigh of a moment passed between us, cupped us in its hands, as we sat quietly and looked at one another. A moment so huge surely he was feeling it too?

Another one of life's opportunities, and what was I going to do with it?

Nothing. I just stared back and waited for him to make the call.

Elijah shook his head, pulling a pantomime impressed face, and chose to end the moment.

"Goddamnit, Miss Super Sifter. I knew that you'd win."

CHAPTER 18

We flicked through the rest of Dickens, reminiscing about watching *The Muppet Christmas Carol* as children.

"Gonzo should always be Dickens, always." Elijah almost knocked over his drink, he was so high on sugar. "It's the best casting of anyone in anything, ever."

I nodded a lot – feeling the effects of my second drink. "My favourite muppet is Beaker," I said.

"Beaker? Which one's that?"

"The really thin orange one who sort of squeaks instead of talks."

"Oh my God – the super nervous one? I love him! Beaker's his name?" Elijah started clapping and laughing. "*Beaker.* That's brilliant. God, you've successfully sifted the muppets too, and found the best muppet. You have a gift."

The cafe emptied out and I got more and more twitchy. The staff eyed our empty cups, checking their watches, making hushed conversations about New Year plans. I couldn't fully listen to Elijah as I was falling down a spiral staircase of neediness.

What are we doing next? Will we just say goodbye? Is he bored of me? Or did he mean what he said about us staying up till midnight? Can he smell how much I want this? Is that off-putting? Am I showing it on my face?

His random rant about Blue Monday was interrupted by a brusque lady telling us they were closing in ten. "Yeah, so, think how much money the drugs companies make off us being sad..." He picked up his phone to check the time. "Woah. That went quickly. I was talking too much again, wasn't I? Time flies when you're being attention-seeking..."

"You weren't talking too much."

"Well you were definitely listening too much. SO rude. All that listening."

"I..."

"Relax, I'm joking." He clapped his hands. "Right. Where next?"

"I...I dunno." I found myself scarcely able to talk.

"Well, it's not midnight for hours yet. But it's also freezing cold. And all the shops are shut apart from the off-licences and they won't serve us anyway. So..." He picked up his empty cup, passing it from hand to hand. "You could come to mine, if you like?"

"Huh?"

"I mean, my mum's having this stupid party, which, as you can imagine, is going to be the worst thing ever. Just a bunch of psychologists, standing around, drinking Malbec, and congratulating themselves on how brilliant they are. There's actual nibbles. That's the word my mum used… *nibbles*." He shuddered. "But, anyway, it means there's food and we can just stay upstairs. But if you're busy, or if it sounds lame as hell, well, we never made any plans, did we?" When he glanced over at me, he was blushing. The tiniest hint of it, but still.

"Going to yours sounds great," I managed.

"Really?"

"Yeah. Warm. Nibbles. What else does anyone need? As long as your mum doesn't mind, of course?"

"No. She won't mind. I mean, she may be a bit weird for a moment because you're a girl, but I'll explain to her it's nothing like that, you know."

Oh…

I mean, I'd assumed as much. I mean, we didn't even really know each other. We'd only met twice. I'd tried very hard not to think of him like that. But still.

"Exactly," I said, not blinking.

"And you don't have anything else on tonight?"

I considered fibbing for a second but a throb of instinct told me to be honest with Elijah. "No, nothing. Usually I stay up and watch Jools Holland. But that's been ruined since I found out he films it in *September* or something and fakes being excited about the countdown."

Elijah's face erupted into a giant grin. "Lies. Lies. Everywhere there are more damn lies. Great, great." He knocked over his empty cup. "Whoops. Sorry. But that's great you can come. Oh shit. I didn't tidy my room. Oh well, never mind. Come on, let's go. I cannot wait to freak out my mum. Can you pretend to have an attachment disorder, just to mess with her?"

"An attachment what?"

"I'll explain on the way there."

It took us several minutes to wrap ourselves back up in the required mounds of winter layers. I arranged my yellow scarf carefully, feeling a swell of gratitude to Mum for buying it, even though I knew hardly any thought had gone into it. As we walked to the nice part of town, I realized I should probably tell my parents where I was.

Paige: Over at a friend's tonight. Back after
midnight. Have a good shindig. Happy
New Year! xxx

Mum didn't reply for over three hours, and then only:

Mum: K. Happy new yr x

Like I was a mate she was sending a generic response to.

"We're here," Elijah said, huffing from our walk up his road.

We stood outside a detached, modern-looking house. He pulled out a key and pushed his way through the green door laden with a tasteful holly wreath. "Honey! I'm home." It echoed around the grand entrance.

I followed him in, trying not to gawp too much. The word *tasteful* could be used about literally everything. Elijah plopped his keys onto the tasteful side table, and we shrugged our coats off and hung them on the tasteful coat stand. We stepped across the tasteful floorboards, following the tasteful jazz music echoing softly along the tasteful vanilla hallway, hung with tasteful art canvases of naked women and then stepped into the tasteful kitchen.

Elijah's mother was at the stove, stirring a pot of mulled wine. She had the same dark hair as him.

"Elijah, darling. I didn't hear you come in. Oh, who's this?"

I found myself practically unable to speak surrounded by all this tasteful tastefulness.

"This is a friend from school, Paige. She's not my girlfriend," he added. "Just a friend."

His mum put her ladle down on a tasteful side plate. She held out a hand. "Paige, was it? Lovely to meet you."

"You too," I squeaked. "Umm. Your house is nice. Very tasteful."

"Oh, is it? Thank you. Well I've tidied, for tonight you see. Having some drinks and nibbles."

It was funny to watch Elijah flinch.

"We're just going to hang upstairs and watch TV," he told her.

"Oh. Okay. You will come down and say hello to everyone,

right?" She picked up the ladle.

"Yeah, sure, whatever. Can we grab some *nibbles*?"

"Go for it. Hang on, I'll get you some from the pantry. You promise you'll come down?"

I watched her pad over to a little door.

"Sorry she's being so weird," Elijah whispered.

"She is?"

"Why's she making mulled wine from scratch? She should just buy bottles of it. It's because she knows they'll ask."

"It smells good."

"It smells phoney."

"Alright."

She returned with a tray of what, as promised, could only be described as "nibbles". Pastry puffs topped with cheese, posh crisps, even posher dips, home-made in an expensive blender.

"You're allowed two beers each from the outside fridge," she told me sternly.

"Oh, that's okay, I don't…"

Elijah lightly trod on my foot, and I realized he might want my allocated beer.

"That's great. Umm, thank you. Cheers. Yeah, thanks."

She examined me again, taking in my yellow knitwear, my make-up free face. "Door open at all times," she said to Elijah, who beetrooted so hard I caught it off him.

* * *

"Oh my GOD, sorry about her. I'm so sorry," he said upstairs on the landing, our feet sinking into the plush carpet. Things were a bit more dishevelled and chaotic up there, and I realized she'd just done a ground-floor tidy to trick the guests into thinking the whole house was like that. There were bookshelves everywhere, half-blocking the entrances to the five doors that led off the landing. All non-fiction wedges with important titles.

The Marshmallow Test, and Other Psychology Lies

Through a Child's Eyes

Naming. Feeling. Healing.

Attached

I plucked *Attached* off the shelf and held it up to Elijah. "Is this the disorder stuff?"

He laughed. "Yeah, that one's quite good actually."

"You've read all these?" I asked in awe – there were so many of them. And they all looked academic and hard.

"I've skimmed through most of them. It's the only way I know what my mum might actually be doing when she's not here." He leaned backwards against a door, nudging it open with his bum. "And, of course, it makes me the most psychologically well-adjusted human ever. Right, this is me. Come on in. I'm warning you, it's generically teenage-boy disgusting."

I followed him into his room. A boy's bedroom. The first boy's bedroom I'd ever been into (Adam's doesn't count). The room was Elijah all over – a haphazard and bizarre creation between four walls. It was painted a calming pale green, which juxtaposed with all the stuff everywhere. He'd essentially made two walls into a pinboard, crammed with a bizarre assortment of papers he must've found interesting – postcards, random quotes from books written out and stuck there, photos ripped from magazines. On his desk he had piles of books everywhere, so much so there was hardly any working space. I spotted a red pen and my heart twinged. Above his bed was the only thing that had any order: a bookshelf with all the books lined up neatly. I stepped further in and realized they were all the same book, different editions of *The Catcher in the Rye*.

"Woah," I said, walking closer.

"My Holden collection? Oh yeah, it's cool, isn't it? I've made myself limit it to English language editions only, not foreign editions. Otherwise I'll get overwhelmed."

"Am I allowed to look?"

He flung out his arm while falling to the bed with a *smush*.

I leaned over and plucked a copy at random. It was navy blue, with the title in silver embossing. I opened it up to see neat, clean pages. "You don't scribble in these copies?" I asked.

"No. I've got one copy I scribble in. The rest I preserve for the sake of…I dunno. Being a bit of a dick, I guess. It's not like I'll ever sell them on."

I opened another edition aimlessly – just giving myself time to digest the strangeness of the situation.

I was in a boy's bedroom.

He was on his bed.

There wasn't really another obvious place to sit, other than the office chair.

"You don't think I'm massively pretentious, do you?"

I put the book back in its spot on the shelf. "Only a tiny amount."

"I mean, you can't be a boy my age and be obsessed with *Catcher in the Rye* and NOT be a little bit pretentious really. If anything, I'm just paying homage to the cliché. Giving it the nod it so deserves."

I put a careful smile onto my cheeks. "You're a true hero."

He returned my smile and saluted. "By the way, I don't smell. And I won't make a move on you or anything. You're allowed to sit on my bed." He patted the space next to him.

"I can't believe you're making a thing about it." I was the colour of ketchup as I reluctantly perched next to him, hugely aware of his body and the exact placement of all of his limbs.

"Naming an issue actually reduces anxiety of the issue," he explained, wagging a finger at me. "I read it in one of Mum's books. Point out the elephant in the room and then everyone instantly calms down about the elephant."

I shook my head. "Not in my household," I muttered – thinking of the Dumbo colony that I called *home*.

"Sounds like your family need to read some of my mum's books."

I didn't know what to say.

"Sorry, I didn't mean to upset you."

"No, it's fine." My hands were suddenly the most interesting pair of hands in the world. I swirled them around each other as I felt guilt plunging into me like an injection. I felt like I'd betrayed my parents somehow, just by offering that stupid joke. "So, umm, what time are your mum's friends arriving?"

Elijah's didn't press further but his energy dropped a few points, like he was scared he'd upset me again. I didn't know why I felt so weird. I blamed the bedroom.

He rolled his eyes. "Mum's very important friends arrive from seven. You'll know when they're here. They make this noise in a group. It's a bit like '*a yah a yah, rah, a yah, ya, rah, rah, yah.*' Jools doesn't start for ages. Have you ever seen *Carrie*? Thought not. Hang on, I'll just download it."

He got up without giving me time to respond and left me alone on the bed. I used the opportunity to claim a little bit more space without worrying I'd accidentally touch him. Elijah picked his sleek laptop off his desk then collapsed back down so we were touching slightly, despite all my efforts. "I was thinking you'd love *Carrie* after you were talking about those dickheads in your year." He pulled up a film still showing a teen girl covered in blood.

"Eww." I scrunched up my face.

"It's great, I promise. They tried to remake it a few years ago, but the original is the best. As always. Right, come on. Can you hit the light switch? You have to watch a horror film in the dark."

"Okay." I nervously got up and plunged us into darkness,

perching once again on the bed, recreating some space. I felt Elijah smile in the dark.

"Right," he said, as he hit the space bar. "Here we go."

CHAPTER 19

Holy hell, there were a lot of distractions getting between me and *Carrie*. I mean, the film was amazing and terrifying, but, Elijah did *not* warn me that it opened on a scene in a school changing room where all the girls were freaking naked. *Naked.* I was watching naked people on screen, WITH A BOY. Even my stomach lining was blushing, though Elijah didn't act like it was weird at all. Then the main character, Carrie, only goes and starts her freakin' PERIOD, so that was fine. Totally fine, watching a girl bleed period all over herself, stark naked, while the other naked girls chucked tampons at her. Did I mention how naked everyone was? Elijah seemed to think this was incredibly normal, just watching the film with his foot slightly twitching, while next to him, I was dying. His doorbell kept going and all the yah-yahers arrived.

Ding…

Clop clop clop…

Door opening.

YAH!

YAH!

Oh nice to YAH YAH YAH…

You too YAH YAH, come in and YAH YAH YAH…

Clop clop clip clip clop clop. *Door to kitchen opening.*

Several YAH!s.

YOU'RE HERE YAH…

I AM YAH YAH YAH…

And then the yahs would merge into one collective auditory mass of yahing.

"They really do sound like all they're saying is '*yah*'," I remarked at one point, when Carrie had thankfully put some clothes on.

"I told you. Don't worry. You'll learn to tune it out."

In time, I sort of did, but there was more distraction in the form of Elijah himself. Him being a boy. It being dark. Us being on a bed. I was highly attuned to the heat that grew in the small gaps between us. To Elijah's breathing. How the laptop moved up and down slightly with his lungs. How I had to lean into him to see the screen properly. I concentrated so hard on coming across chill that two scenes passed and I couldn't tell you what happened.

Then it all started to kick off and I was finally able to focus. Carrie got pranked by the popular kids at the prom so started murdering everyone with her telekinesis. It finished with one final scare, so huge that I yelped and hid behind a pillow while Elijah pissed himself laughing.

He held out his platter of snacks to me while I hyperventilated. "Nibble?"

I shuddered and he laughed again, before chucking two squares of pastry into his mouth, one into each cheek like a hamster.

After the credits rolled and my heart rate had normalized, I turned to watch him finish chewing.

"That group of people in the film," I said. "The ones who pranked Carrie. You're right. They do remind me of Grace and that lot in school."

"That's why I thought you'd like the movie."

I reached out and shoved a pastry square into my face just as jazz music started rising up from downstairs. I glanced down at my phone. It was ten. Two hours until a new year.

"I've been working on the school yearbook," I told him. Wanting to unlock it all for some reason. Elijah sensed it and muted the laptop. "Ms Gordon got me involved because I'm on the newspaper, but the whole thing has been commandeered by the popular people. They're turning it into just this giant piece of…I dunno…propaganda legacy for themselves. They're using it to bully people, to remind them of stories they'd rather forget, to cement their popularity in the pages. It's such bullshit." I shook my head and found my fists clenching. "Really worrying bullshit, and yet Ms Gordon doesn't see it, and well, me…I'm just allowing it to happen too." I looked up to find Elijah listening intently, hamster cheeks full. "I'm letting them get away with it," I said. "Like, I'm on the paper, and sometimes I think I would make a good journalist, you know? I'm quite good at watching people and noticing things, but I'm not doing what you're supposed to do as a journalist. I've never actually exposed anyone, I just cover stupid stories about Comic Relief and stuff. I've even stopped going to meetings cos I'm so angry at myself. But, the yearbook…This is even worse, and I'm just letting it happen."

Elijah finally swallowed. "Why?" he asked softly.

I ran my hands through my hair, even though my fingers were greasy from the pastry.

"Because I'm scared," I admitted. "Because I don't want them to spread stories about me…"

"So you're letting them spread stories about everyone else?"

I winced as he said it so matter of factly. "I guess 'letting' is the right word. Yes."

"Hmm."

It wasn't a judgemental "*Hmm*", more a thoughtful one. He put the platter of nibbles down. His teeth glowed solidly blue from the laptop light as he broke into a grin.

"Want to kill them all?" he asked.

I snorted. "What? Like Carrie?"

"I don't know telekinesis but we can destroy them in another way."

"I think murder might be a bit extreme," I joked to confirm he was also joking.

"No. Let's not actually kill anyone. But there's other ways of destroying nasty people without harming anyone. Kill their story," he explained. "Kill the propaganda. Suffocate out the unkindness."

I sighed. He said it like it was an easy thing to do. Like standing up to people who could ruin your life was as simple as popping to the shops. But popping to the shops didn't pump my stomach with anxiety like the thought of calling out Grace and co did. It was hard enough living in my house: with my dad, being constantly afraid of upsetting him, and constantly upset about him hardly noticing me. I wasn't sure I had the strength to have school get hard too. School was just something to survive.

"And how do I do that?" I asked.

Elijah gestured out to his stack of books. "Easy. You take out a red pen and you start telling the truth from the margins. Keep telling the truth until it's out of the margin and it's mainstream."

I shook my head. "That's anything but easy, Elijah."

"Maybe at first, but it gets easier with time."

Even the thought of doing what he said made me feel sick – the need to self-protect roaring up my throat like sour bile. I was filled with exhaustion from dancing the dance between hiding and then hating myself for it, and also feeling stifled and insignificant and wanting to scream about who I was and what I knew.

"I'm going to need to think about what you just said," I said eventually. "It's a lot to take in."

Elijah smiled. "Well, just as well Jools Holland is about to start faking New Year's Eve for us. How very fitting."

* * *

We sat and watched Jools pretend it wasn't September. I wondered where he was right then. If Jools's New Year's Eve tradition was to watch himself on television? I asked Elijah and he laughed. Gradually, I got more used to us being on a bed together. I leaned back into his pillows and tucked my feet under the cover. I sensed him looking over in the dark and smiling as he saw me unwind. The noises from below us grew louder as the yah-yahers got drunker. They cranked up the jazz music, which is not what anyone should ever do to jazz, and we had to crank up Jools in order to hear over it. At ten to midnight, Elijah's mum appeared in the open door, eyes red and misty.

"I'm not interrupting anything, am I?"

Elijah didn't turn his face away from the screen. "Yep. Right now. In fact, this is how all the kids have sex these days," he replied.

"Elijah!" I showed my horrified eyes to his mum, though she just gave a wry smile.

"We're just watching TV, Mum."

"Well I want you to come down for the fireworks. To meet everyone."

"We're good up here, thanks." He still wouldn't look at her.

"Please. Come on," she pleaded. "They're all asking after you. Just for the countdown, and for the show."

"Your whole life is a show," he muttered, grappling himself out of bed, whilst I followed nervously behind.

Downstairs, we were swallowed into a collective drunken mist. Old people stumbled towards us with bad breath, grabbing Elijah to tell him how much they'd heard about him and asking, "Is this your girlfriend?" while we both shook our heads.

"Outside, outside," his mum bellowed, stumbling in her heels. "Onto the patio. Now please. We only have five minutes."

It was freezing – the sort of air that catches in your lungs, and I folded my arms in a fruitless effort to keep warm. We were ushered onto a tasteful patio, where we waited for "*Darrell from the lab*" to start the display.

"I'm so sorry about this," Elijah kept muttering. "Honestly, I'm so sorry."

"It's fine." I didn't understand why he was so embarrassed. "It's fireworks. Who doesn't like fireworks?"

I was contemplating what he'd said about killing someone's stories. Like so many of his words, the idea had dug into my consciousness, pulling down mental levers.

We were pushed to the front.

"God, this is so boring, I really am sorry."

"Don't be sorry. It's great."

There was a muddle about the countdown. Someone started counting too early.

"No, no, not yet," his mum squawked. "We're going by the BBC." But people had got all the way down to four before she finally stopped them.

"Okay, now now now now NOW!" she orchestrated.

"Ten, nine, eight..." But it was tough to re-rally the troops and we all just mumbled random numbers.

"Happy New Year!" she yelled.

It took a moment for us all to realize that this was it – the key moment. The date had flipped over to a fresh diary within a second.

"Happy New Year," everyone parroted. Then they understood it, and then they said it louder. The celebrating kicked in twenty seconds too late. Kisses were exchanged. A few party poppers unleashed. Fireworks started exploding at rival parties around us.

"Happy New Year, Sifter." Elijah pulled me in for a hug and a quick kiss on the cheek.

"Happy New Year," I stumbled out, shocked by the kiss.

He examined my face for a moment, in all its teeth-chattering glory. "I'm glad we met," he told me. "I think this year's going to be nicer because of it."

"Yeah. Me too."

It was the truest thing I'd ever said, and I didn't want the moment to leave us.

"FIREWORKS."

Darrell from the lab kicked into action and Elijah's lawn exploded into sparkles. Everyone oohed and ahed as bangers flung themselves, squealing, into the sky, before smashing against the night, raining rose petals of colour onto us.

"Should old acquaintance be forgot," a random psychologist started singing.

"And never brought to mind," another added.

The group descended into the inevitable jaunty screeching of "Auld Lang Syne". Two men grabbed my hands, making me cross my arms, then jumped up and down, shaking them. I was lost in a circle of strangers, singing into this unknown new year, with very tasteful fireworks exploding above me, and I hadn't felt so happy in so very long. Sparklers were then distributed. Elijah escorted our hissing flames away from everyone, and my socks got soaked in freezing dew as I stepped onto his lawn.

"So, new year," he said, the sparkler lighting up his face. "Any new year's resolutions?"

I was a bit mesmerized by my firework and how, as I waved it, it left a faint trail behind it, one that died too quickly. I started spelling my name. *P…a…i…g…e* and stamped myself against the blackness for a millisecond before the light trail faded. The song we'd just sung brought back a vivid memory of Ruby and me spending Bonfire Night at her nice house. Waving our sparklers and pretending they were magic wands. Ruby, who made me so happy and feel so seen, and then who betrayed me so utterly.

The look on her face when I opened my front door…

"Not yet, no. I'll have to think about it. You?"

I listened to Elijah's excitable overly-ambitious plans to learn Japanese while I watched my firework reach the end of its short life. I flung it about to get the most joy out of its dying moments.

"Should old acquaintance be forgot…" I sang to myself as we made our way back into Elijah's house and into a new year. I looked down at the charred remains of my dead sparkler, and forced myself to push thoughts of Ruby from my head. "...and never brought to mind."

Year Nine

Do you remember when...

...**Cara** bunked off for a **whole** term and somehow didn't get **expelled**?

...**Sam** and **Grace** almost got **chucked out** of the funfair for **kissing** too **passionately** on the waltzer?

...**Joe** **FINALLY** hit **puberty** and made up for it by pulling **TWELVE** girls in one night at the **Coconuts Club**?

Year Nine was the year when we stopped being kids and started becoming adults. It's when so much young love blossomed. Sam and Grace were SO CUTE back then, weren't they? It's great that they're such good friends now. Shows how mature we are...

WHAT REALLY HAPPENED

Year Nine.

Year freakin' Nine.

I mean, where do you even start with Year Nine?

If life was fair, and politicians knew what they were doing, they'd just give all students Year Nine off.

Everything that is the most awful happens in Year Nine.

Firstly, it's where puberty hits everyone the hardest. Almost daily, someone will come in showcasing a brand-new pair of overnight boobs, or a couple of centimetres of height, or a broken voice. All the mental health problems show up as spontaneously as a dropped bollock. Year Nine – *boosh!* Along come self-harm scars, and clinical depression, and suicide attempts, and people saying they're just doing it for attention, and doctors not quite knowing if they should prescribe SSRIs because you're not sixteen yet. Coincidently, that's why Cara "bunked off" a whole term of school. Because she was so clinically ill she had to go to hospital. And maybe she was safer there, because Year Nine is when girls become… how do I put this politely?

Utter bitches, the lot of them.

Your friends become your tormentors. Although, come on, they're not bullying you, you just can't take a joke! The psychological warfare puts Putin to shame. One day you come into school and you say hi to your supposed friends but, overnight, they've been discussing how terrible you are behind your back and are now freezing you out without admitting that's what they're doing. So they'll go for lunch without you but say they forgot. Or you'll be walking home and they'll all just randomly run off and leave you there, laughing, pretending it's okay. A female friendship group will then hold a little "committee", telling their chosen victim, in grown-up voices, everything that's wrong with them as a person and how nobody wants to be their friend any more, and… why are you crying? We're just trying to be honest, jeez.

Year Nine. We should all get a special medal and six months of counselling on the NHS.

CHAPTER 20

7th January

Everyone in our year is calling Laura Goddard a slut, and she's been socially ostracized.

Something serious went down at the Awfuls' New Year's Eve party. I could taste the gossip the moment I got into school on the seventh of January. The air was ripe and thick with it. Whisperings of suspicion were confirmed when, that very lunchtime, Laura Goddard sat alone in the canteen – staring into her buddha bowl like a punished vegan puppy, while Grace, Amelia and the boys walked past and deliberately ignored her.

By the end of the week, the third most popular girl in my year group was formally christened as "that slut, Laura Goddard".

"What's her supposed crime then?" Elijah asked, on a cold, bright lunch hour two days into term. We'd escaped through the back entrance of school to this little park around the corner, our hoods up to protect ourselves from the bitter wind. I twisted my face towards him and felt my cheeks burn cold.

"Word on the toilet stall is that she got drunk at New Year and got with Sam Hutchins."

Elijah nodded solemnly. "Right. Okay. And that's a problem because…?"

I mock punched him. "Elijah! Don't pretend you're not aware of the huge and historical romantic entanglement of Grace Langdon and Sam Hutchins?"

"Sorry, I missed this week's copy of *heat* magazine."

"Look. I don't TRY to know this information, it just sort of seeps into my life. So, Grace and Sam went out for a month in Year Nine but broke up because Grace said it was too intense. She said it's clear that they'll get married one day because there's 'such a *thing*' between them, but she's too young for that right now. They make out at occasional parties, before Grace doubles down again and tells him they have to wait for each other."

He clutched his heart with a gloved hand. "Oh my God, Shakespeare, you've been usurped."

"Shut up."

He was still cackling.

"Anyway, Sam is off-limits, even though Grace hasn't technically dated him for two years. But, as I said, Laura, '*the slut*', broke '*girl code*' and '*betrayed*' Grace in a way she '*never thought possible*' and so '*she's out*'."

"I like your enthusiastic use of air quotes there."

"I'm using reported speech."

"Always the journalist."

"That's me. God, it's good to be back." I sighed and readjusted my fluffy hood. "Best days of our lives."

What was hard to admit was that the past two school days *had* been some of the best of my life. Because I had a friend again. Elijah had sent me a message the night before our first day back.

Elijah: Lunch tomorrow? Anywhere but the canteen? It's too early in the year for Darwinism.

That started a new daily ritual of sneaking out the back entrance and escaping for one blissful hour.

Elijah turned towards me and I mirrored him, so we were hood to hood. His hair, stuffed inside, needed cutting and fell into his eyes.

"So, will all of this be in the newspaper? Front page news, surely?"

"Oh yeah. I'm going to win the Pulitzer… No. I've stopped the paper for now, I told you. The yearbook is too much as it is. Plus, the whole school knows about it anyway."

"The whole year group," he corrected me. "I can promise you that no one in the sixth-form common room even knows who Lauren Goddard is."

"Laura."

"You see."

I sighed again and the cold air hurt my throat. "I've got yearbook tonight after school."

"You keep telling their stories for them." He said it in such a superior, knowing voice that I felt a jolt of anger.

"Don't. Come on. You make me feel bad when you say stuff like that."

His face softened and he reached out and brushed my hand. "Sorry."

I scrunched up my nose and batted off his hand. Too angry to even enjoy the physical contact. "I get what you're saying but it's just not worth the energy. Nothing I do or say will make any difference to how that lot behave. I'd be throwing myself under a bus for no reason."

"Can you at least put a typo in there? Spell Grace's name wrong or something in the yearbook?"

"Activism by typos?" I smiled, despite myself.

"Hey, it's better than no activism at all."

"Hmm."

His words had been festering in me since New Year's Eve. Making me think I should *do* something about it all, rather than just write about it in my spiteful notepads. But I also felt this shrill anger at him for not getting it. Lack of fear isn't always a sign of a stronger person, it's often just a sign that someone has an easy life.

With that all said, Elijah's judgement was still marinading in my brain later the same day when I was back in the newsroom with Ms Gordon and the rest of the committee.

"Paige, Happy New Year," she greeted me. "This is the first time I've seen you all term."

"It's only the third day."

"Still, I missed you." She was particularly hipster that day, experimenting with a giant pair of red prescription-free glasses, paired with a neon pink corporate jumpsuit. Her hair was pulled up in a bun to showcase a new undercut above her left ear.

I slouched in my chair next to Daisy. "I like your make-up today," I found myself telling her, without thinking first.

Her hand went to her face in surprise. "Oh, thanks. I got the eyeshadow for Christmas."

I had spoken to someone unexpectedly and the world hadn't imploded. Shocked, I continued. "It suits you," I added. It did. It was green and she'd put it all around her eyes the moment the bell had gone.

"Cheers."

"You're welcome."

I wondered where my burst of social confidence had come from.

"They're late again," Daisy muttered.

I didn't need to ask who.

"They won't miss the meeting about Year Nine. Not when that's the year Sam ate the battery."

Daisy smirked. "I'm surprised they're not writing their own screenplay about it."

The door pushed open just as I was sniggering, feeling warm at the unexpected social interaction, and in they came. Minus a Laura but, surprisingly, plus a *Cara*.

"Sorry, are we late?" Grace didn't sound sorry at all. The current drama suited her. She'd made even more of an effort with her appearance. She seemed to have curling-tonged her hair before she'd tied it into a ponytail.

"We were just starting," Ms Gordon said. "Cara! What a surprise! Sit down. It's good to see you. Are you coming to help with the yearbook?"

"Yeah, if that's okay?"

Cara looked slightly shell-shocked at her sudden leap up the social greasy pole. I mean, she'd always been somewhat popular. She was pretty and had developed a weird mystique after coming back from hospital.

"The more, the merrier. Brilliant. Lovely!"

We all moved our chairs to make space and none of them said thank you. Amelia, in particular, seemed to be in total bitch mode.

"Make room, for God's sake," she hissed at Daisy.

Ms Gordon put her glasses on top of her head. "Right," she said. "We've got Year Seven and Eight sorted, so we're pretty much on track. It's looking good. It might be the most polished yearbook this school has ever produced."

Grace and Amelia lit up, taking the compliment for us all. Cara watched them and then sat up in her chair too, pretending she'd had something to do with it.

"So, those pages are all ready to be signed off, and we can move on to Year Nine. Yes, Amelia?"

Amelia had shot her hand up. "Yeah, miss, about those

pages." She spread her gelled fingernails out on the table. "Well, sorry Laura isn't here today because she's not feeling very well. She's gone straight home. But she told us to tell you, urgently, that she doesn't want some of those photos of her used any more. She's got all insecure about there being photos of her before her braces." Amelia was going for best actress and best supporting all in one go. Her performance of *concerned and caring friend* was utterly faultless. "We told her she was being stupid and that she's *gorgeous.*" She rolled her eyes. "*But* she got really upset. So, like, is it okay if we take some of those photos out? Put some of the backups in?"

The room was still. We all knew that Laura wouldn't want her photos to be taken out. We waited, wondering if Ms Gordon would fall for it. "Oh no, of course," she said, swallowing it whole. "We don't want *anything* in there that upsets people. It's supposed to be a happy thing to cherish."

"Cheers, miss." Amelia gave everyone a smirk, confirming we were in on the joke. "Thanks for being so understanding."

I, as usual, did absolutely nothing to stop this. I pondered how Laura might be feeling. She had given five years of service to popularity. She'd sacrificed her kindness, her integrity and her identity to the pursuit of being best mates with Grace and Amelia and being *that popular kid in school.* One drunken mistake at one party, and it was gone. All for nothing. She was being wiped not only from their table and the canteen, but from the very yearbook. Her entire legacy eroded. And I was doing nothing.

"Fine. Well I hope she feels better soon," said Ms Oblivious.

"Thanks, Ms Gordon." Grace smiled serenely like an angel in a stained-glass window. "We don't mind staying behind to show you the pictures."

"Bless you. Right, now…" Ms Gordon looked down at her notepad. "Let's look at the list of submitted stories for Year Nine memories. Cara?"

Jumpy, she nodded at the mention of her name. "Yep?"

Ms Gordon smiled as she lowered her glasses. "It says here that you…er…bunked off school for a whole term?"

"That's a joke, miss. I was away cos I was sick."

"Oh, yes. Sorry. We don't have to have a memory about that."

Cara darted a look at Grace. "It's fine," she said, not sounding particularly fine. "I don't mind writing about going to hospital."

"Oh, really? That's quite a…huge thing to do…"

"Isn't she *so* brave?" Grace interrupted like a crashing truck. "Cara, it's just so inspirational."

Cara swelled up from the compliment. "I don't know…"

"No, it's the actual bravest. Like, telling everyone about how mentally sick you were and what you've overcome, that's just…you're like a *celebrity* or something. It's going to give the yearbook such an…authentic honest vibe."

I saw Cara wince. Like this story didn't fit the horror of what she'd gone through. But she was in the clan now.

And they wanted an emotional tell-all for their project. "Yeah, I guess," she said.

Ms Gordon took that as a yes. "Well, only if you're sure."

"*Are* you sure?" I found myself asking Cara loudly.

I felt the room take a breath.

"*What?*" said Cara.

My voice shook. "I'm just saying, it's a big deal. I mean, if you really want to do it, that's great. But, well, is that how you want to be remembered in the yearbook?"

I had no idea why I was saying this stupid, dangerous thing. Well, I did. Elijah's voice in my head: *You keep telling their stories for them*. I owed nothing to Cara, I hardly knew her. But I could tell she was uncomfortable. Unsure if her mental breakdown was the legacy she wanted to leave behind.

Amelia's face was red with instant anger. "Fucking hell, miss, what is she saying?"

"Don't swear, Amelia."

"But she's being really offensive."

Cara's head twisted around to check their response, trying to figure out if she should be mortally offended or not. I was finding breathing quite hard but forced my face to stay neutral.

"Yeah," Grace said. "You're being so stigmatizing right now."

"I'm not trying to stigmatize anyone." I turned to Ms Gordon. "It's just, isn't it my duty as a journalist to double-check she's really sure she wants this? A whole page dedicated to her illness?"

"What's wrong with having a mental illness?" Amelia practically shouted.

"Nothing at all," I said. "But that still doesn't mean Cara wants it to be the main thing she's remembered for in a yearbook she'll look back on for the rest of her life. It's about informed consent."

"At least she'll *be* remembered," Amelia sneered while the room watched us silently, slack-jawed. "Unlike *some* people. I mean, who even are you?"

"Girls!" Ms Gordon warned. "That's enough."

"It's true, miss," Grace said, her pretty lip curled. "Who even is she? She's making Cara feel bad, when she's being so brave…"

"Stop saying '*Who is she?*'" Ms Gordon clapped her hands three times. "Honestly, girls. Be kind, please." She had that bulging gaze of a teacher out of their depth. Amelia and Grace started laughing nastily, whispering, "*Who is she?*" and descending into hysterics, while Cara stared down at the empty page of her notepad.

"I'm sorry," I backtracked, voice jittery, suddenly terrified of the attention I was drawing to myself. "I honestly didn't mean to offend you, Cara." I turned to her. "I was just checking. I'm not saying it's not really brave, it is. That's why I wanted you to be sure."

And you know what? I could *tell* Cara wasn't sure. She was confused. She wasn't sure if she wanted to write it, and she wasn't sure if she should be angry at me. It must've been a weird week already – plucked out by Grace and shunted up the popularity ladder, given one chance to shine for the last term of school, but on what condition? That she bares her soul in their vanity project? Didn't she want to be remembered for more than this? Like the time she won a prize in Year Ten for her maths coursework? Or the amazing spoken word poem she performed in the school assembly. Grace had never mentioned putting that in the memories section. The stories about the worst things that happen to us always eclipse the good stories. People love to define us by the worst, rather than the best.

Amelia gave her a pointed look and Cara surrendered. She narrowed her eyes at me.

"I think you should mind your own business." She glanced at Amelia again and smiled. "Whoever you are," she added.

I kept blinking, like it would dislodge the pain ripping through me. I'd told myself so many times that I didn't care, but…

Who even is she?

Whoever you are.

Nobody knew.

It was confirmed. Via the official channels of popular spokesperson.

I was nobody.

I knew that already, but it still hurt.

"Girls, please! Or I might have to start giving detentions."

I was blinking so much I basically had my eyes shut. Nobody defended me. Nobody spoke up, or took my side. I couldn't blame them. That was all I'd ever done too.

"I'm sorry," I sighed.

I wished I could unsay it all. Elijah's reassurances about how these girls didn't matter meant nothing. Yes, nobody cared about them outside my year group but, like it or bloody not, I was in this year group, and it mattered, and I didn't matter and that hurt. Also, I'd just broken all my own rules for clearly no reason at all.

"I'm sorry," I repeated, now terrified about my punishment. "I didn't mean to offend anyone."

Cara shrugged. Grace and Amelia looked bored already. Ms Gordon remained useless. "Shall we move on? See who wants to cover Joe's, umm, big night?"

The meeting burst back into normality. Matty put his hand up to volunteer. Jade had some feedback on font choices. From the outside, we had moved on. But I knew differently.

I'd gone from *Who even are you?* to painting a bullseye on my own forehead.

Time would tell which was worse.

CHAPTER 21

The house was disquietingly quiet when I got in. I closed the door, listened. Sent out bat signals to pick up emotional radar readings. I couldn't sense Mum's nervous energy. There was something not quite right though. I slipped my shoes off, careful to tuck them properly under the shoe rack. I went to check out the living room. Empty. Fine. I walked into the kitchen and stopped in the doorway.

A smashed plate on the floor.

My heart cracked – sending fault lines throughout my body. I stared at the smithereens of the plate, like it could somehow grow a mouth and tell me what happened. Who smashed it? Why had nobody cleaned it up? Nightmare stories played themselves through my head…then I was startled by a cough upstairs, the squeaking of floorboards.

Adam. I found him in his room, his rucksack wide open, moving piles of clothes into it.

"Adam?"

"Woah, Paige. You scared me." He flicked me a grim

smile, then went to his wardrobe to remove a pile of scented, folded jumpers Mum had laundered for him. He scrunched them into a ball and stuffed them into the bottom of the bag.

"You alright?" I nodded towards his packing, my heart unable to keep up with all these developments.

"What? Yeah. I'm going to go back to uni tonight."

"I thought you still had another week off?"

"I do."

He removed more clothes from his wardrobe and I was too scared to ask what happened. We never talked about anything in this house. "Right."

I watched him pack with an urgency I hadn't seen before. He kept looking at his ticking clock. He pushed in a few T-shirts, and his going-out shirts. Then he started on electricals, crouching under his desk and yanking out numerous charging cords, wrapping them into a tangled ball, stuffing them on top. I just stood and watched, scared. Waiting for him to tell me what happened. Not wanting to know. Not wanting him to break the code and make it real.

"Adam?"

He paused. He wouldn't look at me, but he pushed his thumbs into his eyes.

"Christ, Paige," he said into his hands. "What even is this house? I can't stay a second longer."

He fell onto the bed and curled into a ball. I took one tentative step into his bedroom. I'd never seen Adam like this. He was always glowing in the spotlight. Happy to soak it all up. Not weak...not scared. He was the lucky one out of the two of us, not the broken one.

"You don't realize how toxic it is until you get out," he told his bedroom wall. "You get used to it. We think it's normal, because it is to us. But then, when you leave... I went to uni and, honestly, Paige, it's like taking my first breath of fresh air. Then I came home and it's worse because being away from it makes me realize how bad it is. How bad *he* is."

The fear I felt. He'd broken the code. We didn't talk bad about Dad. Especially Adam.

"He's not awful..." I gasped – worried somehow Dad would hear. "He doesn't..."

"What? Hit us?"

I couldn't believe he'd said it.

"But you worry, don't you? Don't you worry? I worry all the time about Mum. I make myself sick worrying about Mum."

"She...she loves him."

"Oh my God, you're just as bad. It's because you've not left yet. You need to get out, Paige." He leaped up and grabbed my hands, his eyes wide. "Promise me you'll get out. Promise?"

I squeezed his hands back. "What happened, Adam? Downstairs?"

There had never been mess before. Never been Mum missing before.

I watched the story play out on his face and my breath hardly made it to my lungs.

"Did he?" Asking those two words brought so much pain it was like my entire throat had erupted with blades. I danced on a knife's edge waiting for his reply.

"No," Adam replied, after way too long. "He didn't."

"But..."

"Mum smashed the plate."

Relief gushed through me like a surging tide, though this still wasn't going to be a happy story.

"I woke to the sounds of them arguing. Dad had walked to the train station but couldn't get into work because all the trains were cancelled due to signalling problems. He slammed the door so hard when he got back. Then he somehow made it Mum's fault, like he always does. But he was really yelling at her, Paige. Like, I know he sulks, but I've never heard him yell like that before. They must've thought I was out...maybe they're like this when we're out... Anyway, he was screaming stuff like he '*never wanted to stay here*' and how she'd '*forced him*' to live in the '*countryside*' and that's why he never gets promoted." Adam blinked slowly and brought his hands over his cheeks. "Anyway, he stormed out. Slammed the door even harder. The whole house shook. God knows where he's gone. I was about to go check on Mum when I heard the plate smash. She must've thrown it against the wall or something. Then the door slammed and she was gone. I tried calling but she won't pick up. I've waited for hours and she hasn't come back. I dunno. All I know is none of this is normal, Paige. I can't stay. It's too much, I have to go back."

"But you leaving will make it worse," I said.

I shook my head – still trying to take it in. Dad's temper had been getting worse the last few months. His silent treatments lasting longer and used as punishments for even smaller infractions. Was it because Adam left? My imagination was already swerving direction – away from Adam's story to the story of how terrible it was going to be when they came home to find him gone.

"How can it get worse?"

"You know if you leave it will. Please…Adam. Stay. You make him happy."

I don't know why I bothered pleading with him. Adam wasn't Dad, but he wasn't far off. Adam knew how to look after Adam, and looking after Adam was Adam's top priority.

"You can't put that on me," he said, right on cue. "Whatever happens, it's not my fault. You don't get it, Paige. I can't stay here. I hate who I am here. In Bristol…God, I feel so light. Do you have any idea what that feels like? I promised myself I wouldn't get sucked back in when I came home, and I won't let you make me feel guilty about that." His face was set like it was carved from ice. He zipped up his rucksack with a loud rip and tossed it over his shoulder, while I stood helpless. "Look, I'm going to try and catch the four-twenty train." He spoke to the top of my head. "Don't worry. I'll message them when I'm on the train with a story.

I'll say I got my essay deadline wrong or something. That I need to get back to the library."

"That won't be enough. They'll want you to stay and say goodbye."

"Well what about what I want, Paige?" he snapped, sounding so much like Dad that I found my body shrivelling up in exactly the same manner. "Look, I have to get my train. My advice? Don't be here when they get home." He jumped to set his backpack properly. "Anyway, be safe. I'm off. I'll see you at Easter, if I can stand to."

He winked and saluted. The most inappropriate of goodbyes considering what he was doing to us. I stayed in his room for a while after he'd left, my body held still by invisible forces, thinking of the smashed plate downstairs… Then I stepped out into the quiet of the hallway, ears pricked up for noises of someone coming home.

I brought up Aunty Polly's number, pausing before I hit call. I needed an excuse to go round there. An excuse to go round and an excuse to get her to check that Mum was okay without giving away what I knew. But my mind was too thick with the day's drama to think anything up. My altercation at yearbook felt like it had happened weeks ago.

My phone buzzed with a message from Elijah.

Elijah: Would you rather…

Elijah: A) Have a biography written about you where you had no control over what the writer wrote?

Elijah: Or B) Have no one write a biography
about you at all?

I couldn't smile. Even Elijah's constant need to chat philosophy couldn't shake me out from my terror.

Dad was losing control.

Dad didn't normally lose control. Did he?

Paige: C) Write my own autobiography?

Elijah: Correct! What would the title be?

Paige: I dunno.

Elijah: TERRIBLE title.
Elijah: Mine would be called IF YOU
REALLY WANT TO HEAR ALL ABOUT IT.

Paige: Obvious.

Elijah: But brilliant.
Elijah: People would either get it straight
away or they wouldn't.
Elijah: You need to separate the wheat
from the chaff, Sifty. The WHEAT from
the CHAFF.

Paige: I don't know what chaff is, but it

sounds like a really yummy carb.

Elijah: Stop making me laugh so much.
It intimidates my fragile masculinity.

Paige: Well maybe work on making it less
fragile then?

At this point, I was lying on the hallway carpet, head sideways, shaking too much for it to be called anything other than "uncontrollable". I was trying to formulate a message to Polly that would explain everything without explaining anything at all. Trading quips with Elijah, on the other hand, came quickly and easily. It was relaxing to pretend my life wasn't falling apart. To be the girl I'd been that lunchtime.

You keep telling their stories for them, Elijah had said.

I closed my eyes again. Here is how our family's story usually went. Dad would get upset about something minor and get into a giant sulk and basically ignore us for days. Mum would cry and plead for forgiveness and weep, and now, it seemed, she'd upgraded to throwing plates. Then Dad would forgive her, and he would say sorry too, but, at the same time, he would come up with his own story about how really it wasn't his fault at all, and how actually his silence was what any reasonable person would do, considering all the things that Mum had done wrong. So Mum would end up apologizing for causing it all and then they'd become The Best Couple Ever, kissing and not being appropriate in front of their children. And I would swallow the story. I would never tell Polly what happened because things were better now, and it all felt pretty good so why rock the boat? So Dad would tell us his story about what happened, and Mum would tell it, and I would tell it, and Adam would tell it. And none of us would tell anyone outside our house anything other than how perfect we all were. Everything would get better until something happened that annoyed Dad again.

The pressure in the house would keep building, like filling a balloon with too much air, and I always knew it could pop but I really hoped it wouldn't. And I could keep telling the story and choosing an easy life...except it never worked. He always popped again, because we always somehow messed up again, and again, and again, and on it went, and nothing changed, apart from that Adam had left now, and Mum had started throwing plates all over the kitchen, which implied that telling Dad's stories was making us steadily worse, rather than better.

I pulled up Polly's number again, the thud of betrayal gnawing at my stomach, making me feel beyond ill. I wondered how to phrase it to give enough away to keep Mum safe, but not reveal everything... I felt absolutely sick with fear. For Mum. For myself, if I didn't get out of this house quickly.

If you're not scared, then it's not courage.

She picked up on the third ring.

"Paigey! My darling. How are you? Is everything alright?"

I took a cartoon gulp and rolled over so I was staring at the hallway ceiling.

"No," I said. "Can I come and stay for the night? Mum and Dad have had a bit of a row."

CHAPTER 22

I had Neo and Wick on my lap, both purring so aggressively that my whole groin vibrated. It did nothing to combat the blood-curdling anxiety ripping through me. I checked the time again and stroked their furry sleeping bodies, only for them to kick me off. I needed something, anything, to calm me while I waited for Polly's return.

She'd picked me up a few hours earlier, face fixed in an unreadable expression. When I opened the door, she'd pulled me into a rough hug, then held me at arm's length.

"Are you alright?"

"I'm fine. Yes. Thanks for coming."

"Have you got your things?"

"Upstairs."

I'd run up to collect my overnight bag, hastily packed after her strict instructions down the phone.

"Paige, sweetie, I need you to put some things in a bag and come stay with me. Don't worry, we'll sort this."

She'd taken it so seriously that I was already worrying

I'd been overdramatic. Why had I called? It was just a fight. Couples fight. That's normal. Nothing that bad had happened…though my stomach was telling me otherwise, writhing under my school jumper with fear of what would happen if the front door opened… The threat of danger felt huge, even though Dad had never… When I got to the bottom of the stairs, bag heavy on my back, there was no one there.

"Polly?"

I found her in the kitchen, staring at the plate smithereens. She'd told me on the phone not to clear it up.

"Polly?"

She jerked but stayed staring at the smashed crockery. I joined her, scared of her silence.

"Are you *sure* she was the one who threw the plate?"

"That's what Adam said."

"But you're not sure?"

"He said Dad stormed out, then it was quiet for a bit, then he heard the plate smash, and then he heard Mum storm out too. I swear it's not usually…this bad." I'd only started to tell Polly the truth, by revealing this one indiscretion.

She brought her twitching fingers through her short hair. "Right…hmm…" A further silence. Then she turned to me, a bright smile on her face. "Let's get you to mine, shall we? How do you feel about takeaway for dinner?"

I tried to match her sunny face. "Perfect."

* * *

Her cats greeted us like dogs, piling into the hallway, rubbing themselves around our legs as we hopped to get out of our winter boots.

"Tea! Tea?" Polly took us into the conservatory and made me a perfect cuppa. "There you go, my darling. Are you alright to chill for a bit? I need to make a few calls."

I took the tea from her. "To who?"

"I need to chat to your mum. Just to make sure she's okay…"

"She's going to be so angry. Adam…he's left…now me…"

"Shh, it's fine. We're grown-ups remember? We can sort this out. Don't worry. Look, I've got a new imported issue of *The New Yorker*. I'll let you read it before me." She pulled it out of a pile of magazines on her side table.

I couldn't read it. I just flicked through the pages and tried to make out her muffled voice through the walls. When I heard her footsteps, I flicked over a wodge of pages so she'd think I'd been reading.

"Everything's going to be alright." She smiled but I'd known her long enough to know it wasn't real.

"Is Mum okay?"

A lightning flash of pain rippled across Polly's face. "I've spoken to her. She says she's fine."

"Where is she?"

"Getting her hair done," she said. "She said she had an evening appointment." I shook my head. It didn't surprise me. Though that should be a surprise in itself. "I'm going to go pick her up and take her home. Are you alright staying here for a while?"

"And Dad?"

"She said he's fine too."

Polly ran her hands through her hair again, finding it harder and harder to hide the emotions on her face. "I spoke to Adam too. He's all good. He told me to tell you he's glad you rang me."

I didn't know what to say to that.

"Give me an hour. Then I'll be back with takeaway."

So I let her go and see her sister, worrying so much about what I'd done in telling her about the fight, and what my punishment would be when I got home. My hands started wobbling on my cold cup of tea and I put it down so I didn't spill it. My phone kept going with oblivious excitable buzzes from Elijah.

Elijah: We need to sift again.
Elijah: Like we did last summer…
Elijah: Gettit?

Paige: My turn to choose a book?

Elijah: I have to reluctantly say yes.

Paige: You so bossy.

Elijah: I know, it's awful.

The cats, sensing my discomfort, both jumped up on me and started bum-barging one another for space on my lap. They rotated, purring, and digging their claws in and out of my school skirt, before both finally settling. It was dark outside – feeling even later than it was. I sat still and stroked them, staring out at the blackness, until I heard the sound of the door being unlocked and Polly arriving on the threshold.

"I went for Chinese." She held up two bags like a hunter-gatherer.

"Have I ever told you how much I love you?"

"You get out the cutlery, I'll sort the drinks. Meet you at the table in five minutes?"

I stood, which took some time as both of the cats found this unacceptable. Neo even stayed sitting on my lap as I rose, pretending my lap wasn't vanishing. I clutched up a handful of cutlery from the drawer and met Polly in the small dining room where she'd put music on and poured herself a large glass of wine, and me a giant glass of Diet Coke. The food's sweet smell floated up my nostrils.

"Sit, sit."

I felt nervous around her as we shovelled food into our mouths. Both of us overeating and not chewing properly – trying to stuff the chasms in our stomachs with monosodium glutamate. When we'd finished, she pushed her plate away, and sighed. My stomach hardened around my undigested food.

"That was so disgustingly unhealthy and brilliant."

She leaned back in her chair. "I'm sorry I was so quiet. I just needed to eat and emotionally digest."

I sipped at my Coke and waited.

"Thank you, Paige," she said. "For telling me. I know it must've been hard to make that call. You must be feeling very conflicted right now, maybe like you've betrayed your parents? But it was really brave of you. In the long run, this is a good thing. Though it may not feel like that now."

I gulped another cartoon gulp. "How was Mum?"

"She was…fine. She said she's fine. She was worried about Adam leaving and what to tell your father, but she came up with a good lie, and your brother's agreed to keep to it, to minimize any…damage. By the time I said goodbye, she believed the lie herself… It's hard, Paige, isn't it? When she does that? I struggle watching her twist reality to make it work for her… Sorry…I shouldn't say that. I'm tired. And I should be used to it by now, shouldn't I?"

My stomach was too full. Her words took up too much space. This was the first time Polly had ever talked about my parents and their relationship. I felt this weird relief – that my betrayal wasn't so bad if Polly had already suspected. But also great sadness at the confirmation that things really were wrong in my family.

"Paige, I'm going to be honest with you," she said, wiping sheen off her brow. "I feel a bit out of my depth here. I'm trying my best, but this is all very confusing. The main thing is that I want to keep you safe. I think it's too late for my sister, but hopefully it's not too late for you…"

Then, my Aunt Polly, who never lost her composure – not when she got the diagnosis; not when she lost all her hair; not when Dad made his endless digs – put her head down on the table. Sadly, helplessly, into a plate with two remaining noodles stuck to the china. Shock stuck me to my chair before I was able to go and give her a hug. She yanked me into her.

"Sorry, I'm so sorry. I'm just a bit overwhelmed."

I let myself be hugged and wondered how much harder she'd take it if I told her all of it. About how much we pretended. About how scared we all were. About how Dad didn't need to be violent because we were so scared already. I didn't dare. This one share already felt like a huge infringement.

"Sorry, I'm not being a very good grown-up," she sniffed. "It's all been a lot for one day. Oh my God, bloody cat! Get down!" Neo had jumped onto the table and stolen the last two noodles. "Get down."

Neo looked equally surprised at his own behaviour. He started coughing with his whole back arched, then spat out some cat sick.

"And, instant karma. Oh God, the carpet. Great, thanks, Neo, you furry maniac."

It was funny enough to yank me out of my spiral and we both howled with laughter. Polly collected my plate and returned with a cloth. She squeezed my shoulders then she sat across from me again.

"Okay, so here is how it's going to go, if that's alright

with you?" She sounded together and businesslike again. "You're going to stay here tonight, because I'm not feeling so great, and I'd like some company."

"What?!... Oh, I get it."

"You may have to stay for two nights. I mean, I really am quite upset. You know how dramatic I can get, what with my chronic loneliness and all. If only I wasn't such a weird dyke, I wouldn't have to pull your family into this."

"I..." It was so surreal. It was like she was saying Dad's words – telling his stories. But he'd never said any of this sort of stuff in front of her. How did she know?

"Meanwhile Adam can't believe the stupid university won't let him log in from his home computer. It's disgraceful, really, that he has to travel all the way back to Bristol, just to finish this essay. He's *gutted* to be missing the last week of winter break."

She explained the rest of the necessary lies to get through the pinch point. It was very strange, having an adult tell you to lie, but Polly's stories were perfectly structured, with the ideal reader – my dad – very much catered for. There was nothing about these lies that cast him in any blame, or my mother. In fact, they gave him just what he needed. Smugness – about the mess of Polly's life. Anger – but a manageable amount, safely directed towards Adam's university and their IT incompetence. He could even play the hero with this story – Dad's favourite game to play. How *generous* of him to let his precious daughter stay with her crazy aunt. I drooped with relief.

"Right, I don't know about you, but I need another drink." She screeched her chair back. "I think you're old enough for a small glass of wine. Medicinal. What do you say to wine and a movie?"

"Yes please."

I took my stuff upstairs to her tiny spare room, that had actual commissioned oil paintings of all the cats she'd ever owned on the walls. I changed into my pyjamas and, waiting for me downstairs, was a tiny measure of red wine poured into a glass.

"*Bill and Ted*?" Polly asked.

"That would be most excellent."

The night wound itself in. The stars came out. Polly's whole body shook as she laughed at the movie. No messages from my family, but that was expected. Elijah was still sending messages, and at least I felt safe. That counted for something. My lungs were filling properly, relaxing my muscles as they deflated.

I hadn't felt safe. Then I told my story, and now I did.

That was worth noting, I thought, as my eyelids tugged themselves down, drawing the curtains on my very bad day. I fell asleep to the noise of Polly's giggles, and a cat purring lightly on the rug.

Year Ten

Do you remember when...

...**Teddy** got a full apple **stuck** to his **braces**?

...**Guy** tried to **peroxide** his hair and it turned **neon yellow**?

The days when dreaded exams began. Sets and coursework and soooo much stress. We still managed to have some fun though!

WHAT REALLY HAPPENED...

Year Ten is usually pretty quiet. Or maybe it just *feels* quiet compared to the horror of Year Nine. I mean, if someone shat on you every day for a week it would be terrible...Then, if someone came along and pissed on you every day instead, you'd be thinking, *Well, at least it's not shit.* Maybe that's what Year Ten is...piss instead of shit.

Let's not lie. School is still terrible. And exams crop up and tap you on the shoulder and say, *Oh I'm sorry, were you having an awful time? Sorry to hear about that. Here. Could you hold my bag for me while I punch you in the face?*

If Year Nine is where the battles are fought, then Year Ten is where everyone takes a breather to lick their wounds and count their winnings. Friendship groups ever so slightly calcify. People sort of know where they stand in the grand hierarchical mess and keep their heads down, not wanting to rock the boat or be horrifically bullied any more.

The bullying is a quieter, more sophisticated whisper, so you *really* notice the people who are still total twats. Who are still ruining lives needlessly, because they're right at the top of the food chain.

Don't pretend you don't know who they are...

Ruby came back to me in Year Ten...

CHAPTER 23

I woke in an unfamiliar bed. I was greeted with an unfamiliar "Good morning" from someone who loved me, and walked an unfamiliar way to school.

"Are you okay?" Elijah asked when I met him in the library that lunchtime. It was way too freezing to go to our usual bench. "No offence, but you look very tired."

"I'm fine. Just, well, tired."

"I hope you're not too tired to go sift-hunting with me?"

We scanned through the fiction shelves for a book to sift through together. Elijah's enthusiasm more than made up for my emotionally drained energy. He bounded over to copies of *The Great Gatsby* and started telling me about how the author, F. Scott Fitzgerald, died before he could see how hugely popular it became.

I yawned while he yabbered on, and pulled out a copy at random, opening a page right at the end. Then I smiled the first smile of that day. I held up the page to him, which was covered in red pen.

"Looks like some dickhead has already sifted this."

Elijah went as red as his penmanship, but still looked proud. "Disgusting! Who would do such a thing?"

I turned the page back around to see what he'd underlined.

> *They were careless people, Tom and Daisy – they smashed up things and creatures and then retreated back into their money or their vast carelessness… and let other people clean up the mess they had made.*

I felt Elijah's breath on the back of my neck as he read over my shoulder, and closed my eyes a second to savour the sensation.

"What a quote," he said. "There's no point us reading this. I've already picked the best part. It's hard being such a genius." He took the book off me, inserted it back into the shelf and ran further down the aisle. In the space his body left, something caught my attention. There, sitting in my old nook, was Laura Goddard. It was like seeing a giraffe in Antarctica or something, though she had camouflaged herself to fit in. She wore not a scrap of make-up, her hair hung unstyled around her shoulders, and she was reading a book with her knees pulled up to her chest. How the mighty had fallen… A tingle of fear fizzled down my spine as I remembered my altercation with Grace and the other Awfuls the day before. Would they bother punishing me like they had Laura? I didn't really have the strength for that, not with everything going on at home. Everything I wasn't telling Elijah.

"So, Paige, would you rather write the world's most admired novel but die before it became admired, or enjoy moderate success while still alive?" he asked, bounding up to me like a puppy injected with coffee. Then he paused. "Are you absolutely sure you're okay?"

"Huh?" I turned away from the ghost of Laura Goddard.

"I said, are you sure you're alright?"

I smiled. And imagined saying the words, "*No, I'm not actually. I stayed at my aunt's house last night because I'm so scared of my dad.*" I imagined how that would change how he saw me.

I smiled even wider.

"I'm good, just tired," I replied. Determined not to ruin one of the only good things I had left in my life.

Polly picked me up from school that day and took me to Pizza Express before dropping me back home. It was just as well we had a coupon because we were both so nervous we hardly ate our dough balls. She stood next to me on the doorstep. My entire body quivered as I rummaged for my keys. One, two, three, four… But Dad opened the door wide, grinning.

"Polly," he boomed, like the jolly ghost of Christmas Present. "Welcome." He stepped back, warm and friendly, signalling the start of a new honeymoon period.

"Hi, Glynn," Polly said. "Thanks again for letting Paige stay. I really needed the company."

Polly had hunched her shoulders and spoke meekly, pulling her sleeves over her hands.

"It's totally fine. I can't imagine how lonely it must get sometimes. I can't go a night without missing Jane."

The house was inviting and central-heated. Hoovered, sparkling and fresh. Mum greeted us in the hall, also looking warm and hoovered, sparkling and fresh. She'd overheard his compliment and came up to hug him from behind.

"You're such a dope," she said, burying herself into his back.

"It's true though, my darling."

I watched Polly watch Mum but she stayed in complete character as hapless aunt.

"Aww, you guys. I don't know what's got into me recently. It's just like all my life decisions caught up on me." She shook her head. "Sorry, it's not appropriate to talk like this in front of Paige."

"Paige is a grown-up, isn't she?" Dad's glee was evident. I could sense his need to whisper in my ear, "*See, I told you so.*"

"Maybe you should go upstairs, Paige?" Mum said. "Let the adults talk."

I nodded to Polly, who nodded back. I climbed the stairs, passed the monument of Adam's empty room, and fell onto my bed face first. I listened to murmured voices, discussing things on my behalf, then was summoned back down to the living room.

"Paige, honey?" Dad said, clearly loving every second. "Your aunty has been a bit low recently. How would you feel about staying at hers over the weekends? Keeping her company for a while?"

Polly's eyes met mine and she blasted a silent warning to me. I knew not to react enthusiastically.

"Oh," I said. "Umm...really?"

"She needs you," Mum said, holding Dad's hand over the gap between their chairs.

"I guess... *Every* weekend?"

"Polly, sorry I don't know why she's being so rude."

Polly almost broke and smiled, but saved it just in time. "No, *I'm* sorry. I shouldn't have asked. I'm pathetic...sorry."

"Maybe for a while?" I tried out my own acting muscles, sounding reluctant. "If you really need me to."

A ray of light was opening in my life. An oxygen hole punched into my coffin. I didn't dare believe it, I didn't dare hope. Every weekend. Me, not in this house. A gasp of life. A snatch of my stomach not hurting. Oh God, if Dad knew how much I wanted this, he would never let me go. I was auditioning for my own happiness.

"Good girl. Let's see how it goes." Positively hyper from Polly's great downfall, he stood and wrapped me in a rare hug and, despite everything, I clung to him, wanting it to last longer than it did. I suddenly didn't want to go anywhere. I wanted to stay there and be perfect like Adam and try and make Dad like me. Sensing this, he broke the hug off first.

"Thanks so much, Glynn," Polly said. "I'll sort myself out soon. I promise."

"Take as much time as you need. Paigey doesn't mind."

I winced to show I did a bit, even though I really truly didn't. But I was happy to tell whatever story I needed to escape Dad, despite wishing he was still hugging me.

29th January

Ethan made out with Elise at a party over the weekend and told everyone today that she has "cucumber tits" when they're not in a bra.

6th February

Abi and the rest of the Drama Lot decided they hate Joanie for no reason. They all helped her plan her birthday party and then none of them showed up.

14th February

Grace and the Awfuls sent fake Valentine's cards to about twelve people, including Lily, Karl and Ranj. Everyone apart from them knows the cards are fake.

15th February

Joe did a racist impression of Daisy in a bad mood in the canteen, and Daisy had to pretend it was funny.

Last day of half term

I've experienced no retaliation for standing up to Grace etc. in yearbook. I think I'm safe...

CHAPTER 24

My life changed drastically for the better, with weekends opened up with Polly, and lunchtimes spent laughing and reading with Elijah. Snowdrops pushed themselves eagerly through the frozen earth. Tiny burgeoning buds appeared on the tree branches. Grace and co didn't end up punishing me for my impassioned yearbook interruption, apart from the odd dirty look. Their hatred was still saved for Laura, who now had full-time residence in my old library spot.

"What are you doing tomorrow?" Elijah asked, near the end of the half-term break, as we played cards in his bedroom while rain splattered his windows.

"Nothing, why?"

"Do you want to go on an excursion? It being the last day of the holidays and all?"

I was exceedingly grateful that he was so engrossed in gin rummy that he didn't see my ginormous grin.

"An excursion where? Why?"

"To London. To see things. To do things. To live. Shall we meet around ten? Get the train up to London Bridge?"

I nodded, trying to hide my excitement. We only lived an hour away from London on the train but I rarely went. Maybe once a year if Polly got tickets to some weird feminist play. "Perfect. And what's the plan? Just mooch?"

"What a word. Mooch! Mooch. Yes, yes, let's mooch. Let's not do anything other than mooch. Oh, Paige. Your lexicon is exceedingly impressive."

"Listen back to that last sentence, you literary show-off."

He laughed as he played a card. "I have no idea what you mean."

I couldn't sleep that night, in my tiny room in Polly's house. The anticipation of the next day's mooching fluttered in my stomach, like a tsunami of butterflies. One of her cats mewed in the corridor while I placed my hand on my tummy to calm myself with my breath.

My stomach hadn't felt nervous with good nerves for so long.

It knew what it felt like to twist into knots with anticipation, but that was often associated with bad nerves. Not giddiness. Not counting down the clock because you couldn't wait to see a person, rather than staring at the whirring minute hand, wishing it would slow, because you don't want them back yet.

The last time I'd been this giddy-nervous was the night before I saw Ruby for the last time…

I blinked into the dark.

I dared wonder if he was excited about seeing me. About mooching with me. I smiled as I imagined the answer was yes, then the self-doubt kicked in.

Wait…maybe he isn't? Maybe he's only been hanging out with you because he feels sorry for you? It's a miracle he's spent this much time with you already. Maybe it's a charity thing? Remember what happened with Ruby. Remember how much that hurt. What if it happens again?

A cat meowed again as I crammed my face into the pillow. It always struck me as hugely unfair that you could never take your head off at the end of the day, like an uncomfortable underwired bra, and have a little break from it for a while. I tried not to press the play button of my Ruby memory tape, but I was flooded with bittersweet hauntings of our childhood together. The feel of her hand in mine on the first day of secondary school. Telling her about my dad under the duvet at her house and her reaching over and hugging me and telling me she would always be here for me…

…and then…

The feeling in my stomach when I heard her in my hallway. The searing pain. Humiliation. Betrayal…

"Alexa, how do you know if someone likes you?" I whispered into the darkness.

She didn't answer because she wasn't here. She was back

in my other room, in my other life. My bedroom haunted by the last time I saw Ruby.

"You look nice." Polly smiled as I ran down late into the kitchen. I'd overslept, and rushed around the kitchen, grabbing a glass of juice and a banana for a panic breakfast. "Looking forward to your day in London?"

I stuffed the fruit into my coat pocket. "Yes. It looks freezing though."

Neo twirled around Polly's feet, expecting a second breakfast. "Well you've wrapped up, that will help. And stop to drink a hot chocolate. Hang on..." She rummaged in her bag that was hanging from a kitchen chair and withdrew a twenty-pound note from her purse. "Here, take this." She held it out. "Treat yourself to some hot chocolates."

My heart felt like it *was* hot chocolate when I looked at that note. It wasn't the money, but the thought behind it. Uncomfortable, I joked it off.

"I mean, London's expensive I hear, but surely drinks aren't this much?"

"Well, buy some for Elijah too then." She wafted the money and I relented. "When do I get to meet this boy, by the way?"

"Polly, it's not like he's my boyfriend."

She grinned. "But you want him to be?"

"Polly!"

She cackled so loudly that Neo jumped into the air and

scrambled out of the room in an orbit of fur. "Sorry. I shouldn't wind you up. I'm being an embarrassing aunty. I truly apologize."

"It's fine...thank you for the money."

"You're welcome. Are you dropping back here tonight before you head to your parents?" She asked it casually enough but the air ripened with tension. We kept having these lovely moments where I lived at her house at weekends and most of half-term, and we could pretend this was for always. But then reality tapped us on the shoulder, reminding me Polly wasn't my parent, even though she was the only person who acted like it, and this wasn't my home, even though it felt like one, and I had to go back to my actual parents and actual home, even though they didn't want me there. All so we could pretend a pointless story of being a functional family.

"I have to pick up my stuff, if that's okay? Thanks again for letting me stay."

She ruffled my hair through my bobble hat. "Don't be daft. Any time. Now, go buy some overpriced hot chocolates and pretend you don't fancy this boy."

"Polly!"

She was already walking away, cackling again, following her cat to apologize.

I stared up at the giant green dome, wrinkling my nose. "Madame Tussauds?" My breath came out in puffs of vapour that floated with disbelief into the cold blue sky.

Elijah grinned like the Cheshire cat with veneers. "Yes! I found a two-for-one coupon online and I think we will learn an important life lesson."

We were standing outside Baker Street tube station, inhaling huge amounts of carbon monoxide from the traffic slugging past us. A long snake of tourists stood patiently nearby and he was trying to make me join them.

I sighed good-naturedly. "I thought we were going to mooch. *Mooch.* That is the exact opposite of important life lessons."

"What can I say, Paige?" he said, in a faux arsehole voice. "I'm so disgustingly, consistently, on-brand."

I burst out laughing. "I can't believe you just said the words '*on-brand*' about yourself."

"It doesn't count if you say it ironically."

"Everyone who says it thinks they're saying it ironically."

It felt safer teasing Elijah, deflecting the feelings I didn't want to feel – the pathetic fantasies that had started playing in my head. When we'd ridden the train up that morning, both of us reading, I'd looked over at him, scribbling in his red biro, and imagined him looking up to smile and leaning over to kiss me. The yearning made my blood thicken. I bathed in the heat of this alternate reality for a second, until shame wriggled in, making me blush, telling me off for thinking such an idea was possible. The whole time, Elijah stayed engrossed in his book, oblivious to what I was thinking about him. Thank God. Our friendship meant too much to risk it on something as cliché as a crush, and he gave me no reason to think this was more than a friendship.

We joined the queue and it moved efficiently, with plenty to look at while we waited. London was on such a huge scale it almost didn't seem real. The conversations around us hummed with the symphony of different foreign tongues, as families from all over waited to see famous people carved out of wax. Elijah got his book out and started reading and I copied him. But, like on the train, I kept glancing up – never finding him doing the same.

You want too much, I told myself. *Isn't a friend enough? Stop it!*

My brain was scrambled egg after my sleepless night torturing myself about Ruby. Self-loathing pumped through my blood, making me edgy and nervous about ruining things with Elijah.

Like you ruin everything. You are a pointless slug and nobody likes you.

Elijah, oblivious, kept reading his book.

Quickly enough, we paid with our coupon and stood behind a group of overexcited American teenagers wearing matching neon hoodies, waiting to go into the first room. We were held back by an usher, who kept putting his head around a door to check the room was clearing. Then we were nodded through and everyone around us held their phones up in video mode to film themselves entering.

Elijah nudged my shoulder with his. "Let's go," he

whispered, and we followed everyone into a room filled with frozen humans.

The group dispersed – people shrieking and running towards different celebrities. Clumps formed around each waxwork as people queued to get photos with them. We walked slowly around each clump, trying to figure out who most of the figures were. Some statues I got – like Brad Pitt and James Bond. Some of the waxworks looked remarkably like their subject, and others looked more like a kid's freaky drawing.

"It's not very…consistent, is it?" I said, looking at the shrunken head of a popular TV judge. "The craftsmanship?"

Elijah giggled. "Can you imagine how weird it must feel to be someone famous enough to get one of these? And then meeting it for the first time?"

"Proper disconcerting. A bit like when you hear your voice back on a recording."

"Spot-on metaphor, once again."

Then Elijah reached over and squeezed my hand. It was inexplicable. It was the shortest of moments and yet so much happened in the milliseconds Elijah's hand was in mine. I felt every sensation. The cold of his fingers from reading his book outside, the warmth of his palm, the rough feel of the skin on his writing finger. Then his hand wasn't there any more and my palm was dancing with itself.

And Elijah, being Elijah, acted like he hadn't just squeezed my hand at all.

"It's too crowded in here," I said, feeling way too hot way too quickly. "Can we move on?"

* * *

It was very peculiar, wandering past celebrities but knowing it wasn't actually them. It was even more peculiar watching how everyone still responded like they were real. They gasped and squealed and acted star-struck but then also would do bizarre and dehumanizing things like pretending to pick a celebrity's wax nose, or swearing at them.

We found a quiet bench near Marilyn Monroe – who stood posing with her white dress blowing up from an air vent underneath. We sat in the comfortable silence I was used to sharing with him, and took in the never-ending line of people queuing to get their photo taken with her.

"So…" Elijah said, with his well-rehearsed voice of someone about to start a philosophical monologue. "I was reading last night, when I found the coupon, that Madame Tussauds regularly shifts about their waxworks. They only display the figures they believe are still '*socially relevant*', and '*retire*' the ones that aren't."

"Harsh."

I watched a mother dangle her toddler next to Marilyn – the unassuming kid staring out blankly, held up by the neck of its yellow coat.

"Do they melt them down to make a new one? Or just keep them in storage?" I asked.

"I don't know."

"If I had a waxwork and they decided to tell me I wasn't relevant, I would demand to own it. I'd keep it next to the front door to scare people as they came in."

Elijah laughed and then did it again – reached over and quickly squeezed my hand. "It's such a strange place, right? I guess it's kind of a profound reflection on society though? People elbowing each other to get a photo in front of something that isn't real? Celebrating the fake? It's all very, very weird."

I got very cold then. A chill from the air-conditioning made me erupt in goosebumps.

Fake.

What a word that was.

Fake.

I blinked away a flash of my dad smiling with his whole essence whenever they had friends round. His arm around Mum's shoulder, laughing, relaxed, glowing, the life and soul…until the friends went home and he muttered that he couldn't believe she'd made that joke at his expense and didn't talk to us for two days.

Fake.

A flash of Ruby's face, the last night I saw her. The way she held her mouth open as she stared upwards at the mirror, carefully applying another layer of mascara to this new face of hers that I didn't recognize.

Celebrating the fake.

After a half-term break of authenticity at Polly's, later that day I'd have to return home to the land of fake. The thought made me feel ill. Elijah stood, not noticing my sudden weird chill, and held out his hand, which I certainly did notice. "Shall we head on? Go and pick the Queen's nose?"

I took his hand to heave myself up off the bench, and could therefore hardly concentrate as we entered the regency section. We found the royal family protected by a blue rope so we couldn't pick the Queen's nose. This made Elijah alarmingly cross.

"I mean, what's the point in that?" he muttered. "Why build the Queen out of wax if you can't pick her nose?"

"Do you think she picks her nose in real life?" I asked, as we were jostled out of place by a very enthusiastic American family who could not believe their luck that they were in the same room as a fake Kate Middleton. "She must've tried it, just once? In the privacy of her own palace?"

"You're delightful." Elijah shot me a proud look.

I pointed over his shoulder towards the historical section. "We can pick Shakespeare's nose instead?"

"So we can only pick the wax nostrils of the dead?"

"Duh. Everyone knows that."

We melted into the most marvellous puddle of unstoppable giggles, Elijah temporarily jolting me out of my despondency. Blasts of warmth shot through my body and, in that moment, I honestly forgot what it felt like to be lonely. I let myself feel safe with Elijah again and made myself stay in this beautiful moment rather than getting tugged back into the darkness that was threatening to engulf me. A few passing tourists glanced in our direction, our laughter pulling them away from their excitement at Barack Obama.

"Come on, you." Elijah offered his hand AGAIN to guide me to the next room, and I felt all sorts of unhelpful things dance across my skin. That was FOUR times he'd taken my hand. Was it National Hand-Taking Day? Or was there something in this? The hope pushed my tired mouth into another smile. I stood and he released my grip.

"Do you want to go see how these wax things are made?"

"Sure, why not?"

CHAPTER 25

But something was still building in me as we weaved our way through the statues and adoring people around them. I felt like a supervolcano, one that's been dormant and is long overdue a dramatic eruption. Thinking about Ruby the previous night had started me rumbling. And now, watching all these people throw themselves giddily into worshipping a statue…emotional magma released itself into my stomach.

When we arrived at the *Behind the Scenes* section, we found it much quieter than the rest of Madame Tussauds. With fewer selfie opportunities, most people quickly passed through, only glancing at the projected video explaining how a wax figure is made. But Elijah made us sit through the whole video and we learned how to make a fake version of a real person.

"Can you imagine the patience you must have to do this job?" he whispered in the dark. "I mean, they insert every piece of hair *individually*. It takes weeks!"

"Hmm." I nodded as I learned how they chose a statue's

hair, clothes and make-up. The painstakingness of it all. The accuracy needed to create a believable fake of a real, living, breathing thing. A flawless recreation of a flawed human being. The *effort* of it all, to present a perfect front. All the energy going into the outside, with no care for the empty, waxy, vacant inside. I suddenly felt utter exhaustion at the thought of going home later, of climbing back into the perfect waxwork. I found my eyes getting wet and blinked. The volcano was erupting. Everything tumbling out. *Not here. Please. Not so publicly.* But my body didn't care I was in the middle of a major tourist attraction, didn't mind the embarrassment. It had decided to spew…

"Are you okay?"

I nodded and gulped.

"Are you *sure?*"

My throat was tighter than freshly-washed skinny jeans. I gulped again and stared out at fake Adele meeting real Adele, her mouth falling slack-jaw as she was presented with herself.

"Wanna go get some air?"

I nodded once more, still unable to talk. My skin erupted with prickles; the air was too thick and hot to breathe in. Waves of irritability crashed through me, pulling me into their rip tide. *How are all these people here and in my way, and breathing my oxygen, and being too slow walking in front of me, and being so annoying and hateful and ARGH I need to get out.*

Elijah, sensing something, steered me expertly through the last rooms. The crowds were unbearably slow. Oblivious.

Selfish. I swallowed down the huge urge to shout for them to get out of my way. When we finally emerged into the cold blue air, it was almost worse. Traffic crawled past us, spilling out exhaust fumes, clogging my lungs.

"There's so many cars," I gasped. "The air. There isn't any air."

Elijah's eyes widened and he pulled out his phone. "There's a park just around the corner," he said. "Let's head there."

He led me through the streets. I was so trapped in the buzzing of my own head that I didn't even get gooey about his hand in mine. Every time we stopped at a pedestrian crossing I felt a roaring in my stomach, like I couldn't handle the extra few seconds between me and wider space.

"Not much further," he muttered. "Come on."

Finally we came to the ornate gate of Regent's Park. And though it was still busier than parks at home, the air didn't feel so dense. Elijah sat me down on a bench and I leaned forward onto my knees, my hands shaking.

What was happening? Why could I not cope? Why did my brain feel like it had been chucked into a very aggressive washing machine cycle?

"Just take some breaths." Elijah's voice was calm, like this happened all the time. The crisp air hit my lungs like iced water. "Keep breathing. We're in no rush."

I stayed bent over, taking in breath after breath, eyes closed, listening to the distant thrum of traffic and the gentle honks of nearby ducks. The world crashed and thrashed behind my eyelids and my heart was thudding so loudly I wondered if this was a panic attack. All I could do was ride the wave until it passed.

Which, after a few minutes, it did.

I eventually raised my head. The park blinked into view in all its wintery gloriousness. The sky really was the most shocking shade of blue. Everyone's breath came out in clouds of dragon smoke that hit the light and turned gold.

"Sorry," I said, not looking at Elijah, so embarrassed.

"It's fine. Are you alright?"

"I...think so."

"You don't need a drink or anything?"

"No...not yet. I don't know what happened."

He put a gloved hand on my knee. I turned to face him and Elijah was wearing an expression I hadn't seen before. There was no laughing smile, no glint. Just a piercing but gentle stare, eyebrows drawn in caring concern, head slightly tilted. He seemed about five years older. It was the first time we had ever really sat and looked at each other, and the moment was so intimate, I almost lost my breath again. I'd never felt so *seen*. So solid – like I really existed, like I wasn't just a pointless blur of a person. But it was too overwhelming after everything and I cut it down. I made myself smile like a waxwork model, shrugged.

"What upset you?" Elijah asked quietly. "You were fine, and then suddenly you weren't fine. I feel guilty..."

"What? Why?"

"Well, did I do anything? Say anything?"

I looked back up at him and his grown-up face. "No. You've not done anything...I..." What *had* happened? I wasn't sure myself. I traced myself backwards, to the video, to the wax being made. I opened my mouth to see what words came out, to see if my mouth knew more than my brain. "I'm sorry," I found my mouth saying. "I'm...well... I don't know... It was the fakeness. Of the whole thing. The concept hurts me if I think about it too much." I coughed to clear my swollen throat. "I think it's just..." I paused, letting the truth reveal itself like a rose unfurling its petals. "...I just realized that practically everyone in my life is a wax model." My voice caught as I said it, confirming it as truth. "I mean, apart from my aunty... I don't have many people in my life and the ones I do have aren't real. Honestly, my family may as well be in Madame Tussauds. The smiles never waning, the make-up never slipping off, staring vacantly out at people who are excited to see them because they're perfect; but they're not."

Elijah's hand was still on my knee, urging me on. We'd spoken so much about so much. We'd delved deep into the darker waters of the human experience – sharing books and thoughts and philosophies – but I'd never told him about what it was like to be me. I'd been enjoying knowing him too much to ruin it. I hadn't been able to face the thought of him seeing my messy, lonely life as a contaminant. But now I realized the alternative was scarier. I didn't want to be a waxwork with this boy. I didn't want to be a moulded smile and unblinking eyes. So I told him the terrifying truth of my tiny life.

"My dad...he isn't kind," I said slowly. Choosing each word with painful precision. "But he pretends he is. And my mum pretends he isn't scary, even though he is. We all pretend he isn't scary. But...Elijah...he's *terrifying*." I whispered that word. Scared Dad would hear, even though we were miles away. "He's never, like, hit us or anything but he doesn't need to. I don't know if that makes sense. But it's got worse since my brother went to uni, and now it's so bad I have to stay with my aunty at the weekends. And honestly? I feel...terrified telling you even this much. I can't...I can't talk about it. It's this huge, lonely secret in my life and I don't like betraying my family. Nobody knows. Well, there's only one other person who knows. Ruby...she was my best friend..." I gulped and gulped but it didn't stop the tears as I let myself think about Ruby properly – blowing the top off my volcano. "She knew... She was the only one I trusted to tell. Who I could truly be myself around. But she moved away...and then, when I last saw her, she wasn't herself any more. She'd become a waxwork, like everyone else." Tears ran freely either side of my nose.

Elijah put his arm around my shoulders, hugging me to him. "What can I do?" he asked.

"I can't talk about my family. Not properly. Not yet..."

"Of course, of course."

I sniffed hard but it wasn't enough to stop my nose running. "It's thinking about Ruby that's pushed me over the edge," I said. "I was thinking about her all last night."

"What happened with her? How was she a waxwork?"

I sighed. The Ruby stuff was so embarrassing. It was so… *secondary school*. I wasn't even sure if Elijah would get it. And I didn't want to remind this beautiful boy with his arm around me what a colossal loser I was, but still… It was better than being wax.

"What happened?" I repeated. I took a deep breath of blue sky and shook my head to dislodge the searing pain of that memory. "Ruby got popular. That's what happened."

We'd stood at the school gates, holding hands, staring at the imposing building like it was an alien spacecraft that had arrived overnight. Backpacks high up our backs, uniform fresh and worn exactly within the rules. Summer had taken us from the top of the school food chain as boastful Year Sixes and dropped us right back to the bottom again.

"Oh my God, look at them. They're so tiny and cute," some older girls said, as they sauntered through the gates, ties loosened, non-regulation eyeliner smeared under their eyes.

Ruby and I looked at one another. *Cute*. We were cute. It could be worse, we guessed.

"So, this is secondary school," Ruby said, staring after the girls. Maybe she was looking after them wistfully. Now I look back on it, she probably was.

"Indeed it is."

"How hard can it be?" she asked.

It turned out – with Ruby by my side – not terrible.

I mean, we got lucky. They put us in the same form, and we clung to one another like lifebuoys amongst the sea of new faces. Because our school was religious, it had a wider catchment area, and there were only three other people from our primary school in our year. In this ocean of unfamiliar, it was so much easier to just hang out with each other rather than embracing the opportunity of making new friends. Easier to just sit together in the canteen to share a plate of chips. Easier to be each other's partner in PE. Easier to ignore the new food chain building. When Grace came in on the first ever mufti day, wearing a miniskirt so mini that every boy declared himself in love with her – launching herself as leader of this new world – Ruby was more enamoured by it all than I was.

"Did you hear," she asked, as we sat together on the bus home one dark, rainy afternoon, "that Grace and Sam tongue-kissed at Amelia's party over the weekend?"

"Eww." I wrote the word *eww* in the steam of the window.

"Do you not think he's good-looking?"

I pulled a face. "No. And I bet you didn't think he was good-looking until you heard that Grace kissed him."

She was quiet the rest of the journey.

"Want to watch TV or something?" I'd asked her as we stepped out into the bus shelter. I kept my voice neutral but I was always hopeful. She knew I used her home as a Safe House.

"Actually I've got too much homework. Sorry. Maybe tomorrow?"

But other than the odd burst of interest, and the odd tiff when I wouldn't gossip with her, Ruby seemed just as happy as I was to weather the storm of secondary school quietly, side by side. We claimed a little spot in the library each lunch hour. Saw each other at the weekend. We were just those two girls – always together – nothing to be bothering with.

Then the unthinkable happened.

Ruby: Can I come over? My life is
ruined!!!!!!!!!!!!!!!!!

The message appeared one evening while I was hiding upstairs because Mum hadn't put enough butter in the mashed potato.

Paige: Better if I come to you. R u ok???
I'm sure it will be fine.

Ruby: Let's meet at the bus stop.
Can't be in my house a moment longer.
PAIGE IT'S SO TERRIBLE.

I was greeted in the night-time drizzle by a Ruby-shaped ball of snot and sobbing.

"We're…we're…moving away," she heaved and there was a moment's delay before I realized what that meant. For me, as well as her. And my heart fell out onto the grimy, damp pavement, where it's never really been picked up from since.

It wasn't just moving away. It was moving *far* away. To the Isle of Man. An island. An *island.* Something to do with her dad and tax. You had to fly there or get a ferry. She'd try and come and visit but the reason they were moving was because there was no family here – not since her gran died. As leavings go, it was the most far and dramatic and huge and terrible, and I hardly slept for weeks leading up to it as I was sobbing so hard, alone in my bed.

I stayed over at her house on the last night, cocooned in sleeping bags laid on yoga mats, surrounded by her boxed-up life. We didn't sleep, only cried, and made promises to stay in touch and always be best friends and for her to come and visit whenever she could.

"It was awful, the first day back at school without her," I told Elijah, on a bench in London, through falling tears that stung the coldness of my cheeks.

I had no one to talk to. No one to sit with. No one to co-conspire with. No one to protect me. No one to roll my eyes at. It was Year Eight. Friendships had already been made. No one was in the market for anyone new to hang out with. Nobody wanted to befriend that weird girl who sat alone in the library. There would be many days when I'd go without saying literally anything out loud. Sometimes I'd sit in my room and speak to Adam's old Alexa, cradling my voice box in my hands, reminding myself how to talk. Reminding myself I could still form words. Saving them mostly for Ruby.

Paige: How was your first day at school? OMG I miss you SO MUCH. COME BACK NOW, THIS HAS STOPPED BEING A FUNNY JOKE.

Ruby: School was awful! Everyone is a small-town nightmare. Like, they've all known each other since they were babies. So weird. Screw this. I'M ON A PLANE, COMING TO SEE YOU AND LIVE IN YOUR WARDROBE.

Paige: AMAZING! I've put some cushions down in there.
Paige: OMG. Gossip all over school. Grace and Sam got off again at the school disco. I didn't go, of course, but it's all anyone is talking about.

Ruby: WHAT??? But she's like three metres taller than him! Could he even reach her face to kiss her? Or did he just have to suck on her chin? I hope for both of their sakes he reaches puberty soon.

Paige: I dunno. But if he did suck her chin, I know that everyone will be doing that in a week's time rather than kissing the regular way.

Ruby: LOL. God, everyone here does sooooo much more than kiss. Boredom bonking is what I call it. Very weird. They bypassed chin-sucking in Year Six.

But as time went on, Ruby seemed less and less interested in my second-hand tales of her old secondary school. I'd listen out in toilet cubicles, keep my ears pricked up whenever someone gossiped in a quiet maths lesson. She was always so much more into all that than I was. Until she wasn't…

Paige: So Grace has declared all-out war on Lisa Heartly for no reason. She is a shunned person. No one is talking to her.

After two days…

Ruby: Typical I guess.

Then nothing.

Months blurred to a year. A YEAR. Promises to visit got fewer and further between. We both knew it would be hard for her to come see me. She'd have to pay for a plane ticket, and then where would she stay? I mean, that implies there was even a question. I would never have dared ask. Time did that thing where it both moved super slowly and super fast – individual days feeling like drawn-out torture, combined with sending messages saying, *How is it Christmas already? How has it been a year already? How is it Christmas again?! How has it been two years already?*

My window to absolve myself of my loneliness passed. I was too scared of everyone around me to be friendly. Ruby was the only one I could trust. I morphed from being *That girl who's always with that other girl* to *Who? Oh that one? The one who works for the paper but never speaks? What'shername?*

Paige: How are we in Year Ten now? How have I not seen you in so long? WILL WE EVER SEE EACH OTHER AGAIN?

After several days…

Ruby: I know. Weird huh?

I pretended things weren't different. Deluded myself that we were still best friends. That Ruby wasn't clearly moving on. I needed her too much… And then, the perfect opportunity arose to win her back and remind her of how great we were.

Paige: OK. Sit down. Put a nappy on. Because you're about to pee yourself. GUESS WHO HAS A FREE HOUSE THIS HALF-TERM? AND GUESS WHO HAS

LOOKED AT FLIGHTS AND SEEN THEY ARE LESS THAN FIFTY QUID THAT WEEK?

I refreshed my phone. Refreshed again. Fizzing and whizzing with excitement. There were two ticks. She'd seen it. She'd read it. Why wasn't she replying? Was she booking her ticket first so then I'd have to be the one peeing myself?

Paige: Are you alive? Or have you died from excitement?

Ruby: I'm alive. Soz. Cool. I need to check what's happening that week tho.

No caps lock. No reaction gif. No delight at the thought of seeing me. That should've been my first proper warning. A reason to build a fence around my heart. But loneliness does weird things to a person. You build a sandcastle out of hope, with turrets made of denial and desperation, digging a deep moat of longing. You collect crumbs from minor social interactions and squeeze them together and pretend it's a cake. Then you scarf it in one and are starving again instantly. Eventually, I got a crumb of a reply from her, and lo and behold, I got out my cake tin, sprinkled the crumb into it, and put it into the oven, preparing icing to top it with once it had cooled.

Ruby: So, actually, Mum and I are coming

to London that week to see some shows, do some shopping. There are no decent shops here. We're staying in a hotel, but maybe I can come for a night? Got anything exciting going on we can do? x

It was my turn to take a while to reply. I stared at my phone and said, "Huh?" out loud. A night? Only one? We had so much to catch up on, even a week wouldn't be long enough. I'd lied to my parents, telling them I was staying at Polly's while they were away, to get the week free for her. And *anything exciting we can do?* What the heck did that mean? Surely our reunion was exciting enough? So many red flags were flapping but I was in my castle of loneliness, squeezing my crumb as hard as I could. So I wrote, *I can't wait!* and we agreed Wednesday, and I decided we could try out the new pizza place in town, which would give us plenty of opportunity to chat. Once she got here, Ruby would be glad I hadn't planned anything more extreme. I wouldn't be able to anyway. She knew this. She knew who I was and why… She…

…she arrived three hours late.

She arrived not looking like Ruby.

I ran downstairs, jingling with nerves from waiting so long. I pulled the door open and there she was. My best friend. My missing piece. My everything…

Oh my God, she did not look like her at all.

I mean, we'd sent each other photos and, yeah, I'd

noticed from the selfies that she wore make-up now. But I was never on social media, so hadn't witnessed the extent of her transformation.

"Oh my God," she said as we clasped eyeballs on one another. "Paige!" She seemed happy to see me, and I exploded with relief, dragging her in for a hug.

"Oh my God oh my God oh my God," I squealed into her perfectly-blown-out hair.

We jumped up and down in the hallway, squealing squeals not even dogs could hear. When we broke apart, we both really looked at each other, and I think we were both surprised.

Ruby could've walked right off a catwalk. Her whole face was plastered in expertly-applied make-up. Even her nose looked slimmer, which I later found out was because she "contoured" it. She redid it before we went out. Her body was long, lean and firm – like a yoga teacher's. And, despite the cold, she had no coat on and wore a cropped top to show off her perfect stomach, with low jeans so tight she might've spray-painted them on.

"You look so different," I managed.

"You look exactly the same."

There was awe there too, but not good awe. Judging awe. I touched my make-up-free face, with no foundation to cover my blush.

"Umm, do you want a cup of tea?"

"Do you have green tea?"

"Umm. Maybe. I'll have a look."

"Thanks. Regular tea's not good for you. The tannins."

"Right."

We left her giant bag in the hallway and made our way into the kitchen, neither of us knowing what to say.

"We've not got green, but we've got peppermint? No. Oh, okay. Decaff? No, it's not loose-leaf. Okay, sure. Yeah, I can just put some lemon in hot water."

We took our steaming mugs up to my room and Ruby wandered around it with more judgemental awe. "Oh my God, this is exactly the same too," she said.

I tried to see my room through her eyes, shame joining my self-consciousness. I guess it hadn't changed a lot. My bedroom was plain then and it was plain now – she knew why. I couldn't do much without it drawing a nasty comment.

"I've still got our photo up." I gestured to my desk where a framed photo of us stood. It was taken at our Year Six leaving disco – both of us mid hysterical laughter as we did the Gangnam Style.

"God. I wish you didn't have that up. I was so fat back then."

"*What?* You weren't."

"Puppy-fat-tastic. And our hair! What were we thinking? Trying to ombré it ourselves with that kit from Superdrug. God, we were losers." She laughed and took a sip of her lemon-wedge tea.

We sat and sipped our drinks in such a painful silence I'm surprised our eyeballs didn't start bleeding.

It was bound to be awkward, I told myself. *It's been years.*

It must be weird for her to be back. Make an effort.

I put on my brightest voice. "So, what's going on on the Isle of Man? You like school and stuff?"

At that, Ruby sat up on her cushion. Her eyes came alive for the first time since she'd walked in. "Oh my God, yeah, school is great actually. Okay, so you know that girl, Delta? The one I used to hate?" I nodded even though I wasn't sure. "Well, it turns out I was being silly, cos we're best friends now, isn't that funny? I mean, it was a bit touch and go last term when she got drunk at Lexi's party and told me she fancied Jimmy. You know? That boy I had a thing with in Year Nine? But I reminded her of the girl code and she backed off. And yeah, we're great. And then there's Zara. She's nice. A bit desperate, but harmless. I think she might be gay. Delta said that she's always doing this heavy breathing when we get changed for PE. I mean, if she's gay, fine. But, like, just admit it, you know? Don't be all weird and heavy-breathing about it?" She laughed, flinging back her perfect hair and sinking again into her monologue.

I sniffed hard, as I relayed all this to Elijah on our bench. He was listening patiently and wonderfully, arm still around me. "It was so, so weird," I told him. "She was being cruel about people. And she'd lost all self-awareness. She just kept blah-ing on about all these people I didn't know, and all these dramas I didn't care about." I shook my head into the cold, looking over at him sadly. "You know how you say nobody else cares about our school year? Well, none of those names meant anything to me. Delta, Zara, Jimmy… it meant nothing. And yet, to Ruby, it was everything. She talked about herself solidly for about an hour. She even pulled up photos of everyone to show me…and God, that was the first time I saw her profile. It was like…well…it wasn't Ruby. It was all photos of her basically in her underwear, arching backwards to show off her body, acting like a semi-porn model, with flame emojis as captions that she had written about herself, and everyone underneath it had replied with more flame emojis."

Despite how upset I clearly was, Elijah still laughed at my description.

"Sorry, I sound really judgemental. Maybe I am. It just… it wasn't the friend I knew. Or maybe I didn't know her at all…that's what hurt so much. Maybe this was what she'd always wanted and, now she was free of the shackles of unpopularity, she was able to be herself…" My eyes pinched in more tears. A year ago now and just as painful.

I told Elijah how the wretched night progressed. How much Ruby's nose wrinkled when I told her about the new pizza restaurant. How, once she'd got over that disappointment, she'd spent an hour in our bathroom, and come out looking like she was dressed to go into the VIP section of an exclusive nightclub. How she'd asked me to take photos of her, but didn't ask me to be in them. Then, throughout dinner, how she'd spent most of the time on her phone.

"She did ask me the odd question," I explained, "but she'd be checking likes as I replied."

And, over my *capricciosa*, I came to the haunting realization that I'd been waiting *two years* for this one evening. Holding my breath, putting my life on hold, until she came back to me. Putting no effort into meeting anyone new. Whereas Ruby had moved on, maybe become the person she'd always wanted to be. She'd moved forward while I had stayed just the same, nursing a shrine to what we used to have. And even though I was in a bustling restaurant, with a queue of people waiting for a table by the door, I felt utterly alone. The humiliating isolation in realizing you don't only have the wrong end of a stick, you're holding a different stick entirely, and you're the only one holding it…

We made small talk while she ate her superfood salad. She had come, I reminded myself. She was still here, and trying, and had got on a plane and given up an evening in London to see an old friend, even if I had let her down by staying myself. The stupid pointless slug.

Well, that's what I thought.

"We went to bed weirdly early," I told Elijah. "She said she was sleepy. Honestly, it was lights out at eleven. Then I was woken by the sound of her whispering in the hallway. She was on the phone to someone. I know it was wrong but I went to the door to listen, and…she said…she…"

Elijah's arm tightened around me. It was so embarrassing to tell someone what had happened – especially a boy who

I kept thinking about kissing. Yet I couldn't not share it. I'd wanted to tell someone for so long. To not carry the burden of hurt alone any more.

"She was complaining. To that girl Delta. She was saying things like *'Oh my God, it's so boring here. I wish I hadn't come. My friend is such a loser now. It was so embarrassing to be out with her. She's, like, so pathetic.'*"

I closed my eyes and felt my heart break once more as the memory played out. I had never felt pain like it, with my ear against the wood of my door. Pain like a white heat. Too painful for colour. My family had always seen me as a boring loser, but Ruby never had. She'd seen more in me. Loved me. But now she saw what they saw. What everyone saw.

"I cried quietly on the floor as I'd given her the bed," I said. "And I came to the realization that maybe I *am* a loser. If it's the popular opinion, maybe she's right? Maybe they're all right?"

Elijah interrupted me for the first time. "No! You realize that *she's* the loser, right? You must realize that."

I shrugged. "I don't know. I was stupid enough to hold onto her, even though she clearly wasn't holding back. Too naive. Too pathetic. Too..."

Desperate, I wanted to say, but I didn't dare. Not wanting to put that particular word out there in connection to me.

But Elijah was still shaking his head. "It's not pathetic to want to keep connected to the people you love," he said, sounding a bit like he'd swallowed one of his mum's psychology books. "Or to want to be loved for who you are, rather than some weird act you put on."

His words worked and the grip around my heart loosened a little and I was able to smile.

"You know what? I do know that," I said, turning to him. "It's taken a while but I'm getting there. But that's not the only thing that's sad about it. What upsets me is that girl wasn't Ruby." I shook my head. "She wasn't real. She was this weird…recreation. Like a wax model." I shrugged, remembering the air vanishing in Madame Tussauds. "It's fake. The whole thing is fake. Ruby. Everyone at school. My dad… It's like, in order to get on in life, you have to be wax. Perfectly carved, and staying relevant enough to not be shoved into storage. Kicking everyone else down so you're not the one being stored away. But all of us have imperfections. We all know this, yet everyone's so desperate to hide them so they can be important, feel superior…" I sighed and watched my breath spiral into the blue sky. "We prefer fake," I said, thinking, painfully, of my mother for a second before quashing it. "We prefer fake stories to the real ones. The wax to the reality. Like, in Madame Tussauds…nobody minded that none of it was real. Like Ruby didn't seem to mind that none of her was real. In fact, she seemed to prefer it. And she also didn't seem to mind that she hurts people…that she hurt me. It's so messed up. It's like, let's all turn ourselves to wax and be terrible to people who point out that we're made of wax so we can feel superior, even though our whole existence is a lie…

God, what am I going on about? I'm sorry. I'm babbling."

Elijah hugged me so hard that I could feel the beat of his heart through his coat. "Don't be sorry," he said, releasing me. "Don't be sorry at all. You're talking sense, as always. So much sense. In fact, I don't think I've met anyone who speaks as much sense as you. Which is strange considering how very little you speak, on the whole."

I sniffed again and wiped my nose with my coat sleeve. Not very attractive, but I'd let everything out anyway – it wasn't like he would find me attractive after this. Not when he knew what a contaminated loser I was. "You're being very kind."

"Not kind. Honest."

"I think I shut down after that night," I told him. "I mean, I'd left it too late to make friends at school but I was still sort of myself. But last year, when she did that, it hurt too much and I died a bit. Ruby was the only person who knew what my family was like. Who knew the truth of what it was like to be me, and therefore why I am the way I am. She understood why I'm so quiet, so scared, so closed. And then she rejected it…she became like my dad…more interested in power than the truth."

The cold started to sneak in – finding gaps in my winter clothing and flooding through. I began to shiver. The only part of my body not freezing was my knee, which still had Elijah's hand on it.

"I'm sorry about your dad," he said, with such honesty and intensity I almost fell off the bench. "And I'm here whenever you want to talk about it. It's nowhere near as bad in my house, but to some degree, I do get how it feels when it's your parent causing you pain." He withdrew his hand to run it through his hair and my knee turned cold. "When it comes to my mum, I just feel constantly conflicted. I'm so angry at her for being such a hypocrite. But the moment I get angry, it hurts, because it's my mum and I love her, and I want her to love me. I've read enough of her books to know that need isn't something you can easily override…" He laughed even though he didn't mean the laugh. "You're trapped in this endless cycle of wanting more from them, and then hating them for not giving you more, and then feeling guilty and defensive of them, because you love them and don't want to feel badly about them, so you want them to change, you want more of them…but then the circle starts again…"

There will never be words to describe how much this landed. No adjective to adequately depict the feelings I got sitting on that freezing bench and hearing him say that. I started crying, and he teared up too.

So much for mooching, I thought.

"Things with your dad sound a lot worse than things with my mum," he continued, wincing at the thought of my home. "But I do get it. Especially the fake thing. You know that my mum actually lectures in attachment theory? She's considered an expert. She sits in labs all day, experimenting on kids to prove to society how important it is to be there for them, so everyone can give her a giant tick and a slap on the back and a well done, but at home, behind closed doors, she's hardly there. She's only Mum of the Year when she's having one of her performative parties." He took a long deep sniff. "I know why, too. It's because I remind her of my dad. God knows what the hell he did to her to make her hardly able to look at me. She never talks about him. It. Their divorce. She's supposed to be a psychologist, but we never go into the deep stuff. We never talk about anything that isn't totally plastic...or wax," he added, looking back at me and smiling.

I smiled too, despite the huge sadness we both felt as we snuffled. I felt weirdly calm, and good, and freed. I might be a loser. I might never be perfectly carved from wax. But this...now...it was the realest moment I'd ever lived in. And the realness of it was so much more beautiful than a fake, perfect shine. The telling of the story of what it's actually like to be you, and someone telling you their story back, and both of you realizing your story is kind of the same...it was the best few minutes of my insignificant life. And I only got to this moment because I'd told the truth about what it was like to be me. The imperfect, scary truth.

I turned to Elijah and tried to be as nourishing and comforting to him as he had been to me. "I'm sorry about your mum," I said, with full sincerity. "It's a shame she doesn't know you very well because you're pretty awesome, Elijah."

In the coldness of the weak winter sun, his cheeks grew hot and red. "Well, I'd say the same for your dad too. And this Ruby girl, whoever she is. She's missing out. It will take her too long to realize it, but she will realize it one day."

I rolled my eyes and he laughed.

"So wise and yet so lacking in self-belief."

I could feel our moment waning and wanted to end it before it soured. I needed it to stay perfect and unblemished for ever. "This is hardly mooching," I joked. "I don't think mooching involves butt cheeks this cold."

Elijah laughed widely and followed my lead without question. "You're right. Let's go warm up somewhere. We're letting the mooching side down. Lord Mooch is going to have to discipline us for crimes against Mooching and take us to the Highest Mooch Court in all of Moochland for a trial."

"What the actual hell are you talking about, Elijah?"

"I don't know. I've got frostbite of the head. Let's please go inside somewhere."

CHAPTER 26

We descended into the depths of the tube network and were soon warm again. The blast of central heating mingled with the warmth of mushed-together bodies, and soon I was shrugging myself out of my coat, and taking my hat off to fluff my hair.

"What is it?" I caught Elijah looking at me from where he was holding the pole. "Do I have hat hair?"

"No, nothing."

He looked down again, smiling at the filthy floor. I added this to the hand-taking and the knee-grab and the arm-around-me on the bench – put it all together and came up with hope. But not enough hope to do or say anything about it. It would kill me to ruin the pearl of a moment we'd just shared.

He navigated us to a part of London called the South Bank. It was right on the side of the Thames and teeming with people bundled up to enjoy the gorgeous day. Elijah pulled me to this open-air second-hand bookshop under a bridge and we searched for marginalia together. I found a battered copy of *The Catcher in the Rye* that was filled with pencil annotations and underlines. When I showed him, he honked with delight, and drew me in for a hug, before running over to the bookseller and buying it immediately – boring me by reading parts out loud as we walked down the river.

It was packed. Street performers demanded applause as they tottered on stilts, food huts pumped out fragrant steam, and the hot chocolates I bought us cost a fortune. We perched on the bench, next to a grumpy looking man sitting with his arms crossed, and slurped at our sugary drinks, staring out at the water. There were so many people here. So much life. I didn't know a single person walking past us, whereas, back home, you couldn't really even go get a milkshake at McDonald's without seeing at least twelve people you'd grown up with. No one here cared about school or who got how many photos in the yearbook. I allowed myself to think about Adam for the first time in a while, and a word floated into my head.

Perspective.

Adam had left the suffocating smallness of our town, gone to Bristol, and met loads of people who didn't know about our family and his school and our general lives. He'd realized how…unimportant he was, maybe, after years of Dad making him feel like a god. And that had given him the perspective to see what was really going on. Whereas Ruby had left our small town for somewhere even smaller and probably more suffocating and her perspective had got smaller, narrower. Her need to be important had been made greater by the fact that, in a tiny pond, you *feel* more important.

I took a deep breath, the cold air hitting the warmth of my tongue from the hot chocolate, and felt my lungs fill to full. Maybe in time, I pondered, I could escape to a city too? I could live somewhere busy and crowded, filled with people who didn't care about me in a way that was good for me?

"What are you thinking?" Elijah asked.

"How great it is to feel so insignificant right now, in this busy city."

He laughed. "Well, it's funny you should say that, because we are moments away from the third stop on today's magical mystery tour. The stop I like to call the 'legacy' part of the day."

I turned to him, confused. "Huh?"

He smiled sheepishly, reached into the pockets of his long chequered coat, and held up two padlocks.

"What are they for?"

He pointed to the water's edge behind me and I followed his finger. Chained to the railings were hundreds of locked padlocks, jammed onto every available space. It was the first time I'd noticed them.

"What the hell?"

I got up and wandered over to take them all in and Elijah followed. "They're padlocks," I said, unnecessarily, considering he had two in his pocket. I bent down to get a better look at the nearest one. A heavy-duty padlock, inscribed with the initials *HT* and *WG* and the date of only two days ago, had been clicked into place on the metal. It was one amongst a sea of padlocks, all carrying two sets of initials.

"It's a love lock," Elijah explained, reaching out and looking at one. "I read about them online. People leave them on landmarks in cities all over the world."

"Why?"

"They throw their key into the river afterwards apparently. It's to leave proof of their eternal love. And it's good content for social as well." He rolled his eyes, smiling. "It made me think of the messages you left behind in books, and I thought you'd kind of like the idea."

I crouched down and examined more of the locks. Lots of them were pretty new, the date only within the last year or so. But some were at least ten years old. I wondered where those people were now, whether they were still in love, whether they ever came to visit the padlock they'd left here over a decade ago.

My blood started sparking.

"They're great."

I felt Elijah's smile on the wind. "I knew you'd like them. Now, I know we are not a couple in love, so I thought I'd buy two, so we can do one each. Does that break the rules, do you think?"

When he said the words "couple in love" something lurched in my heart like it had just woken up from a lifelong nap.

"It's better than the rules," I managed to get out – unsure of what that giant emotional sneeze was about. I levelled him with a determined stare to throw him off any potential scent. "We will be declaring eternal love to ourselves. Your psychologist mother would LOVE the idea."

Elijah laughed. "Oh my God. She really would. Careful now, otherwise she'll get her laboratory rats to come up here with little rat padlocks and measure their serotonin levels afterwards."

"What a highly specific and very odd image."

Elijah bowed, then held out one padlock and a Sharpie pen. "Here to serve, as ever."

We returned to our original bench and each wrote our initials on our padlocks. It was beyond cold now, and getting darker as I wrote out *PW.*

"Are you ready?" Elijah held up his finished padlock. He'd written his initials, the date, and then added, *I exist*.

I held up mine, and we laughed when we realized we'd written the same thing. Two separate *I exists* on two separate padlocks. "Ready?"

We returned to the railings. "Let's stand close, so it looks like we're just nuzzling," Elijah said. "I think this might actually be a tiny bit illegal after all." He enveloped me in his coat, his smell and his warmth and his Elijah-ness, and my heart sneezed again, but I closed my eyes to block it out. This moment was about *me* – not anyone else. I felt so much lighter after telling Elijah about Ruby and Dad, the shame of it lessening with his understanding and his hug. I turned my padlock over in my cold hand and thought about what it represented. The tiny pieces of myself I'd left scattered around my small life – scribbles in the margins of books, flickering images on a security camera, a scrawled message in the steam of a window. I was telling the world I was here, but that was all I was telling it. Maybe I needed to tell the world a little bit more than the bare minimum? I squeezed the padlock and felt the cold metal seep through my gloves. This padlock was the bit of me, deep inside, that knew my story was worth telling. That maybe it would be good for me to start telling it. If I could just find the courage…

Elijah pulled his coat further around me. "Ready, steady, go."

We clicked our locks into place overlooking the river and the city lights and people who didn't know who I was, or what it meant to be me. I pictured the years rolling past. My life changing. My hair growing. My face becoming lined. The journey of my life, constant flux, constant changing… and yet this padlock would stay put. And I wondered who that girl would be, all those years in the future, coming back to visit her padlock.

I wanted her to be someone brave enough to tell her story. To have the lightness that comes with that.

I exist.

The sun was blobbing down, tucking itself under the river. I felt the winter wind lift my hair and the squeak of who I am became a roar. The voice that tells me I'm nothing faded to a soft whimper.

I wiped my eyes with my coat sleeve, punctuating what had just happened, and turned to Elijah. He was holding up his padlock key and grinning. Always knowing when I needed time.

"Ready?" he asked.

And I was. Ready to become the person I felt I was blooming into.

I nodded and, together, we chucked our keys as far as we could into the grey Thames water. They fell with unremarkable plops and were lost to the currents. I felt the hugest urge to rest my head on his shoulder – to breathe him in and take everything this meant deep into my lungs.

And Elijah, oblivious, unwrapped his coat and acted totally normal. "Can we read old books the whole way home and share the best bits we find in the margins while eating mint Aeros please?"

I nodded. Not disappointed. This moment had been about me, and him – not us. "Sounds perfect."

It was pitch black by the time we got home, our breath frosting, my knees shaking under my jeans as we got off the train. The barriers swallowed our day tickets, and we stood facing one another.

"Thank you." I glanced up at the announcements board rather than him. "Today. It meant a lot."

"Right back at you. Seriously."

The way he said "seriously" made me look at him and he

was staring at me. All laughter gone. A look of…intent on his face.

"I'd better go," I said, choking it. "I need to get my stuff from Polly's before I head home."

"Me too. I've been pretending I don't need to do my philosophy essay but I actually really need to do it."

We stood still, neither of us leaving.

"So…"

"So…"

A robotic announcement bleated in the background. The barriers pinged with the noise of accepted tickets and the *boosh* of them flinging open. People rang taxi companies because it was too cold to walk. Still neither of us moved.

"See you at school tomorrow?"

Why was it always me breaking the tension, especially as I didn't want the tension to break?

"You will indeed." Elijah opened his arms to hug me goodbye. The second I was enveloped in his arms, I found I couldn't let go, even though we were in the middle of a train station. I squeezed him around his back, feeling his chest pressed to mine, his heartbeat thudding against my own. My nose was in his neck and the smell of him was like a tailor-made perfume. He hugged me tighter and I felt this *feeling* coming from him. An energy he'd only briefly danced with all day. He didn't let go and neither did I. We hugged past the point of it being usual. It would take only one of us to tilt our chin and it would become a kiss. Was he thinking this too?

…And, yet again, it got too much for me. I slackened my grip.

"Better go," I said.

Elijah didn't miss a beat. Or maybe there was no beat to miss in the first place. Maybe it was just a hug between friends and I was reading too much into it?

"See you tomorrow."

He waved goodbye and walked in the direction of his house…not glancing back. And I watched him not glance back and, just like that, the hug became something less. A projection rather than a reality. A lovely memory.

A memory that would soon be tainted because, of course, someone had seen us.

Year Eleven

Do you remember when...

...**Charlie** got **everyone** a year-group **detention** for ruining the school photo?

...**Everyone** thought **Paige** was one half of a **devil-worshipping** couple?

How has time gone so quickly? How is it almost time to say goodbye to this school, these corridors, the memories? We all grew up. Older, wiser. No longer scared of the big kids in the canteen – we are the big kids in the canteen. They say school days are the best days of your life, and who's ready to say goodbye to that? We're not sure we are. But life keeps going, and at least we get to wear our own clothes in sixth form.

WHAT REALLY HAPPENED...

Beware of anyone who tells you school was the best time of their life. Chances are, they are a massive psychopath. Anyone willing Year Eleven to *slow down* is usually the reason the rest of us are praying it will hurry up. The truth is, by Year Eleven, you're tired of it, bored of it. You've had to cope with it all for so long. You want to be free.

To some degree, things loosen. People are too tired to care. Exams take up so much mental anguish. Growth spurts settle. Braces come off. Tribes solidify. The end is in sight. We just want to get through to the other side. To drop the subjects we hate, and let go of the labels that we can't shake.

The labels we can't shake because *They* won't let us.

They. The ones who don't want any of this to go away. They. Who maybe know, on a subconscious level, that this is the best it's going to get for them. They sharpen their fingernails and dig in, holding on tight, reminding us that it's not over yet. It's not over until the night of the Leavers' Ball, where they will literally reign. Know your place till then. Don't you dare mess it up. Don't you dare, don't you dare...

...whoopsy!

CHAPTER 27

The first day back after half-term break had already been brutal considering it wasn't yet nine a.m. Dad woke up with a cold, which stopped him going to work. A cold that, of course, was Mum's fault for letting her disgusting friends into the house last Friday, who'd deliberately infected him. I'd got dressed silently upstairs, trying not to make any noise on the floorboards, wincing at the grovelling apologies downstairs, then the slam of Dad's retreat into his bedroom and his sick bed. Mum cried in the kitchen and I realized it would be another day of slipping out without breakfast.

Was it getting worse? I asked myself as I disappeared, unnoticed, out of the front door.

Had me going to Polly's made it worse? Or was it just the fresh air of Polly's house making me realize it was actually quite bad, rather than normal?

I hadn't thought to worry about school. It had been weeks since my outburst in the yearbook meeting and nothing had happened. I'd assumed the Awfuls considered me too insignificant to take on, which was a relief while also vaguely hurtful. Anyway, my brain was busy digesting my long hug with Elijah, alongside worrying about Mum but knowing I'd only make it worse if I tried to talk to her about it.

The stares were the first sign that something was wrong.

Nobody had ever, *ever* stared at me before, so I noticed it immediately with a fluttering heart.

As I passed the school gates, I sensed people from my year turning their heads to look at me. My stomach, already a rock lined with lead and wrapped in a coat of barbed wire, dropped into my knees.

No no. Not today. *Please*, not today.

Maybe it was just toothpaste around my mouth? I patted my butt self-consciously to check my skirt wasn't tucked into my tights. No. Maybe it was a one-off? The stares continued as I made my way to form room. Then came the accompanying whispers. And the odd terrible giggle. My face turned red. My lungs to cement. My knees jellified and I could hardly make it past the lockers.

Then, up ahead, there they were. Grace and her rearranged trio, leaning against her locker, looking perfect and unflappable. Her eyes actually lit up when she saw me. She turned to Amelia, whispered something, and they both let out cruel laughter.

Payback.

For challenging her at the yearbook meeting, even though it was weeks ago. Now I had the horrific wait to find out what the rumour was. Because they never tell you. That's part of the game.

I ignored them as I walked past. Mouth set. Emotionless despite the tsunami crashing around my body.

"Be careful," Grace whispered. "Don't want to piss her off. God knows what they'll do."

Hang on...*they'll?*

A cold fear cocktail exploded around my body, and, as I slunk into form time, the room hushed.

They'll.

I'm not a "they"...am I?

No.

Not Elijah.

Mrs Collins arrived right after me, giving me no chance to overhear the whispers.

"Calm yourselves. Jesus. It's Monday morning. How do you have the energy?" She clapped her hands but everyone carried on chatting. She raised her eyebrows smugly. "Well, fine then," she said. "If you *don't* want to know more about your Leavers' Ball, that's fine. Chat away."

Everyone fell quiet in feverish anticipation and Mrs Collins's eyebrows got even smugger.

"Tickets go on sale this week," she said. "You can buy them from Mr Clarke's office. There's a leaflet here, explaining the dates and prices."

She passed out a flier and people leaped on them like they were Willy Wonka's golden tickets. I didn't even glance at mine as I'd had to proofread it before it went to print.

It was a generic school-ball poster: a clip-art illustration of a couple in evening wear twirling above the ornate font that said, *A Night to Remember. A Night to Say Goodbye.*

"Sounds like some kind of suicide pact," Elijah had remarked when I'd sent him a photo before half-term. "With limos."

Elijah… Oh God. What was going on?

I felt the classroom's eyes return to me as Mrs Collins started to bore people with small print. The price of the ball tickets. The behaviour expected. The date of the Leavers' Assembly. How much the yearbook cost. When you needed to bring money in by. Then, as if things weren't terrible enough, she gestured to me, a stupid smile on her face.

"Of course, you can talk to Paige here if you have any questions. She's been really involved in the yearbook. Let's thank her for her hard work."

I shrank into the sweaty plastic of my chair as the class gaze intensified.

"Before she kills us all," a male voice said, to surrounding laughter.

"Yep. Her and her psycho boyfriend will probably curse us all at the ball."

Further laughter while I closed my eyes and tried to regulate my breathing. Elijah. They'd dragged him into this. The one good thing about school. It hurt so viscerally I felt I was having an allergic reaction. Then my phone buzzed in my pocket and I checked it under my desk with shaking hands.

Elijah: Can we meet at break? Something weird is going on.

No joke. No sarcasm. No warmth. The bile in my throat started roaring. Sitting in my chair was practically unbearable. Regret pulsed through me, stinging my insides with each heartbeat.

Why did I have to say something? Why was I so stupid? Why did I bring this on myself? What is wrong with me? Have I learned nothing from keeping those notebooks all these years?

Mrs Collins answered a few questions about the ball (*No, you can't drink, Daniel. Yes, you will be expelled. No, Daniel, I will not be DJing*) then shooed us out to assembly. I pulled my sleeves over my hands and blended in as best I could as we spilled out towards the main hall. Then, as we passed the girls' toilets, I ducked in, gasping as the door swung shut. I let out a weird groan of pain and went into the end toilet, put the seat down, and sat on it with my legs up.

I hated myself more than I hated them. So stupid. So, so stupid. I wanted to scream and rip my skin off at the same time. I banged my head against my knees multiple times, remembering the stupid words falling out of my mouth in that yearbook meeting. "*What if Cara doesn't consent? Yadda yadda yadda.*" What the hell had I been thinking? And I hadn't even freaking jumped in front of the car for a very important reason. So what if Cara was happy to write something for the yearbook? I'd ruined my life for that?

Not for Charlie when they threw a nut at him? Not for all the other horrific things I see every day?

The corridor outside fell quiet.

The whole school fell quiet.

I still wasn't entirely sure what the rumour was that they'd started about me. How bad could it be?

Assemblies were held. The bell rang and I locked myself in the cubicle, and sat with my head between my legs, as girls used the toilet before lessons. Some of them tried my door, but I held firm. I would stay there for the next hour. I would stay until I could see Elijah and figure out how bad this was. The bell went again. The toilet emptied as girls hurried away to avoid getting a late slip. I heard two girls chat quietly as they washed their hands in a rush.

"...someone saw them kissing at the train station. I know, right? It's always the quiet ones."

"Woah. But Elijah's really fit. Weird. But fit. Plus, he's a sixth former! And she's like..."

"Nobody, I know. But I heard that they're like this crazy, witchy voodoo couple. Worshipping the devil and that. Into all sorts of weird sex stuff. Makes sense. I mean, he's good-looking, but he is strange. And her...well...nobody really knows much but..."

Their voices were lost as they left. Now I knew what the rumour was.

Because Elijah and I hugged at the train station, we were, of course, a couple that worshipped the devil and did crazy sex things.

So stupid. Oh, it was always so stupid, but hats off to Grace. It was good. Stupid enough to spread like a virus. Stupid enough to stick like superglue. So many joke opportunities. This was it. From this moment, I would always be the sex cult girl… And Elijah would be the sex cult boy.

Elijah…

I let out a weird moan again. With panic. With rage. At them all, but mostly at myself. Because no matter how careful I'd been, I'd let myself slip once. And you only needed to slip once to be ruined for ever…

CHAPTER 28

I read once that humiliation is the most powerful human emotion. We fear it the most, avoid it the most, and find it the most unbearable to sit with. It's the humiliating memories that haunt you most aggressively when you're trying to sleep – still recoiling in your skin when your brain hits the *replay* button. My dad certainly feared humiliation, probably even more than he feared indifference.

Now I was going to be a humiliation to Elijah.

I was going to taint his life with the tang of social judgement. He was going to be embarrassed to know me. Just like my dad found me embarrassing. Like Ruby found me embarrassing. I cried quietly as I tortured myself with how humiliating I was to everyone.

The hour of my bunked-off lesson inched by as I told myself stories of how Elijah was going to react. At the very best, he'd find it pathetic and childish. At the worst, he'd be repulsed. Disgusted at the idea of being romantically linked to a loser like me. Humiliated to be associated with something so childish when he was so mature and above such things.

"Look, I'm sorry, but maybe we shouldn't spend time together for a while," he would tell me without meeting my eye. *"It's just a bit much. You know?"*

I shouldn't have said anything in that yearbook meeting. Why had I said anything? I'd have to sit alone in the library every lunchtime again, and Laura had taken my spot. Shrivel my way through to the end of the year.

When the bell went, I ran to our quiet patch and sat shivering – waiting for him and his verdict.

Elijah appeared with a beanie hat pulled low, face grim, long coat wrapped around himself. I wondered how it was possible my heart could beat so hard without exploding into dust.

"I'm sorry, Paige, if you got the wrong idea. I didn't mean to lead you on. I don't feel like that about you. What have you been telling people?"

Elijah folded his coat under his butt as he sat next to me.

"I'm sorry," I told the half-frozen ground instead of saying hello. "I'm so sorry."

"What the hell are you sorry for?" His voice was warm and comforting – not defensive. I looked over to find not a trace of humiliation on his face – just concern.

"It's all my fault. I stupidly challenged the stupid popular girls in a yearbook meeting and this is their revenge. Someone must have seen us at the train station and started a stupid rumour… Sorry. I didn't even think people knew who I was…"

Elijah smiled grimly. "Well, we were sacrificing all those babies, to be fair," he said. "We can't be surprised we brought attention to ourselves."

He was joking. I laughed with a large shocked "Ha!", melting into glorious relief.

"So you've heard then? How we basically worship the devil?"

He rolled his eyes and shook his head. "Yes, I was informed when I got into the common room this morning that I was a) dating a Year Eleven, and b) having a threesome with Beelzebub."

"I'm so, so sorry."

He held up his hands. "Don't be! Christ. I'm not mad. Did you think I'd be mad? I was worried about you. I mean, if it's got to the sixth-form common room, I figured it was the most dramatic thing *ever* in your year. I wanted to know you were okay?"

His words were hot chocolate. A shocking slurp of it that almost burned my tongue.

"Oh, yeah. I'm fine," I lied. "I mean, it's obviously ridiculous."

"Yeah, but this stuff upsets you."

"It's not fun, being socially annihilated for no reason. No."

"Oh, it's not for no reason," he said. "Be certain about that."

"What do you mean?"

"You challenged them. You made them look at themselves and, *of course*, they didn't like it. So they're doubling down. Trying to let you know who's in control of the story." He reached over and patted my shoulder. It was nice, but it was also distinctly unsexual compared to the lasting hug of the other day. He was being kind, certainly, but he was also reasserting the boundaries. The rumours had maybe spooked him more than he was letting on. An icy pang of hatred shot through me, at the girls who did this to me, who took it upon themselves to alter the dynamics of my life. "It means it's working," he reassured me. "It means you got through."

"Well, they're being worse than ever." I put my fingers to my temples. "What am I supposed to do? What are *we* supposed to do? Everyone thinks we're out here, like, sacrificing pigeons and God knows what else."

He shrugged. "So?"

"So! That's all anyone is going to see in me until I leave school."

"So?"

"So! That's not fair. That isn't me. It's ludicrous, and everyone knows it's ludicrous, and yet they'll say it about me anyway."

"Okay then. So…why not tell them who you really are?" He put his fingers under his chin. "The worst has happened now, and it's not that bad. Why not keep telling the truth? Keep telling the story about who they are? Keep challenging them?"

"It'd be easier just to leave school."

He laughed. "Leave school if you want, if that's the best decision for your future. But don't leave because of something as dumb as this."

"It's…not fair!"

His head fell to one side. "No, it's not fair. It never is…"

I did more furious under-eye wiping. "And sorry you're being dragged into all this…childishness. It must be embarrassing for you."

He shook his head. "It's not. I don't care about stuff like this, you know that."

"You MUST care a little bit."

He shook his head again. "Nope. Caring is how you give them your power."

"Well, you must be a psychopath if you don't care what people think about you." With nowhere for my anger to go, it landed on him and I shot him a dreadful look. Plus, he was lying. He said it hadn't impacted him but I could sense the change of vibe between us already. He was distancing himself from me because of it. I'd ruined this. By following his advice I'd ruined it.

His eyes widened, wounded. "That's not fair, Paige. I do care what some people think about me. But I decided to only care about the opinions of people who I care about. Other people can tell whatever stories they want about me. I can't control that. And I don't care what they say any more. Everyone, everywhere, is going to have an opinion about you. The important thing is learning whose opinions are worth listening to. Plus…" He let out a jet of breath that turned to frost. "Let's be honest about it. I'm a boy. Any rumour that I'm screwing a pretty girl is always going to be a good look for me. Even if I don't agree with that. Even if they're saying we're screwing slaughtered lambs at the same time. I'm sorry that's how the world works, but that's how it is."

He'd just called me "pretty". It was the first glow of warmth I've had all day – pathetic as that may be. Elijah had never commented on my appearance before and now I knew he thought I was pretty. But it was ruined. I couldn't pretend there wasn't an edge to our interaction now. An uneasiness in how we related. Naming the elephant in the room can be powerful at the right time, but awful at the wrong time. We knew we'd hugged for too long. It had been there between us, hovering, waiting to be named, unparcelled and examined. But now it had been named not on our own timeline and in a whirlwind of teenage patheticness. The gust of social turbulence had blown out our flicker. And I knew we wouldn't hug like that again. Grace and her friends had taken that story from me. They'd snuffed out the flame of my own life narrative in revenge for me throwing a thimble of water onto theirs.

It wasn't fair, it wasn't fair, it wasn't fair.

"It still isn't fair," I told Elijah. My own frozen breath carved a trail through the sky next to his.

"I know. I'm sorry."

I felt the literal and metaphorical distance between us on that bench and I started to fill it with rage. It had been too unfair for too long. Injustice after injustice, going unpunished and uncorrected – rewarded even. Scribbling the truth in my sad little books at home and then coming into school and filling the yearbook with lies. I was no longer humiliated that everyone thought I worshipped the devil. No, I was humiliated by my own cowardice. The bargain I'd wagered with the devil. A zipping of my lips and a pact to stay silent about the truth, in exchange for a quiet life. Yes, I was angry at Grace and the rest of them. But I was even angrier at myself.

"I…I…want to do something about all this," I said, lifting my chin. "I want to start telling the truth."

I glanced sideways and saw Elijah's face had transformed. Like he'd overheard the conversation I'd just had with myself. He gleamed with pride, his smile so wide it split his face. "Do you want to do a blood sacrifice for revenge?" he joked. "I've got two skinned cats in my bag, but the spell won't work unless you pour some of your virgin blood on top of them?"

"How can we be virgins if we're also having weird satan sex with one another?"

His eyebrows raised and there it was again. Our spark. The tiniest splutter of it. But I didn't have time for that now. Not with my anger and sense of purpose raging through me, making me feel strong for the first time in my life.

"Seriously though," I said. "You're right. I need to do something. I need to finally fight back. I need to tell the real story…" Then I thought of the feeling of walking through the corridors that morning with everyone's eyes on me.

The sickness in my guts. The giggles that would now follow me wherever I went. The gross comments made behind my back. And I put my head on my knees again, losing the will as quickly as it had come, wanting to run back into my security blanket of passive silence. "But I'm scared," I told him, turning my head to one side to look back at him. "I'm really, really scared."

Elijah tilted his head. "Of course you're scared," he said. "But you don't have to do it all at once. And you don't have to do it alone." He patted my back platonically. "I'll help you."

3rd March

Grace etc. started a rumour that I worship the devil with Elijah, and we are a weird sex-cult couple because we hugged once at a train station.

10th March

Everyone's saying Laura Goddard has incurable "super gonorrhoea" after we had a school assembly about it.

15th March

Joe took out Patrick's chair just as he was sitting down in biology today and he hurt his back falling to the floor.

22nd March

Now, apparently I'm a prostitute!!??

CHAPTER 29

One of Charles Dickens's most-sifted quotes is, "*It was the best of times; it was the worst of times*" and it certainly rang true in the month following the devil-worshipping rumour. I started living the thing I'd been dreading for years. I was a laughing stock. A target. People snorted when I walked past. But I also had Elijah at my side, making it weirdly enjoyable.

He'd come into school the next day with a pentagram drawn onto both cheeks with his red pen. It caused pandemonium, with Reverend John asking to speak to him immediately, and the news going through the school like a superbug.

"What the hell are you doing?" I asked, when I met him for lunch with freshly-scrubbed cheeks.

He laughed. "Well, one, it's hardly fair for you to go through this all by yourself, is it? And two, the rumour is ridiculous. Everyone knows it's not true. So we may as well have fun with it." He got out his red pen and took the lid off with his teeth, a glint in his eye.

"Elijah, no."

"Come on. It will be freeing, I promise you."

"We go to a religious school."

"Yes, but it's also a human right to respect people's religious identities. Reverend John can't argue with the Human Rights Act." He moved forward, his breath tickling my face. "Come on."

And I embraced the weird liberation that comes from a nightmare coming true – in that, things can't get much worse – and I leaned in, trying not to swoon too much at our physical proximity, and let him decorate my cheek. When we walked into school after lunch, he picked up my hand and squeezed it, and the crowds parted for us, staring, whispering, laughing, getting that we were in on the joke. I'd never felt freer. The shackles of the rumour loosened and I giggled non-stop, even when Ms Collins made me wash my face in the bathroom.

"How's Satan?" someone asked me in the corridor one morning, a week later.

"Your mum's fine, thanks for asking."

They didn't ask again.

Then another rumour went around about someone else, and the heat died down for a while. Spring arrived right out of nowhere – shocking everyone with weird hot days likely caused by climate crisis, but enjoyed nonetheless. I heard that Sam had commented that Laura had good legs, and thus Laura was punished for having legs by being exposed as having super gonorrhoea. She practically lived in the library now. She'd stopped wearing make-up altogether and actually looked much prettier – younger, innocent. I wasn't fooled however. I still had pages of the awful things she'd done in my books at home. I knew she'd happily claw my eyes out, poke them onto sticks and eat them like lollipops, if it meant winning her popularity back.

"I mean, when you make up metaphors like that," Elijah remarked, grinning as always, "you can kind of see where the devil worship idea comes from."

I hit him over the head with the book I'd been reading.

"Also, have you considered she might have learned from the whole thing? Grown?"

I pulled a face. "Yeah, right."

"Ask her if she's okay. She might surprise you."

"Come on, Elijah." I picked up another book at random and forcibly changed the subject. But, as bloody usual, his words burrowed in and I wondered how Laura saw everything now she was on the other side of it. Later that afternoon, while popping to the loo to change my tampon, I found new graffiti about her scrawled in Tippex on the back of the stall in large writing.

LAURA HAS SUPER GONORRHEEA

I stared at it for some time, imagining what it would feel like for her to read this. To know it was here for all to see. To be so punished for something when the boy involved, Sam, had got off totally scot-free. It wasn't the largest bit of activism in the world, but, after I'd flushed, I got out my pen and added an arrow to the graffiti and the words:

Whoever wrote this is a nasty person who can't spell.

I laughed as I read it back, at how pathetic it was. A bleat of protest that was unlikely to ever be noticed, but it was something. It wasn't in my notepad for one. And it was the simple truth, told without malice.

A week later, I'd done the same to a piece of graffiti every time I went to the toilet at school.

What sort of person writes this about another person?

Whoever wrote this needs therapy.

Writing this is bullying. And if you wrote it,
then you're a bully.

"Do you think I'm pathetic?" I asked Elijah one lunchtime in the library, as we were reading *Noughts and Crosses* together to sift it for the best line. "Just scribbling on a toilet stall."

"I would never think you're pathetic," he replied, putting his book down. "This is all new to you. You've got to start somewhere." He put both hands under his chin, to make himself look all cheesy. "As my mother would say to somebody else's child she's helping rather than me, 'You're learning a new language here, be patient and kind to yourself.' This is a muscle you haven't used before."

I laughed, while also feeling a pang of sadness for how he felt about his mum. I wanted to reach out and console him, but we still hardly touched since the rumour.

I was getting better at speaking the language of activism though, and caring a tiny bit less about the consequences.

"Do you think she's paying Elijah to go out with her?" Joe asked one morning when Mr Sanders was out of the room, loud enough for everyone to hear.

"Maybe he's paying me?" I said.

There was then a further flurry of rumours that I was a prostitute, and it hurt less than the first burn. Especially as, that very week, I found some more graffiti on the loo door. Somebody had written *Sophia D is a slut,* which must've been about someone in another year, as I didn't recognize the name. But, under the graffiti, I almost cried when I saw somebody had copied me.

Whoever wrote this is trash.
PS. A slut is a social construct.

I held my heart, traced the words, and let it give me strength to continue living down all the untrue things about myself. I checked on other graffiti and saw people had added to that too.

Why doesn't the school stop this? someone wrote.

Another had said, OH, I SEE SOCIOPATHY IS STILL A THING. PATHETIC.

One more had just scrawled, BE FUCKING KIND. JESUS.

As spring continued to spring, I felt brave enough to go back into yearbook meetings.

In the first I'd attended since it all kicked off, the Awfuls arrived late as always, and Grace smirked at me as she took her seat. A smirk of victory. A smirk of *How about you shut up now?*

My hate bloomed like the blossoms on the trees outside. The smirk may as well have been two tonnes of high-quality compost.

"We've been thinking," she said, before they'd even sat down, "that we should save a page at the end of the yearbook for photos of the Leavers' Ball. I know there's only two weeks between the ball and the Leavers' Assembly, so, Ms Gordon, can you have a chat to the printers or something?" She gestured to Ms Gordon like she was her employee. "But we thought it would be such a great ending to the book, you know? To tell the *full* story."

Her eyes found mine again and she raised one perfect eyebrow. I received it as the challenge it was. Grace was daring me to disagree with her, seeing if I'd learned my lesson.

I opened my mouth, wondering if I dared say anything I wanted to say. Things like, *Seriously?* and *Don't you think your narcissistic personality disorder has had enough enabling in this yearbook?*

But I bottled it the second I started speaking. "I actually *love* that idea," my stupid scared mouth said. "It would mean a very last-minute turnaround, but Grace is right. The Leavers' Ball is *such* a rite of passage. Even if it leads to a tight deadline."

Grace nodded, accepting the truce, and turned away from me.

While I spent the following two days hating myself for being such a coward.

"It takes time," Elijah kept saying. "Give yourself time."

The devil-worshipping prostitute rumours died over the next few weeks, and I was vaguely safe again. Forever tainted, but safe. Petals continued to erupt on previously bare tree branches. Teachers couldn't breathe without mentioning revision timetables. Easter eggs dominated supermarket shelves, and the yearbook really started to come together. We soon had all the memory pages laid out, and could move onto the most treasured section of all: *Most Likely to*. The closest thing you'll ever find to a social version of the Olympic Games.

"Okay, gumshoes," Ms Gordon said in the week before Easter. "Here is a shortlist of the *Most Likely to* categories. We need to pick which ones we think will work in the yearbook. Then each form will nominate one boy and one girl candidate – and we'll put it to a vote." She handed out a list of the sterile topics the school had approved.

Most likely to be a film star.
Most likely to win an Olympic medal.
Most likely to be a head teacher.

They were all pretty neutral, allowing the obvious people to win all the most obvious categories. Fulfilling the destiny of how *Most Likely tos* worked.

"I bet you win model AND film star," Cara stage-whispered to Grace.

Grace simpered and pretended to blush. "Don't be stupid. I can't act!" Her fake modesty made that very clear. She would win regardless.

At the edge of my vision, I saw Daisy roll her eyes, and I smiled and looked downwards, so they didn't see.

"We also need to finalize the questions we're sending out to students to put with their Year Eleven headshot," Ms Gordon said. She distributed two hardback books each around the circle. "Here are the last two yearbooks to give you some ideas."

We all quietly flicked through the pages of earnest school photos of past students. My eyes were searching for him from the second I opened last year's yearbook. It seemed insane that Elijah existed within something so conventional. And yet there he was. I flattened the page down to get a better look.

His Year Eleven portrait was Elijah personified – dishevelled, unkempt, oozing energy. He had both eyebrows raised and stared directly into the lens, face deadpan – all like, *And what?* He looked attractive, as usual – though younger, obviously, and his hair was longer last year. I reached out to stroke the photo before remembering where I was, and pretended to stretch my hand instead. I glanced up to check I hadn't been caught, but Grace, Amelia and Cara were poring over the photos of an old Leavers' Ball, laughing and taking the piss out of girls' dresses.

"I mean, who wears an actual ballgown to a school Leavers' Ball," Amelia whispered, jabbing some poor girl on the page. "Does she think she's in a Disney movie or something?"

Grace vibrated with laughter beside her. "Do you think she got a horse-drawn carriage too?" she added and they honked like geese.

I tuned them out, returning to Elijah's segment.

I hope people remember me as...
favourably as they'll no doubt remember themselves.

My favourite thing about school was...
the excitement of seeing Darwinism be proven in real-time.

In the future, I hope to...
work everything through in therapy.

A little voice wiggled into my heart, curled up, and made a bed in there.

I love him, the little voice told me, like a mewing kitten. *I love him. I love him, I love him.*

I held my heart through my jumper to try and shut it up, grinning until my face strained.

I couldn't help myself. I was so proud of knowing this boy. I tried to make my face and heart calm down so I didn't draw attention to myself.

After we'd all looked through, Ms Gordon got out a pen and stood next to the whiteboard.

"So, guys, what questions did you think worked?"

Grace didn't bother putting her hand up. "I like the first one," she said. "We should keep that. '*I hope people remember me as…*'"

Amelia poked her in the side with her elbow. "I hope people remember me as hot," she muttered and they all giggled.

I'll remember you as being a brutal bully, I thought.

I found my arm going up in the air and everyone noticed.

"Could we change the last question maybe?" I suggested. I looked down at what I'd scribbled. "I was thinking… '*What would you like to tell your future self?*' Then it's sort of like time travel for everyone. We're all leaving messages to our future selves, and, because it's a shared artefact, all of those messages hold us accountable to what we say?"

An impressed nod by Ms Gordon. "What do you think, guys?"

There was a room full of more impressed nods, and even reluctant ones from the Awfuls.

"Brilliant. In it goes. Right, anyone else?"

I leaned back in my chair as the conversation moved on and thought wistfully about Future Me for a moment. The one living in a city, and being brave, and telling the truth – with friends and purpose and laughter. Going back occasionally to visit the padlock by the river and reflect on how much she'd grown and changed. I was in such a state of deep reflection that, when my phone buzzed, I jumped in the air like I'd sat on a pin.

"Paige, you know you're not supposed to have your phone on during meetings," Ms Gordon scolded.

"Sorry." I pulled my phone onto my lap to check who it was – the only two options being Polly or Elijah. Or so I thought, because…

It dropped to the floor with a clatter.

"Paige! I told you. No phones."

"Sorry."

I bent down with wobbly hands. The message was still on my screen.

A message from my brother.

A message from my brother who never sends me messages.

Adam: Look, sorry, but I've been thinking about it and I'm not coming home for Easter. I'm doing this Slum it to Slovenia charity hitch-hike thingy, which is a good cover and, to be fair, sounds like a laugh. I know Dad will be Dad about it. Not told them yet, but thought I'd give you a heads up.

My selfish prick of a brother who only thinks of himself.

CHAPTER 30

The meeting was finished. Everyone scraped their chairs back and filtered out into the empty school, but I couldn't stand.

"You okay, Paige?" Ms Gordon asked. She took a photo of her whiteboard notes then packed her stuff into her feathered handbag. "It was nice to see you contribute today."

"Hmm."

"I can't believe it's almost Easter. Where did the year go?"

"Hmm."

"Paige?"

"Yeah?"

"I need to lock up the classroom now."

"Oh, sorry." I knocked my chair onto the carpet in my haste to get up. "Sorry." I straightened it and it wobbled before settling.

"Are you okay, Paige?"

"Yep. Brilliant. Bye, see you tomorrow."

Why, Adam? Why? *Why?* Stupid selfish brother. Never,

ever thinking about anything other than HIMSELF and what is best for HIM and how to make HIS life easier. He was just like Dad. Which wasn't surprising, as Dad had raised him to be just like Dad. Oh God. I couldn't go home. What would Dad do when he found out? I couldn't. Couldn't. But Polly was away for two nights for some cat mental-health conference, which, she'd said, had a disappointing number of cats actually attending.

I paced the empty hallways, lockers smudging to a blur. What time did school close? I could hide here for a while? I honestly contemplated climbing into a school cupboard and stowing away there overnight.

My phone went again.

Elijah: How was the yearbook meeting?
Have you won most likely to be a total
legend yet? Or do I need to rig the votes?

I typed out and deleted the same message twice – wondering whether to tell him about Adam. Still aching with that self-protective urge to come across as perfect to him. Then I sighed and tapped out the truth.

Paige: Meeting over. Fine. Not so fine news
about my family though. I've just got a
terrible message from my brother.

Elijah: Yikes. You okay? Obviously not.

Sorry. Are you still in school? I'm just
leaving the library. Can come fine you?
Elijah: *Find. Stupid predictive text.
Being fined is the last thing you need.

I stopped in the maths corridor and let out a hiccup of love. At this kindness. This friendship. This life raft of a message. I wasn't alone in this. I had someone.

Paige: In maths block.

Elijah: I'll meet you by the side exit in five?
Take you for a milkshake?

Paige: See you in five.
Paige: Thank u xxx

Oh God, Elijah's face when I found him at the side exit. I was overcome. He may as well have been riding a white horse and fighting off a dragon, rather than slouching with his hands in his pockets and a worried expression.

"Paige." He pulled me in for a hug, and his smell was so restorative they should provide it on the NHS.

I could've easily glued myself to his coat, but I reckoned that would give away my growing feelings. "What were you doing in the library?"

"Philosophy revision. There's blossom on the trees, Paige. That means, exams-wise, we are screwed."

"Yep. Spring is here. Wanna know how I know? Because we've just agreed to delay the printing of the yearbook to include a double-page spread of the Leavers' Ball. I, of course, just nodded like the freaking nodding dog coward that I am throughout the meeting."

Elijah looked at me intensely for a second, and clocked that I wasn't quite ready to talk yet, so he followed my conversational lead. "Ahh, yes. The all-important ball. That non-clichéd rite of passage. Got your dress yet?" he asked, as we fell into step towards town.

"Oh yeah. I've been getting all my animal friends to help me make it for ages now. Who knew mice were so good at sewing? On the big night, all I need to do is shower and then let some birds drop it over my head and I'll be good to go."

Making Elijah belly-laugh should also be prescribed on the NHS. Though he shot me one more anxious look. The dark cloud of my brain turned to a slightly lighter shade of grey as we walked. I looked up, enjoying the magnolia adorning the passing trees.

"Did you go to your Leavers' Ball?" I asked him.

"Umm. No." He shrugged. "I didn't see the point."

"It is a rite of passage though, isn't it? It's part of the school story. Even if you don't go, that's still part of the story. It says something about you regardless. We are still defined by the Leavers' Ball."

He reached up as we passed a magnolia tree and yanked out a pink-tinged petal. He held it against his cheek for a second and then handed it over. "Do you want to go to yours?"

I turned the petal over in my hand, not fully able to concentrate on its velvetness or even the ball chat, as Adam's message kept flashing into my brain. "I don't know," I replied, honestly. "Going has never really been an option. Maybe I would've gone with Ruby if she hadn't left. She would've wanted to go…" I held the petal to my lips.

"Do you ever think about calling her?" he asked. "Asking her what happened? Saying how much it hurt."

I snorted. "She's probably forgotten I exist. Plus, remember the giant coward thing? I told you, I just sat mute through yearbook today. So much for wanting to speak up…"

"Okay, so I'm going to try this thing where I ignore you whenever you're being a dick towards yourself."

"It's true though. I'm all talk, no action… I'm not even talk. I'm just—"

Elijah started whistling loudly to drown me out, and I laughed.

"Thank you," he said. "No more of that please."

As we got to town, people in our school-uniform colours merged with students from other schools in different colours, until the precinct resembled a paintbox of teenagers shrieking, and getting dirty looks from passers-by for the offence of being young. We got to McDonald's and the usual post-school queue had died down as we were so late.

"Strawberry?" Elijah asked, remembering. I nodded and went to get some money. "Don't worry about it. Just grab us a seat somewhere."

I found a little booth at the back, cluttered with empty Big Mac wrappers. I shoved the rubbish onto another table and he arrived moments later, clutching one strawberry and one chocolate milkshake. He found me with my phone out, rereading Adam's message, and I jerked when he offered me my cup.

"So...you okay?" He nodded towards my twitchy hands.

"Yes. No..." I took a slurp of my artificially sweet drink. "My brother, Adam, just told me he's not coming home over Easter. That's all. Well, that's not all. It's just, that's everything."

Elijah nodded and held his straw to his mouth. "Right. I see. Well, I'm not sure I do."

I sighed and tried to explain the weird rules of my life. "My dad worships my brother. So it...won't go down well that's he's not coming back. He'll...make it our fault somehow."

"That doesn't make any sense."

"My dad's responses tend not to make sense...from the outside." I took a sip too quickly and my brain jolted with brain freeze. I winced. "They make sense to me though. To Mum. To Adam. We know the rules. Adam knows what will happen and he's choosing to do it anyway."

Elijah was quiet apart from the slurp of his straw, thoughtful. "Maybe he's just trying to protect himself?"

"Oh, that's definitely what he's trying to do. But he doesn't seem to care that it comes at a cost to us."

Elijah reached over and gently put his hand on top of my hand. My skin exploded with sensation, forcing me to look up at him. It was the first time we'd touched like that since the hug all those weeks ago.

"I'm sorry I can't make this better. I'm always here if you want to talk about it. And I'm happy to distract you if you don't want to talk about."

"I don't think I do...but thank you. Please, feel free to distract me."

Elijah smiled. "I've thought of the perfect distraction. I can take you to your ball."

I snotted out a pink fountain of milkshake. "Oww," I said. "Oh my God, gross. I'm sorry." Strawberry flavouring burned up the back of my throat as I grabbed a tissue, dying.

"That was one of the most disgusting things I've ever seen," Elijah marvelled, watching me mop milkshake out of my dripping nostrils. "Can you do it again?"

"Shut up! Sorry. Oww, it hurts. And it's your fault. What do you *mean* you're going to take me to the ball? That's insane." I wiped away the last of it, dabbing at my school jumper.

"I'm trying to distract you and cheer you up," he said. "Though, now you've responded by snotting up milk and calling me insane, I think I'm the one who needs cheering up. Thank you, Paige, for rejecting me in the strongest possible manner."

"I haven't rejected you. I'm just surprised. I thought… well, you said, the ball isn't your sort of thing?"

"Yeah, but you said that thing about how me not going is actually a thing and now I want to reject that thing because I don't like a thing like that defining me."

"You just said the word 'thing' a lot."

We laughed again. An atmosphere of ease slurping up our milkshake straws. I couldn't understand how someone could pull me out of the pits of despair so very easily. I popped the top of my milkshake lid off and stared into its thick bubbled texture. I hadn't ever considered going to the ball. The ball was made specifically for girls like Grace to be the belles. For them to achieve the American high-school fantasy. Part of that fantasy was knowing we all longed to be in their dress, wearing their glass slippers, in their Hummer limo. For regular teenagers, our role was only to provide the social backdrop for them, the envious looks, to be the ugly sisters…

"I don't know," I said, when we'd laughed our nerves out. "I mean, won't it be terrible? Isn't the ball just going to be everything that's wrong with school concentrated into a toxic pulp?"

"Oh, yes, most definitely." Elijah's straw gurgled as he slurped up the rest of his milkshake.

"So why would we want to go to that?"

"Because, as you said, it's a rite of passage." His gurgling noise stopped. "Also, I've never had someone I wanted to go with before."

When I looked up again, Elijah had turned beetroot. He tried to style it out, waggling his eyebrows, like asking me meant nothing, but we both felt it. A zinging between us. An anxiety from him, that I'd say no. My blood started dancing with energy. With hope. With the fear that always accompanies hope – the usual two-for-one package. And even though this was all I'd wanted for quite some bloody time now – for us to get our zing back – I found myself softening it.

"I mean, I don't have the money for a limo or anything," I said.

"Neither do I. We can get a cab."

"I don't have a dress."

"Have you considered buying one?"

I guessed maybe Polly would give me the money. She'd howl with excitement if she found out what I needed it for.

"You won't know anyone there."

"I know you."

"The music will be terrible."

"We can appreciate it ironically."

"The food will be a buffet."

"Great. I love catching norovirus from people who don't wash their hands properly. It's good for your immune system in the long run."

"I hate everyone there."

"Surely you don't hate me? Not after I bought you such a yummy milkshake."

"We can't pull a Carrie. The rumours about me have only just stopped."

"Aww, dammit. No telekinesis? That's it, I withdraw the offer."

It didn't make sense. None of it did. Elijah was anti-establishment. And yet, he wanted to go with me. And I really wanted to go to the ball with him. Like a switch had been flicked, the world's most basic fantasy started playing out in my mind. How his face would look when he first saw me in my dress. How his body would feel pressed against mine as we danced. People seeing us arrive together. The potent allure of the teenage secondary school fairy tale. That tale as old as time. I guess no matter how hard you try to resist, there's a part of you that longs for that.

"Okay, let's do it," I said, pushing my empty cup away. "Let's go."

His face was like someone had turned on all the lights. "Are you sure?"

"No."

"I will say it again. You really know how to turn the screw when rejecting someone."

"I'm not rejecting you, I'm saying yes."

If only he knew what it meant that he'd asked. If only I was brave enough to tell him that story.

"You're saying yes quite reluctantly."

"I'm not... Honestly. Elijah..." I made myself be serious. I made myself be brave enough to give him a crumb of the truth. "I would love to go with you. Sorry. I was just shocked, but...like...it sounds great."

I closed my eyes, waiting for the universe to punish me

for being so needy and desperate. But there was no rebuttal, no *It was just a joke*. When I reopened my eyes, there was only a grin on his face and a flush in his cheeks.

"I mean, this won't help the rumours that we're a couple."

"School is basically over anyway."

"And what about the devil worship? Can we fit that around our thriving social calendar?"

"We can bring him with us. Get Satan in our limo. He can pay for it."

And for a blissful five minutes, my Dad anxiety faded. Because sometimes just five minutes of a nice storyline can help you through the dense chapters of a nasty one.

CHAPTER 31

I essentially danced home as the sunset finally came out to do its job. I hummed "Once Upon a Dream" under my breath and ballet-stepped from street light to street light. I took the usual shortcut through the dodgy tunnel and waltzed past the security camera – waving as I went. But, as I neared home, my stomach started aching and I dropped my dance steps, and everything about the ball and Elijah was forgotten.

It took multiple attempts to get my key in the door, and I opened it as quietly as I could. Dad's coat was on the hook.

He was home.

I closed the door behind me.

No yelling. Good sign.

"Is that our ever-absent daughter?" His voice boomed from the living room, followed by a jovial laugh. *Laugh?*

"I'm home," I called cautiously. "Sorry I'm late."

"We should put a sign above the door," he boomed. "The Vickers' Hotel. Come and go as you please."

I inched my way to the living room, further surprised to find the air filled with warmth, humour and affection. Mum and Dad were sharing a bottle of wine on the sofa, entwined. They both smiled as they saw me. Smiled.

"I dunno, Jane," Dad said. "But I'm starting to feel old. With Adam at uni, and Paige so grown-up, caring for her poor aunty…where did time go?"

Mum was like a cat who'd got the cream, and the thicker part of cream at the top of the cream bottle, and had been given a spoon to get out the last of the cream. "Don't!" she said. "I refuse to get old. Age is an illusion." She was allowed to smile as Dad had set the evening's precedent. "I've not started on dinner yet, sorry, Paige. Your dad came home early and we've just been chilling."

Dad gestured out to the good armchair. "Come. Sit. Tell me about your day?"

"Oh okay." I shuffled over and perched lightly on the edge. "So, I had a yearbook meeting after school, and—"

"Have you heard Adam's news?" Dad interrupted. "He's hitch-hiking all the way to Slovenia over Easter, raising money for charity. Him and his hall housemates are all doing it. It's a race to see who can get there quickest for free. Isn't that *hilarious?*"

I felt my eyes widen. He knew. Dad knew and he was… okay?

"He messaged me earlier, yeah."

"And he's coming home for Easter Sunday," Mum said. "He said he wouldn't miss my roast for the world."

Ahh, so Adam had done *some* damage control then. I wished him a silent thank you. Though I was still furious at him, and waited for Dad to sour as inevitably as milk left out in a heatwave.

"Shame he's got to get back for exams," Mum added, sipping more wine. "Otherwise he could've stayed a bit longer..."

"For Christ's sake, Jane, he's THERE to LEARN. We should be glad he's revising."

Mum's face had that slapped look, but Dad pulled her into him and kissed the top of her head and it faded again.

"It's lovely that you miss him. We all do. But we have to let him get his degree. Don't we, Paige?"

"Huh? Oh, yes."

"See, she gets it. I get it. Maybe if you actually worked, Jane, you'd understand responsibility."

Ah, the souring was coming. I twisted in my spot on the chair and watched Mum sense it too. She blinked a lot and put her wine glass down.

"Oh, come on. I was only joking." He laughed and was the only one laughing. "You know I love having you here, keeping everything nice. It's just a shame it gives you time to think too much, you know?" He leaned over and retrieved her glass of wine and held it to her lips, jokingly trying to make her drink. She giggled and went along with it. "I do wish I'd had the chance to go travelling," he said, settling back into his chair and swerving into a new topic. "Can you imagine? Hitching all the way to Slovenia? What an adventure. The people he's going to meet...the things he's going to see..." Dad looked away forlornly, out into the blackness beyond the living room window, and hushed his voice a fraction. "I never got the chance, you see. Family life came too early...although, of course, you know what I always say...family is the most important thing..."

Something strange shifted in my head in that moment – watching him, watching how he delivered his sentences. It occurred to me so strongly that I almost fell off the chair...

...it was like Dad was reciting a dramatic monologue.

I'd never realized it till then. But, as he sighed and looked further out the window, I knew so truly that, in his head right then, he was imagining himself in the play of his life or something. That a camera was focused close to his face and was live-beaming his speech to everyone's TVs across the world. He was performing the leading role in the film of his life and believed it was a blockbuster smash hit.

So many people do this, I realized. So many people behave like they think a cinema orchestra is following them around to give them backing music, that they're the superstar of the universe...and the people who behave this way, they're the people who tend to hurt others the most. They think they're the hero of their own story, but, actually, in the pursuit of being so important, they're often the villain of everyone else's.

Dad was in full-blown monologue mode right now. A soliloquy on all the sacrifices he had made. My only purpose in that house was to be his audience when he demanded one. It was Mum's purpose too. And, to some extent, Adam's. Though Adam had the extra requirement of being Dad's legacy. Of taking the baton, of keeping the story alive, keeping Dad immortal.

"Yes...I think I would love Thailand too. The beaches... the culture...the food..."

Sitting nervously on that chair, listening to Dad drone on with his red-wine smile, I felt everything shift around me, like I'd put on a new pair of spectacles after wearing the wrong prescription my whole life. Dad came into focus for the first time.

He will never care about me the way I need him to, I thought, as he made a racist joke about Thai women. He physically, actually can't. There isn't the capacity there. He only has room for himself, and his story, and his legacy, and for the feeling of the camera lens always on him. And another realization wiggled into my skin and bashed a sad, sorrowful gong in my heart.

He is never going to change. The moment's not going to come. He's only going to hurt me more the more that I crave his love. And I could choose to keep trying and keep getting hurt. Or I could choose to accept it for what it was, and take back my sad, lonely and desperate heart and tend to it myself.

Grief spasmed throughout my skin while I sat there, politely nodding when he said Australia is overrated and all koalas have chlamydia.

"I've got revision," I said, when there was finally a natural pause for him to replenish his wine glass.

A slight head nod. "Oh, right. Yeah. Anyway, Jane, so I was thinking, we should get Adam a special backpack as a present, what do you think?..."

It was safe enough. Mum was safe enough. It could've been so, so much worse. I climbed the stairs, thinking there are certain thoughts you can't unthink. Realizations you can't unrealize.

The end of childhood = realizing adults don't know what the hell they're doing.

A small part of me knew this was a good revelation. Maybe the start of a tiny shoot that could grow.

But the girl who just wanted her dad to love her... The girl who needed that... The girl who'd been begging to matter since she drew breath... The girl who woke up every morning with hope that this would be the day...

That girl?

Well, that girl needed to go cry in her room.

CHAPTER 32

The *Most Likely to…* ballots went out. The votes were cast and then collected up by each form tutor and delivered to Ms Gordon for consideration. With Easter looming, she held a last-minute yearbook meeting for us to finalize who won what.

"I know you're going to be slammed with exams after the break," she said, handing out the list of contenders with spring sunshine streaming behind her, making her neon yellow outfit glow even yellower. "So if we can just do this now, then I can type them in. Then we only have the ball pictures to add. Apart from that, we're pretty much done."

We were handed the shortlists. There was no point disputing the obvious fact that Grace and co would get the final say on who won what.

Most likely to be a supermodel…Grace Langdon.

"Oh my God, guys," she said. I didn't know it was possible to fake a blush, but Grace managed.

Most likely to be a C.E.O.…Amelia.

"I feel like I already am one," she said, not even trying to fake a blush. The list went on. Any category associated with a) being attractive, or b) being good at sport, went to the populars. Sam even got voted most likely to win an Olympic gold, despite the fact this guy, James, in our year, was quietly an incredible gymnast – hardly ever in school because he was too busy travelling the country and winning tournaments. As I scanned through, I knew there was no chance I'd be nominated for anything. Yet it still panged, not seeing my name there. Not even for *Most likely to write a novel*, which went to this girl, Bella, who always performed questionable slam poetry at the school talent show. I'd done nothing in five years to make a name for myself, apart from working really hard to make sure I never made a name for myself. I'd achieved my goal and it hurt.

I sat back and let them pick their winners. I raised my hand to vote for whoever Grace and co voted for. I thought they'd be beaming with joy and milking every atom of this moment, yet they seemed weirdly uninvested as they made their obvious choices. In fact, they seemed almost *distracted*. Amelia kept whispering in Grace's ear, who giggled and whispered back. I watched them suspiciously but didn't question anything.

"Voila! Guys, we are done!" Ms Gordon punched the air with her yellow sleeve. "That's the yearbook finished! Well done, well done. I've got us some chocolate to celebrate."

She reached under her desk and pulled out a decorated Easter basket filled with foil-wrapped bunnies and started passing them out. I'd made it. The yearbook was officially done. My involvement in it officially over. Though, as I unwrapped a foiled chocolate, ready to take a bite, I saw Grace whisper to Amelia again, and an odd feeling stirred in my stomach. The relief didn't arrive, just trepidation. An instinct this wasn't the end.

On the last day of term, we had our Easter assembly to remind us, in explicit detail, of all the terrible stuff Jesus went through on the cross, and how he did it for us, and how we should remember that Easter is about so much more than chocolate eggs and remember his sacrifice, but also remember that these exams are the most important ones we'll ever take in our whole lives so be sure to revise. The final bell rang, and we were dismissed for two weeks.

I met Elijah at the gates. The air was warm. He stood under a blossom tree with his jumper off, T-shirt sticking closely to his chest.

"We're free," he cheered, as I walked to meet him.

I handed him a chocolate rabbit I'd saved from the yearbook meeting. "You can say that because you don't live at my house."

"Sorry, I forgot."

"I'm joking! Well, I'm not, but it's fine. I'm going back to Polly's tonight anyway. Going dress shopping tomorrow actually." I felt myself go red. "You know...for the ball."

Elijah raised both eyebrows. "Oh really? Whatcha gonna go for?"

"Something simple, you know? Maybe a train that's only four metres long? And I want there to be some kind of electrical component? Where the dress lights up? It'll need pockets for all the battery packs I'll have to carry around."

He barked out a laugh. "I can't wait to see it. Cripes, I'll need to hire a suit, won't I?"

"If you want to conform, yes. Which, let's face it, is your favourite thing to do."

"I'll get a tie that says *I'm wearing this ironically.*"

"Damn. I was going to get that for your birthday."

We laughed together, walking home in the sunshine, the air easy. Whenever I thought of the ball, I couldn't help but hope something might happen between us that night. If anything ever was going to happen, it would certainly be at the ball. In posh clothes, surrounded by fairy lights, perched on the hinge between the past and the future.

It could be something amazing.

But I needed to get through the holidays first.

CHAPTER 33

Luckily, Adam continued appeasing Dad over the break. The day he set off, he sent a selfie to the family group chat, grinning with all his new uni mates, thumbs up, a gigantic bag teetering on his back.

Adam: What the hell am I doing?
Miss you guys x

It was enough. Dad came home from work acting like Adam had announced a pregnancy. "Did you see the pic? Looks so excited, doesn't he? What an adventure, eh? What. An. Adventure."

The updates continued. A minimum of one a day. Selfies of him looking glum as he waited by a rainy roadside in France. Photos of the weird food he was trying for the first time. He even knew to give regular stats on how well his team were doing on the challenge (*second since you're asking*) so Dad had even more material to beam at.

Paige: Thank you for sending all the messages. I can't tell you how much easier it's making everything.

Adam: I thought it might. He's so fucking predictable.

But none of Adam's anger at Dad was evident in the group chat. He played his part of perfect son, on a perfect adventure, totally perfectly. My shoulders loosened whenever my phone pinged with a new update. And they provided the perfect amount of safe conversation topics for the nights I ate at home. Mum seemed relieved too, her shoulders a foot lower as she brought in the dinner plates. Sometimes even recreating the dishes Adam had sent us messages about.

"I made ravioli, so we can pretend we're in Italy, like him," she said. And, excited to strengthen the bond between father and son, Dad lapped it up, sometimes literally. Greedily slurping up the last of the sauce in his bowl with the last bit of garlic bread.

Regardless, I spent as much time away from home as I could, attempting to revise. So many subjects seemed utterly hard and utterly pointless, especially as I wouldn't be studying them ever again after the year ended. I mean, did I really need to know about the nitrogen cycle? Especially when I could just google it if life required me to know it? I'd quietly looked up the local sixth-form college online and started filling out an application form with my four chosen subjects. It made the rest of my curriculum seem pretty pointless but I made myself work nonetheless. I revised at Polly's, who kept asking me test questions while pumping me full of "brain food" (chocolate biscuits dunked in tea). Occasionally, Elijah and I would revise together at his house, lying on his bed, our feet sometimes brushing as we lay on our fronts, blushing and pretending they hadn't. But when that got too distracting, I hid upstairs in my house, chatting to my old pal.

"Alexa, seriously, what is algebra?"

"Alexa, how come I need to know about shanty towns for geography but I haven't been shown where anywhere is on a map?"

"Alexa, do employers really look at GCSE results for the rest of your life? Or is it a conspiracy?"

On Good Friday, two days before Adam was due home for a whole twenty-four hours, I went to the park with a library copy of a poetry anthology. Apparently "wider reading" got you better marks and English was my only safe-ish bet of getting above a seven. I turned to the section on Simon Armitage, a poet we were studying. And then I smiled so brightly I'm surprised I didn't short-circuit the sun.

The pages were filled with red pen in familiar handwriting. One poem was called *It Ain't What You Do, It's What It Does To You* but it had been garishly retitled in red ink.

It's all about what you do, and what it does to people around you.

I shook my head and laughed into the surrounding symphony of chirping birds and kids playing football. I ran my fingertip over the dents his pen had made in the paper and felt so much love run through me. Towards this boy, towards his words, towards how meeting him through the margins of other people's stories had encouraged me to start telling my own. Slowly, quietly, but getting there.

I reread his annotation and let the red pen work its magic, feeling way too emotional all of a sudden. Two young girls ran past as fast as their legs could manage, giggling into the warm breeze, one yelling at the other to wait. I smiled as they blurred past in the giddy joyful deliriousness of children in summer. Then I got a giant pang remembering Ruby and the summers we'd shared together. I blinked and saw us running together, playing together, learning from each other, in this very same park. We grew up together and now we hadn't messaged in over a year.

It hurt, it hurt so much and yet I had never said anything.

It's all about what you do, and what it does to the people around you…

I closed my eyes and inhaled the warm breeze and the lasting memories and Elijah's words, and when I opened them, I knew what to do.

Her number was still one of only seven on my phone.

I heard it ringing, the pause before our two storylines connected again, taking up stage-space in the play of each other's lives once more. Though something told me this would be the final scene.

Ruby picked up, and there was giggling down the line, followed by a "*Shh*". She was with people. "Hello? Who is this? Shh, I'm on the phone. Sorry. Who is this?" she repeated.

I shook my head in the park. I still had her number, but she didn't have mine.

"It's Paige."

"Oh…" A long, shocked pause. "Oh my God! Hi! It's been ages. Sorry. I dropped my old phone down the loo when I was drunk and lost all my numbers. Paige. Wow."

"Are you free to talk?"

"Umm. Sure. Hang on, I'm just out shopping with Delta. Give me a second." I heard her make excuses and step away and I kept taking deep breaths, gulping in air like it was courage. It was so strange hearing her voice again after so long. I loved her still. I wanted to hug her. I'd forgiven her everything the second she'd said "Hello", but, also, I needed to say what I needed to say.

"Right, sorry. I'm outside now." Ruby sounded shaken too. There was no snideness like the last time I'd seen her. I'd shocked her out of it. "Is everything okay, Paige? This is…er…a bit out of the blue."

"I'm fine. And you?"

"Yeah, good. Great. I was just shopping for last-minute ball stuff. I don't like the shoes I picked any more, and my dress is gold so it's kind of tricky to find another pair that match, but, you know, otherwise I'm all good."

I chewed on my lip. "Sounds like quite the challenge."

"Yep. But I think I've found a pair on ASOS. The shops are crap here, to be honest. You're so lucky to live near London."

Here we were, chatting about shoes, when I was supposed to be having some grand kind of moment. I wasn't sure how to steer things back to what I wanted to say without it sounding dramatic and mad…but then we both knew I hadn't rung to talk about shoes. And, Ruby, to be fair, called it.

"Why have you rung, Paige?" she asked quietly. "It's been for ever. I never hear from you."

"I never hear from you either."

"Well, that's life sometimes, isn't it? It's not my fault I moved away."

There it was. The defensiveness. The spiky shield. She sensed criticism was coming and was mentally running to the barricades. I closed my eyes once more and told myself there was nothing cruel about telling the truth as long as it was only your truth you were telling. I wasn't going to make it hers. I wasn't going to make her story my story. But I needed to say…

"Last time I saw you, you really hurt me," I said. Just saying it – a year of pain and humiliation and self-loathing and anger condensed into one sentence. I almost laughed at how easy it was, how much lighter I felt. "That's why I stopped messaging. Look, Ruby…" I paused for another breath and, probably stunned, she let me continue. "I get that you moved away and it would be hard to stay friends. And we've obviously become different people…or maybe only you have, I don't know. But you hurt my feelings when you came to stay. I felt very…judged, and then I heard you…" I swallowed and forced myself to keep going. "…calling me a loser to your friends on the phone that night, when you thought I was asleep. And that was very painful to hear, and I needed to tell you that."

A long pause. Just the sounds of her Isle of Man shopping centre down the line. I longed for an apology, or a reconciliation, a reconnection, and dared myself to hope for the five seconds my old best friend was quiet.

"O-kay…" Ruby eventually said. Her voice was patronizing. Cold. And the hope died. "Well, maybe you shouldn't listen to people's private phone conversations if you're not going to like what you hear."

I raised both eyebrows as the bullet hit.

"Look…I'm sorry if I hurt your feelings, but I wasn't doing anything wrong. You were the one skulking about and listening in…spying on people, like you always do."

It hurt so much less than it would've done six months previously. I mean, it still hurt, but it was expected, lesser, an obvious response. Just like that, my friendship with Ruby ended for ever – but I'd already known this, already grieved for this. This phone call was just the autopsy to confirm the cause of death – and I was sure both Ruby and I would come to different verdicts where we weren't the one to blame.

"Ouch, Ruby," I replied honestly. "Look, maybe I

shouldn't have listened in, you're right. I was just so confused when you came to visit, as you didn't seem to like me very much when I thought we were best friends, so, yes, I eavesdropped to find out what was going on."

"Well, yeah, that is quite creepy."

"Come on, Ruby! We used to be best friends. What happened? You know why I'm quiet. I've told you about my dad. Look, you don't owe me your lifelong friendship just because we were childhood friends, but it hurt for you, of all people, to speak about me like that, when you know what my home life is like. You were the only person I ever told..." My voice cracked up and I thought about trying to hide it, but I didn't. Let her hear my grief. I was not ashamed of my emotions.

Further silence down the line as my old friend tried to find her own words. Her own truth. I could picture the exact face she'd be making as she figured out what to say. She always used to chew on her bottom lip while she thought things through. Finally she said, "You're being very weird." I knew then the conversation was over. There would be no great redemption arc, no realization and apology, no Scrooge waking up in the morning and ordering a giant goose for everyone in the village.

"You're being incredibly defensive," I countered. Never in the history of my life had I ever countered, but out it came, quick and sharp.

"What am I supposed to do? You just ring me up, after years, to tell me I'm a horrible person?"

"That's not what I'm doing at all. I'm just telling you how I feel."

"Like a weirdo."

I laughed so loud that the two girls playing in the park turned to look at me. "Cheers, Ruby," I said. "That's so kind of you to say."

"Since when did you do sarcasm?"

I could hear tightness in her throat. I knew her so well. A tiny part of me had got through, but not enough. She was too far gone in her own story to want to listen to mine. And, you know what? That was okay. Because at least now I'd scribbled in her margin with the red pen of my own experience. She couldn't forget what I'd said, and it was important that I'd said it.

"Look, Paige. This is all a bit...much, and I really have to get going. We were kids, okay? People grow up and change. I'm not going to apologize for that. And I'm not going to let you make me think I'm a terrible person."

I laughed quietly again and shook my head. The words fell from my mouth effortlessly. "People always believe they're nice in their own heads," I said. "That's what makes it so scary when you look at the state of the world."

Then I hung up.

I chucked my phone to the grass for a second and slumped forward, putting my head onto the scratchy warmth of the ground. Within five minutes, I was upright again, the sun on my face.

I'd told Ruby how I felt.

Finally.

And Ruby had revealed who she really was now.

The most important thing was…I didn't believe what she'd said about me. I wasn't creepy, and I wasn't weird. Everything about me made sense, considering the story of my life, and she was in on that whole story, so it was horrible of her to say such a thing. If she wanted to be a worshipped wax model, so be it. I wanted nothing to do with someone who used my own story against me. It was surprisingly easy to let her go. I shook my head one more time, and she faded. Leaving space for better people and better things.

moving forward

Speaking of which.

I turned over on my stomach and got out my poetry anthology again. It had only been fifteen minutes since I'd found Elijah's inking, yet it felt like years. A deep smile relaxed its way through my body, and I held up my phone to take a photo of the page.

Paige: Some idiot has trashed this book.

Elijah: Oh my God. Simon.
My old pal.

Paige: How am I supposed to pass my exam when you've done this?

Elijah: I will have you know, actually, that my critical analysis of his text got me a

freakin' NINE last year. You are
SO welcome.

Paige: Anyone ever told you you're smug,
Elijah?

Elijah: Only every day.
Elijah: Anyway…
Elijah: What are your thoughts on
Armitage's stuff?
Elijah: Oh, favourite sifter of my heart?

Paige: I would say that his poetry is the opposite of your approach to sifting. I think what he writes about is how you can never really condense one person down into one action, or one sentence. How we are all more complicated than that. It's reductive to even try.

Elijah: FFS.
Elijah: You're so going to get a better mark than me. A ten? Do they give out tens yet? Can you come over and lend that pretentious brain of yours to my philosophy revision?

Paige: Won't I distract you?

Elijah: You're distracting me now. I may as well get the chance to look at you as you do it. X

I read and reread that message till I knew it by heart. Melting into a puddle of hope and longing.

As I said, if something didn't happen at this ball, after he sent me a message like that…

Well…

I stood up, brushed the dried grass off my arse, and walked towards the house and heart of someone deserving of my time, leaving Ruby in the past, where she had already left me. I couldn't wait to see Elijah's face when I told him.

CHAPTER 34

Adam arrived on Easter Saturday, in a heap of stinky exhausted backpack and dark purple rings under his eyes. We lined up to meet him in the hallway, like we were the royal family greeting an ambassador.

"Oh my God, it's so weird to be home." His eyes landed on me. "Paige, dude, it's been too long."

He pulled me in for a smelly hug, rucksack still on his back, and clutched me tight while I tried not to inhale. Why was he being so friendly all of a sudden? Guilt?

"Hope you're okay, dude," he whispered in my ear, before releasing me, and giving Mum a hug next.

"Darling, you absolutely stink."

Dad laughed with a bark. "Let him smell! He's been on an adventure."

Adam and Dad did that weird man hug thing where they kind of clutch each other's forearms. And Easter began.

The following twenty-four hours seemed picture-perfect from the outside. Adam was treated like a returning war hero, and had so many travelling tales we never wanted for conversation. Mum, as usual, outdid herself with the cooking, bringing in roasted chicken and rosemary potatoes and endless home-made tarts, alongside the giant Easter eggs she'd bought everyone. Polly joined us for Easter dinner and we sat together in the corner, cramming thin chunks of Easter egg into our mouths, watching the Dad and Adam show play out.

"How's your application to college going?" she asked quietly, while Adam described this "*totally epic*" moment in Italy where he'd "*totally thought we were stranded*". "You sent it off yet?"

I smiled at her. "Not just yet. I need a reference, and I'm going to ask Ms Gordon, I think. The due date is still a few weeks away."

"And revision? You getting enough done here?"

"It's okay. I've just been staying upstairs. They've been distracted with Adam coming home."

She raised both eyebrows. "I bet, I bet." We turned to where he was delighting my parents, arms waving madly as he told his story, Dad beaming with pride. Polly's eyebrows drew down again. "I worry though...after he leaves...you know you can call me any time?"

I leaned my head briefly against her shoulder to let her know what that meant to me.

Her prediction was right. Easter Sunday came to an end, completed with a family viewing of *The Sound of Music*. We stayed up late to drag out the enforced joy. Dad was drunk again, resembling a smug tomato – his eyes kept straying to Adam in delight that his son was home. But as it got later, his manner hardened.

"Off early then, tomorrow, are you?" he asked Adam, after the von Trapps had climbed over a mountain to flee the Nazis.

Adam sat up straighter in his chair. "Not too early," he said delicately. "It would be nice to have breakfast with everyone."

"Surely you need to rest some more before going back? You must be knackered after all that hitch-hiking?"

"I am… I wish I could stay. But I need the library facilities."

"For what? You can get books out, can't you? That's the whole point of libraries."

Adam kept his voice calm. "It's more than that. It's the computer software and stuff…"

Polly stood up. "Right, guys. I'm off. Thanks for such a lovely day. The food was amazing, Jane."

Mum, vibrating with newly arrived anxiety, stood up so they could kiss cheeks.

"Lovely to see you, Adam. Good luck with your exams." She hugged him but she only waved at Dad, knowing he wouldn't stand to say goodbye. "Bye, Glynn." She turned to me. "Remember, call me anytime," she whispered into our last hug.

* * *

After Adam left, I could feel the thickness of tension hanging in the air of my house. I wondered how long it would take for the explosion to come, my stomach tightening. Hours? Days? Weeks? It was like being able to smell a thunderstorm before the downpour hits.

The thickness in the air hung around school once we went back too. Wide-eyed teachers stampeded through the syllabuses, shoving practice exam papers at us desperately, reminding us over and over that we DID go through this and they DID teach us properly and we DO know this and, no, they DON'T know what exam questions are going to come up which is why we need to revise. There was this weird mix of *end-of-school-screw-it* vibes, and *oh-my-god-exams* vibes – congealing together to make a big mass of stress and relief, curdling like oil and water. After-school clubs were replaced with revision sessions. Even Grace and the Awfuls seemed to be taking it hard. Elijah and I did a double-take when we saw them holed up in the library one lunchtime – making revision timetables with an assortment of glittery pens and taking up too many tables.

Rumours about their elaborate ball plans were released into the public one by one, like a marketing strategy.

"Have you heard Sam's dad has hired a Hummer limo?"

"No, that isn't it. Grace's dad has shelled out for a helicopter to take them to prom."

"Amelia got her dress in Paris so no one else would have the same one."

In fact, the ball dominated most of the conversations

I overheard. Chats about how much the limo cost, and how long it took to save up for it, and who was going in which limo with who, and whether they were just friends or a couple now. Chats about dresses and checking no one had the same one, and booking a hairdresser slot in town, and how there were no slots left because we have the same ball date as Grange School, so which YouTube tutorial was best for fancy up-dos? Then there was the Leavers' Assembly prep, and the accompanying "muck up" day – sharing whispers over what was planned, and how to outdo previous years. Everything mattered and nothing mattered. The end was in sight but it was still just a horizon blob. A blob no one knew quite what to do with. The future seemed earnest and right up in our faces and yet still too far away and unmanageable.

I just wanted my last few weeks to be lived out in peace. To go to the ball with Elijah and let the magic of expectation lull us into whatever was supposed to happen between us. And, yes, I had a dress too. Polly had taken me out shopping over Easter and forced me to buy a dress made of golden sequins which was so not me, and yet I couldn't stop looking at it hanging in my cupboard.

The night before the ball rolled around and the dress was hanging on the back of my door. I watched it twinkle from my bed as I tried to sleep, smiling as the sequins caught the moonlight. I told myself the fairy tale of how my Leavers'

Ball would go… Elijah's face as he saw me. The perfect song playing through the speakers at the perfect time. The perfect look he'd give me before he leaned in for the perfect first kiss.

I curled up in the warmth of my self-written fantasy – completely indulging myself. Using it to comfort the gnawing ache in my gut that told me I would never get a story like that.

That I didn't deserve one.

The ache that knew that trouble was coming.

The Leavers' Ball

Do you remember...

...**Sam** accidentally dropping the **c-bomb** during his Prom King acceptance speech?

...**Mr John's**...umm...**interesting** moves on the dance floor?

...**Grace** arriving on the back of a **motorbike**?

What a night to remember. What a night to send us all off. Everyone looked so beautiful – even the teachers! We danced, and we laughed, and we made so many wonderful last memories of this incredible time of our lives.

EDITOR'S NOTE: Congratulations! You won a tiara. Tell me, now it's over for ever...was it worth it?

CHAPTER 35

Polly: Paige, my darling! Have an amazing night. Send so many photos! At least twelve an hour, for your pathetic aunty. So sorry I can't see you head off. Stupid cat conference emergency. They should let cats organize it, I reckon. They'd do a better job. Anyway, have the night of your life xxx
REMEMBER PHOTOS. ON THE HOUR.
EVERY HOUR.

Elijah: I'm wearing a suit, Paige. A SUIT.
What have you done to me?

Paige: Dude, it was your idea
to go.

Elijah: Oh yeah. See you at six x

* * *

There was a girl looking at me from the mirror and I didn't know her at all. She...shone. She was unmissable. She was the new Paige. A dress like this made it impossible to hide in the margins. But this Paige had survived the rumours. Had learned to care less. Learned to stand out.

We'd been allowed to leave school early that Friday afternoon. There was no point trying to teach with everyone so giddy.

The house had been empty when I got home, though the air still hung thick. I'd showered – taking my time to properly shave my legs, singing and enjoying the sensation of being home and free to be myself. When I'd dried off, I pulled up the YouTube videos I'd saved. One taught me how the hell to do make-up properly, and the other taught me how the hell to do hair properly. I carefully copied the chirpy girls on screen. At one point, I tiptoed into my parents' room to steal my mum's curling wand. The air was even thicker in there. Tension laced the wallpaper. The room was immaculate, each fold of the bed linen a perfect crease. Mum's existence was hardly evident – all her clothes were stowed away, her make-up, her jewellery. I really had to rifle to find the curling wand. Whereas Dad's residue was everywhere...framed photos mostly of him and Adam, his tie collection on its special hanger on the back of the door, the giant stack of books he never really read piling up against the wall. I felt my skin break out in goosebumps, and curled my hair quickly, desperate to return the wand before anyone came home. Dad had taken the day off to attend some barbecue thing with Mum for his friend's fiftieth. They were unlikely to be home till the evening, but I still rushed.

I came undone a few times. Who knew liquid eyeliner required the hands of a surgeon? But, after a few urgent saves, I wiggled into my golden dress, and stood on the landing to see myself full-length.

Who was this girl?

It felt incredibly narcissistic, to be this obsessed with my own image. But I honestly couldn't stop looking at myself. I twirled, jaw open, catching myself from different angles.

I couldn't stop smiling.

I checked the time on my phone. Less than forty-five minutes to go before I was meeting Elijah. I was going to his, rather than risking him picking me up here. I just needed to brush my teeth, pack my clutch bag and wobble into my new heels before I could head off. The extractor fan whirred itself on when I pulled the bathroom light. I caught my reflection and smiled again. I brushed twice, wanting my breath to smell nice. Then, smiling at myself one more time, I turned off the light, shutting off the fan noise, and walked out into the hall...

It was there, I heard it.

Dad's voice. Bad. His bad voice.

They were home. I had no idea what they were doing home early. I froze like a cartoon on the landing.

"...embarrassing me, yet again. Why do you do it? Why are you OBSESSED with embarrassing me?"

"Glynn, sorry. I'm so sorry. I didn't think."

"What a surprise. You, not thinking. Why would you even say that?"

"I said I'm sorry. Maggie just asked about Adam, and I didn't think my answer through properly..."

"What does it mean, when your own son can't bear to spend the holidays with you? They must think we're terrible."

"It was a throwaway joke. They knew that."

"They didn't. I saw the way she looked at us..."

"I'm so sorry."

"Well, it's too late now."

I stayed suspended, one foot raised in the air. Too scared to lower it in case I made the floorboard creak.

"Everywhere I go, you make me look like an idiot. No wonder Adam left as soon as he could. He's probably enjoying being able to walk around Bristol without feeling like a walking joke."

"Glynn, please." Mum started crying. Full crying. I'd never heard her like this. My own eyes filled with tears as I digested this violent shock of an afternoon.

"Oh God. Here we go again. Stop crying, you pathetic bitch."

I audibly gasped. My blood freezing in my veins. He never said things like that...

They don't realize I'm in, I thought.

Then I had a worse thought.

Maybe it's always this bad when I'm not in?

"Look at you. Look at the actual state of you. Do you have any idea how disgusting you are?" His voice was louder and louder, Mum hysterical. I couldn't really breathe. What was happening? What was…

"God knows why I put up with you. What are you doing? Don't walk away from me. Jane!?" His voice turned into a shout as his footsteps followed Mum's into the living room below. "Come back here. Come. Back. Here."

A scream.

A crash.

A bolt of trauma shot through me like lightning.

I fell to the carpet, shaking.

"Now look what you've done."

Mum's sobs were guttural, like an animal about to be slaughtered. I had never felt such primal fear in my life. I wanted to run down to protect her, but I was stuck to the carpet.

"I can't do this." Dad's voice was calmer now, calculated. The total opposite of Mum's hysterical shrieking. "I can't be with someone so obsessed with showing me up."

"Glynn, if you'd just listen…"

"What's the *point* of you anyway? You can't be a very good mother, if your son can't bear to stay in the home you've made. And your daughter is just as useless."

Fear and sadness rushed into my lungs as I gulped for air.

"I said I'm sorry," Mum pleaded through whimpers. "I didn't think. It was just a joke. Maggie will know it was just a joke."

"The only joke here is you."

Another time-freezing scream. Another smash. Violence. Fear. Danger. I flung myself down the stairs, with no thought, no plan, just a need to make it stop. Whatever it was, it had to…

"STOP!" I yelled, running into the living room, arms waving.

My parents froze in shock at my sudden arrival and I took in the awful freeze-frame. Mum was on the floor. She wasn't bleeding. But she was on the floor like she'd been thrown there. Dad was red-eyed. Two ornaments lay scattered like china ashes over the carpet. Had Dad thrown them at her? At the wall? One was only slightly better…

"STOP! Stop stop stop stop STOP."

Dad turned. Slowly. Calmly. "Paige, what are you doing here?"

"I was upstairs. Mum? Mum! Are you okay?"

And just when I thought it couldn't get worse…it did. Because Mum didn't jump up and hide behind me. No. She caught Dad's eye instead. Time slowed as I watched them share a look.

Not just a look, a collaboration.

A whole silent conversation danced between them. An agreement was come to without uttering a single word.

"I'm fine, Paige," she said in a breezy voice. She shrugged with her feet in china dust. "We were just having a bit of a row, and I accidentally knocked these over." She got up and joined Dad's side. United.

"More to the point…" Dad looked me up and down.

"What in God's name are you wearing?" His gaze registered my curled hair and sequinned dress.

"*What?* Er…it's my Leavers' Ball tonight…I was about to head out."

"Let me guess, Polly bought it for you?" He managed to say it in a way that made it clear I looked disgusting and Polly was disgusting and everything about me was disgusting.

How were we talking about my dress?

I crossed my arms, going into invisible woodlouse mode. Withdraw. Retreat. Apologize. Don't say anything. Don't make it worse. Placate. Allow. Vanish. Disappear. I stepped back and crossed my arms further. Retreating into my factory setting. Letting it happen. But as I stepped back again, I felt a jolt. Like I'd stood on one of the sharp shatters of china. A flickering of something in my heart, travelling down my arms, twitching down my fingers. I found myself standing straighter. I rolled my shoulders back and looked at Dad. Really looked at him. Taking in the redness in his eyes, the scowl on his face, the smashed crockery on the carpet, my mum cowering and covering for him. The dance we all danced to keep him happy, with the steps always changing, and it was never enough and he'd never be happy and he'd never, ever see us, because he was so obsessed with seeing himself. The sad…patheticness of him.

And, with that, I felt an entirely new feeling stir.

I felt *sorry* for him.

My dad. The bully. The loser. The fraud. The sad state of him.

And I found my power.

"Why are you so cruel?" I asked.

"I beg your pardon?"

"I said, why are you so cruel? I mean, most fathers would be proud of their daughter leaving school. Would want to take photos and ask who they were going with. But you… you didn't even know I had my ball tonight…and now you're making comments about my dress." I forced myself to look right into his reddened eyes. "It's cruel, Dad," I said, as calmly as he had spoken. "It's horrible."

It took a moment for him to metabolize what I'd said. I watched as, for the first time since I was born, he listened. My hands were shaking but I didn't drop eye contact. Then, initially, a predictable response.

"Oh my God, I was JOKING! You're just like your mother. It was a joke."

"It wasn't funny."

"It's not my fault you have no sense of humour. Also, love, if you're going to dress like…" He gestured to me. "… like Laa-Laa the Teletubby or whatever, you have to accept some backlash." Then he started laughing. He actually started laughing.

My heart tore apart like someone breaking open an empty fortune cookie. "What's wrong with you?" I asked, in genuine astonishment. "I don't understand what's wrong with you… I'm your daughter…I mean…"

Dad then rolled his eyes. "Paige, please do shut up."

It hurt so much. I don't think there's anything more cruel

than someone rolling their eyes when you tell them you're hurting. Especially when it's your own father. Every atom of me burned and yet I wasn't surprised. This is what villains do when you dare suggest they're not the hero. That other people, and their feelings, are important too.

"I EXIST, DAD!" I yelled, right into his face so he actually took a step back. "I wake up every morning and I exist. Because *you* made me. I didn't ask to be here, in this world, in this house, but you guys made me and I'm here and I exist, even though you pretend I don't. And you know what? It really hurts. It hurts that you treat me like nothing and treat Adam like everything. It hurts how we're all scared of you. Literally everything about you hurts me, and you don't even care that it hurts."

Out it poured. My story of what it felt like to be me. The truth tumbling out as gold as my dress. My bravest moment to date. Everything to lose but I was saying it anyway.

If you're not scared, then it's not courage.

The most pivotal scene of my life to date...but not to my father.

In fact, as I spilled out my soul, Dad looked like a man tolerating a boring TV show.

He turned to his wife – the one he had thrown to the ground. "What the hell has got into her today, Jane?" he asked, like I wasn't there.

"Paige, please," Mum pleaded. "It's been a long day..."

"No!" I yelled again, holding up my hand. "I'm allowed to speak. I'm not scared any more. Mum?" Her face...her face sending me desperate *Please stop* looks, begging me… I started crying when I saw her face. "Mum…why do you put up with it?" I asked. "You don't have to…it's not fair…"

"That's quite enough now." Dad wasn't laughing any more. Wasn't rolling his eyes. "Paige," he said calmly and dangerously. "I don't know why you're being so hysterical, but you need to stop."

"Mum?"

Dad held up his hand like he might strike me. "Paige!"

If he was raising his voice then I was getting through. My father was noticing me for the very first time. Listening for the very first time. Why? Because I was telling the truth – my truth – my story – rather than accepting his. There's so much power in that. I felt it pulse through my bones, no matter how scared I was. I could feel the power in me – I felt untouchable and light and free – though my heart hurt at how painful my story was. I kept speaking.

"Rather than blaming Mum for why Adam isn't here any more," I said, staring him down, "have you ever thought it may not be about her? That maybe it's because of you? Because Adam hates it here. He hates how you treat everyone, he hates—"

A charge. An attack.

I ducked as an ornament flew right towards me. It smashed on the wall behind me. I gasped.

"Shut up!" he shouted. "Shut up shut up. Get out! Get out. GET OUT."

There was mess everywhere. Mum sobbing. I couldn't

believe what he'd just… Fear raced through me, filling every limb. And Dad was only gearing up for worse. I could see it – the monster unleashed, wanting to smash, destroy. The mask pulled back. I had to get out.

I ran to the door, barefoot, across the smithereens of normality. Then I thought…*Mum*…

I turned back. Dad was screaming all the swear words. An incomprehensible ball of abuse, his fists flying around himself, calling me a bitch and a whore and a mistake and *the reason we never talk to you is because we never wanted to have you anyway*. The poisoned darts of his words stapled my skin, spread their toxicity. Tainted a bit of me for ever, but I could pick out their venom later when I was safe.

"Mum!" I held out my hand like I was trying to pull her from a burning building. "Mum, come on!"

If I left her, God knew what would happen. If I left her, she would take the fall. If I left her, I couldn't even imagine the consequences. She was staring at the smashed china, and then at my hand, and then at my dad, and then at my hand again. For a second, I told myself a story of what would happen now. The story of her taking my hand, and us running off together. Hugging on the pavement in relief and love. We'd go to Polly's and Mum would break down into tears and tell us everything, and Polly would say, *Shh, shh, you're safe now.* It would be awful but it would be the start of something better. A new chapter. A fresh page. One where we got to tell the story, rather than comply with Dad's. Late nights drinking tea. Laughter. Her pulling me onto her lap like I was a child and saying, *Thank you, thank you for getting me out*. The delusion danced briefly before my eyes as Mum reached out her hand... But then she put it on Dad's shoulder. They stood, side by side. And the actual story came back into focus.

Mum's voice was as cold and controlled as my dad's. "If you can't respect your father," she said, "then get out."

CHAPTER 36

This was not how I pictured Elijah seeing me dolled up for the ball.

"Oh my God, Paige, what the hell's happened?"

His mouth fell open as he opened his front door – finding me sobbing and shaking in my gold dress. I flung myself at him like a terrified animal.

"Elijah."

His name was all I could manage before the grief hit. I slumped into him and drowned his suited shoulder with snot and howls and tears, with relief that I was okay and safe, but guilt that I'd left Mum behind. Also rage at her for not coming with me, for surrendering herself to whatever the hell was happening to her right now.

"It's okay," he said, rubbing my back. "It's okay, it's okay, it's okay."

He managed to kick the door closed, and sort of walked me into his house. My brain was still stuck on a replay loop.

The look they shared.

You were a mistake.

Get out…

He managed to get me into a squashy chair and I huddled like a hedgehog, legs up, showing my knickers, crying into my knees.

"Sorry…the ball…sorry…it's just…"

He kneeled down. "Paige. Don't worry about that. What happened? Can you tell me what happened?"

But I couldn't. Not yet. My vocal cords had cat-cradled themselves. All I could do was gulp for pitiful bubbles of air between sobs.

"Shall I call my mum?"

I shook my head.

"Paige, I'm…I'm a bit scared. Please…"

I looked up into his helpless face and all Elijah's usual bravado was gone. He just looked totally panicked. We stared at one another for moment after moment until my breathing calmed down.

"Sor—"

"Please don't talk until you can breathe properly."

I nodded and focused on opening my throat. Taking breaths into my stomach, forcing oxygen into my ribcage. Every inch of me hurt but still I breathed. My body kept me alive while I digested it.

"My dad…" I said, after a while longer. "I'm okay… but they came home early…it was…it's worse than I even thought…I tried to stop it…I tried to tell him to stop but…

I had to run away... My mum...I left her...I left her when he was that angry."

I went again. Eyes buried into the palms of my hands. Imagining what the hell she was going through. The panic and the fear and oh God...my life. Why was my life like this? Why? It was so unfair. So hugely unfair. In the town around me, everyone my age was getting their hair done, putting the finishing touches to their outfits, messaging friends, taking photos with their parents, awaiting their limos, anticipating the evening and living a normal life, but I never got given one. I was stupid to think I ever would.

"Do I need to call the police?" His question added huge gravity to the already-leaden situation.

"I...I don't know," I replied, honestly.

The police would make everything worse, surely? Mum was already going to pay the price for my behaviour. This would make it even more dangerous. But...*did* he hit her? Did he hurt her? Could he? I never thought it possible. Surely Dad thought too much of himself for that? Surely that was a line he couldn't cross and still be able to look at himself in the mirror? And Dad's favourite thing to do was apply a mask over his darkness, look at himself in the mirror, and tell his reflection what a great man he was.

"My aunt," I said. "Polly will know what to do."

He nodded with urgency. "Right. Can you get me her number?"

I scraped around for my phone and he took it from me. "Polly, wasn't it?" he asked, searching through my address book. I heard it ring in his ear and watched as he waited for her to pick up. He was wearing a suit and bow tie – all pressed and crisp and clean-cut. He smelled of aftershave – something I didn't know he owned. Elijah looked amazing, and I wasn't sure what was wrong with me that I could still have a thought like that with everything else going on. But that's how amazing Elijah looked.

"Hi… No, it's not Paige. I'm her friend, Elijah. Yes, she's safe. She's here. Umm…can you come to my house? Something happened. Paige is very upset. She told me to call you."

I heard the tinny sound of panic echo around Elijah's ear.

"Yeah, yeah. No, she's safe, I think. She's crying a lot. Hang on, I'll ask." He held the phone up. "Are you okay to speak to her?"

I snotted and nodded.

Polly's voice was sharp with worry. "Paige? Oh my God. What's happened? Are you okay?"

I only needed to say one word. "Dad."

Then, if possible, my heart broke even further, because I heard Polly start to cry down the phone. "Where are you?" she asked.

"At Elijah's. On…um…"

"Grovehill Crescent," he provided.

"Grovehill Crescent."

"Okay, look, I'm on my way. I'm in London, so I'll be an hour or so. Oh God, I had a feeling about today… And oh my, it's your ball! Why aren't you at the ball? No. Never mind. Just stay there. Is it okay if you stay there?"

Elijah must've heard because he nodded furiously. "Of course."

"I'm on my way, hon. You can tell me then."

I squeaked one more word. "Mum."

A loaded, terrible pause. "Is she alright?"

"I...I don't know..."

"I'll call her and make sure she's safe. Stay put. It's okay, Paige. I'm going to take care of you."

I hung up and that's when I broke completely.

I'm going to take care of you.

Someone, finally, was going to take care of me.

A sentence I'd never heard. A feeling I'd never really felt – not from the people I was supposed to feel it from. Nurtured and noticed. Seen and responded to. Loved unconditionally.

And it wasn't just Polly taking care of me. It was this boy in the suit, kneeling next to me too. The one rubbing my back as I cried, saying it was going to be okay, even though he wasn't sure it would be. Though I was terrified and grieving, in that moment I was also filled with love, smiling, as I cried.

CHAPTER 37

The birds chirped outside. Time went on. The Leavers' Ball started. Elijah called his mum to check what time she'd be back from the lab. Not till late, she was afraid. How come? No reason, he said. Polly called again to say the trains were a nightmare but she'd be back in two hours.

"Your mum was okay on the phone," she reassured me, melting me into a giant puddle. "She doesn't seem in danger for now. I'm coming for you as quick as I can."

As time passed, I found you get to a point where you can't cry any more, no matter how sad you still are. So it was just Elijah and me, in his giant living room, dressed for a ball we were no longer attending, listening to the tick-tock of a grandfather clock.

"I'm so sorry," I kept saying.

"Please stop saying sorry."

"You missed the ball."

"Because it's always been my life's dream to go."

"I'm sorry I'm such a mess."

"Please stop apologizing."

"Sorry."

We both giggled. Elijah gave me such a huge, sad smile that if I wasn't already sitting down on the squishy squashy chair, I might've swooned.

"I hate that you've seen me like this."

"Like what?"

I pointed towards myself. "All train-wreck extraordinaire."

He shook his head, let out a breath.

"I like how you usually see me. All strong, and good at sifting, and smart, and honest and…not like this."

Elijah bit his lip. I folded my hands into themselves, worrying this was all too much for him. He'd think my life was too messy to want to know me any more…

"I want you to be okay." He chose his words carefully. "Not because I think you're strong or whatever, but because I want you to be okay and happy. Because…well…I care about you, Paige. That's the only reason I don't like seeing you like this."

I closed my eyes. Each word felt like a drop of honey plopping into my heart. Life suddenly appeared a tiny bit more bearable.

"I…I care about you too."

I twisted to look at him, still perching on the floor so he was eye level. He stared back and something huge dropped between us. The impossible happened and everything fell away. There was no fear or pain, just the delicious wonder of two hearts connecting; an understanding being come to.

It was so beautiful that I was about to crack a smile, but Elijah stood abruptly and walked towards the kitchen, breaking it off.

"We need a cuppa while we wait," he called over his shoulder, leaving me in the squashiness of the chair.

I listened to water being run into the kettle, the click of it being turned on, the clatter of tasteful mugs being taken out of tasteful cupboards. And I wondered. I wondered if he'd just felt what I'd felt. I wondered why he had stood and left. I wondered how I had the capacity to care about any of this when my family was ripped apart…and yet I did care… and crave…and need…and I stood up, and followed him into the kitchen. And though it made all the sense in the world right now to preserve the shattered pieces of my broken heart, I had a taste for honesty. It crackled on my tongue like fizzing candy. Elijah was watching the steam pour out of the kettle, his gelled hair already wilting over his forehead, his shirtsleeves rolled up.

"Hey," I announced my arrival.

"Oh hi, I was going to bring them in."

He dropped teabags into two mugs and wouldn't look up at me.

"What just happened in there, Elijah?"

"What do you mean?"

"I know you know what I mean."

"Paige…" His hands went to his face. "Come on, now's not the time."

"Not the time for what?"

He buried himself further into his palms. "Come on. You're going through a lot. You don't need to know..."

"Know what?"

"Nothing. Forget it."

"I don't want to forget it."

"Paige!"

"I'm okay," I told him. "I mean, I'm clearly not. But I also really think we need to talk about this."

"Look, come on. Let's just have a cup of tea, and wait for your aunty and..."

"Elijah!"

"What?"

"I want to know what you're thinking."

"Paige."

"Tell me!"

"Oh my God, Paige!" He dropped his hands, shook his head and turned to face me. And there it was again. The glow in the air. The full feeling between us. "Tell you *what*? What would be appropriate to tell you right now? That I'm a terrible person because you came here clearly in an utter crisis and yet I can't stop thinking about how amazing you look. Tell you that I'm trying to adjust to how terribly our night has changed – yes, *our* night. Because, oh my God, would you look at me? I'm wearing a suit. I'm going to the Leavers' Ball of a year group I'm not even in. I literally have no idea who I am right now, you know that? I mean, I had to rent this. I didn't even know renting a suit was a thing. And yet I found myself doing it and found myself actually looking forward to it because…well…we've been skirting around this, haven't we, but…well you heard what I said… I care about you, Paige."

I blinked slowly. Then again. I kept thinking I'd reopen my eyes after each blink and find the blink would've blinked everything away.

Elijah went bright red. "Sorry, I'm being a selfish prick. Even more so than usual. I'm trying to do the right thing. You don't need this. Not tonight…not now."

My body propelled me forward, made me cross the cold tiles on my bare feet. I stopped right in front of him, reached up and put my palm on his face.

He sighed. "What are we doing, Paige?"

"I think we might be about to kiss."

God, it's the easiest thing, telling the truth, once you've started.

"Are you sure about that?"

I nodded. "I'm sure."

"But I've never kissed a girl before," he said. "And you're crying."

"I've never kissed anyone either, and I'm not crying any more."

"You still have mascara everywhere."

"Oh, Elijah, if only you'd seen how pretty I looked an hour ago."

"You look so pretty right now."

Then he lowered his head and his lips were on mine. My eyes closed. The world went quiet and suspended and wonderful. I had no idea how to kiss, and hadn't thought to ask Alexa, and yet it was like I'd always known how. Or maybe it was because it was us. *Us.* And this is what we were supposed to be doing. This was why, out of all the books in all the library, I found his book and his words, and he found mine, and then we found each other. Elijah kissed me gently, carefully, still aware of all the things that had happened that evening. And all the things yet to come. When we broke apart, we leaned our foreheads against one another's, held palms against palms, breathed in one another's breath.

"I thought you thought love was a trap?" I whispered, remembering his cynical red pen and its cynical red message in the margin. Trying to match that with the way this boy was staring at me.

"You're allowed to red pen yourself," he said. "To scribble out your past beliefs if you've learned better."

We kissed again. Hands moving up into one another's hair, down our backs, tracing the lines of one another. I'd never felt so close to another human. Never touched someone this much. *This was life,* I thought. This. Love. Connection. Kindness. Acceptance. If only the world could run on this. If only the people running it behaved like this.

Then my phone went in my dress pocket – jerking us back to reality. We jumped apart, ripped back into the horror of my present.

"Hi, it's Polly," my aunt told me needlessly. "I've just got off the train so I'm in town. Look...I've been thinking.

I need to go see Jane. I have to triple-check she's safe. Then I'll be over. Is that alright?"

The words she was saying, the fear in her voice. Everything felt awful again. "That's fine. I'm at Elijah's. I'm…good."

The phone call had the same impact on Elijah. He was listening intently and smiled sadly at what I said.

"I'm so glad you're not alone. Tell him thank you. And his mum. I'll be there soon."

I put my phone back in my pocket – feeling the most contradictory pile of emotions it's possible to feel.

"She's just checking on Mum," I said.

He nodded. "You okay?"

"Yes…no…" I let out a huge breath and put my hand through my tear-wet hair. "Elijah, I'm glad that just happened. I don't want you to think it happened for any other reason than because I wanted it to."

His sad smile was still sad, but it was bigger. "I'm glad you've said that."

"Tonight is really weird."

"Really weird."

"But good. But also terrible and…"

And, very quickly, the evening regurgitated on me, and I started shaking again. Elijah hugged me tight and guided me back to the chair. I started crying while he shushed me, rubbing my hand and kissing my forehead.

"What's going to happen?" I asked him, even though I knew he didn't know.

"You're going to be alright. You're going to be safe."

"I'm so scared."

"I know. But I'm here."

"And my mum…"

"Your aunty will make sure she's safe."

"We're supposed to be at the ball!"

"Screw the ball."

We stayed huddled on the chair. Him stroking my hand, my hair, telling me over and over the story I needed to hear. That it would be alright. That I'd be alright. That he was here. That I wasn't alone. That I'd been so brave. It became a mantra, and it sank in a little, calmed me enough to get through the waiting.

And not so very far away, Grace Langdon was declared prom queen and given a tiara, while the school applauded. And my classmates were dancing, and kissing, and making memories, and saying goodbye to this chapter of their lives – in floor-length dresses and penguin suits and with smiles on their faces.

But not in this room, this house. Not in my life.

The doorbell went.

"That's her," I said, leaping up. I flung the door open, and we hugged instantly.

"Oh, Paige," Polly whispered, clutching me like I was a life jacket. "I'm here."

"Is Mum okay?"

"She's fine."

"She's safe?"

"As she can be. As she'll let herself be." She released me and held me at arm's length. "Honey, how would you feel about coming to live with me? Full time? I can't force you, it's your choice. But I...I don't want you back in that house, if I can possibly help it."

I nodded, blowing out a snot bubble. Nodding into the inevitable. "Yes. Yes. I will."

She flung herself at me again, while Elijah stood, watching us, silently, patiently. When we broke apart, she turned to him. "So you must be Elijah? Thank you for looking after Paige. Honestly, I'm so glad you were here."

"There's no need to say thank you."

"Well, she's lucky to have you."

"The feeling's mutual." He reached out and took my hand, lacing his fingers with mine. When he squeezed it, I felt a pulse of joy wave through my body.

Polly noticed our hands, raised her eyebrows, but said nothing.

"Let's get you home," she said. "We can talk more then."

She held out her arm but I hesitated. "Can you just give us a minute?" I asked her, glancing back at Elijah.

Through her strained face, she smiled. "I can give you as long as you'd like. I need to make a quick call anyway. I'll see you outside."

She closed the front door and Elijah and I were left, awkward again for a second. The distance between our two bodies was only a metre, but it felt like a mile. With Polly there, our magical little bubble of the last two hours had popped. What had happened? Did we mean it? What was going to happen next?

But he opened his arms. "Come here."

We hugged and he kissed the side of my head. "I'm sorry this is all such bad timing," he whispered. "But I am here for you. We have all the time in the world. Don't worry about us. I'm here."

I wept into his shoulder. "Thank you."

"As I said, no thanks necessary."

We broke apart and kissed clumsily, still getting the hang of each other.

"I'd better go."

"Let me know how you're doing. When you get a moment? No pressure."

"I will, I promise. I'll see you really soon."

As I turned to get the door, he called me back.

"Yes?"

"Just keep telling the truth, Paige," he said. "I know it's hurting, but it's working."

CHAPTER 38

The cats greeted us in the hallway, like they knew we needed them. As we stepped inside, exhausted and deflated, they mewed and rubbed themselves against our ankles.

"Okay, okay, I'll feed you already. Calm down."

I stepped into the kitchen as Polly turned on the kettle and tended to her flock. It was so warm in there – the glass from the conservatory wall baking it slowly, the sun still in the sky outside. The weather was taunting me with its gloriousness.

I collapsed into a chair, my dress making a tinkling sound, and felt every limb go heavy. I could hardly take the mug of tea Polly handed me.

"Home sweet home," she said, sitting on the chair opposite.

"I'm so sorry."

"Don't be. But please tell me what happened…I need to know."

So I told her the painful truth of what I'd overheard. Of

the violence. The fear. Of the look Mum and Dad had shared when I stumbled in to stop it. At that, Polly started crying.

"When I went over, your mum was fine," she said. "Like last time." My aunt paused, her eyes spilling over again. "This won't be easy to hear, Paige, but...she was blaming it on you. I know that's so painful to understand, but at least you know she's as safe as she can be. Both of them said they're happy for you to stay here as long as you want. Oh, Paige...don't cry."

Every single floodgate inside me flung open and I disintegrated into grief. I cried so hard that the cats ran out of the room. I cried so hard the tea went cold. I cried so hard I couldn't see. I couldn't do anything other than cry. I cried because they were still my parents and I loved them, but they didn't love me. Couldn't love me, for whatever reason. I cried for the years of my life knowing this but not wanting to believe it, for hoping it would be different. I cried because I'd never done anything wrong, and only ever followed the rules, trying to get loved in return. And the moment I broke one rule, I was out, proving the love was never there in the first place. I'd been playing a game that was impossible to win. For a prize that didn't exist. And then I cried for the kindness that had been shown to me. For the cold mug of tea in my hand, lovingly made by my aunty who didn't need to take this on, but who did. I cried for Elijah's hand stroking mine, for him believing in me, and encouraging me to tell the truth, even if it led to this. This now. This present. Because, even though I was terrified and hurt, I didn't regret it. My life had changed irrevocably and my dreams had been blasted from the sky, but at least I had only the truth left around me. Some of the truths were painful, but others were wonderful. Some hurt. Some soothed. But at least all of my life, in that one moment, was completely true. There was a magic in that.

But Mum...

"I still don't get it," I told Polly, when our tears had dried enough for us to be able to talk again. "Mum...she was so scared. She's so unhappy. Why? Why did she defend him?"

Polly held her own cold mug to her chest and looked into nothingness before replying. "That's hard for me to say, Paige," she said. "Because I don't understand it either...not fully. But...well...I was there when your mother met your dad. I saw firsthand how he dazzled her with this story about how amazing he was, and how amazing they were, and how our school rewarded this story and worshipped them as a couple. I was actually jealous at the time. She went from nothing to everything – because of him. She got a life because of him. She got to be important." Polly was almost smiling at the memory...almost. "But then it all changed. Within a year, I reckon. The story stopped being about how great they were, but how great *he* was, and how crazy it was that he would put up with her. It started with jokes and playful digs. Little things, like him always teasing her about how he got better exam results or something... but the story got stuck like that. Over and over, year after year. The narrative was always that your mum was nothing before your dad and she was only something now because of him. Her whole life was only about how she related to him. She had nothing of her own to say… Paige, it was devastating. If only you'd known her like I knew her, the way she was before…" She wiped a tear from her eye and put her mug down as it was shaking. "It's hard to make sense of it. But I believe that if you're told the same story over and over about who you are, even if it isn't the truth, it starts to *feel* true, and therefore it starts to become true, and then it becomes your own story."

I stared at the darkening sky through the glass walls. The sun had left a smudge of red across it before it sank for the night, like Elijah's pen. My aunt's words rang so true, her wisdom so acute that she should've really been surrounded by owls rather than cats. I thought of the story my dad had told me my whole life, about who I was. The story about how I didn't matter. How I wasn't important. Didn't really exist. And I reflected on how, like Mum, I too had made that story my own – had made it come true. No friends, no attention, no achievements – nothing to make anyone notice me. I was told I didn't matter and so I became the story of not mattering. Until that book, and Elijah… Sometimes it only takes one person to tell you a different story. A person you love and respect. And with hope, and love, and encouragement, you can start to believe a different tale about yourself.

"And Dad?" I asked, still staring at the red smudge stamped across the skyline. "I don't understand Dad. Why does he do what he does? He also seems so…unhappy."

"Oh, he is." Polly nodded. "Deeply. In fact, I think your dad is the unhappiest person I know." She raised her eyebrows. "Though, of course, he no doubt thinks the same thing about me." As she said it, Neo mewed loudly, feeling safe enough to return to us now I'd stopped wailing. He jumped on my lap and headbutted my chest until I started rubbing under his chin.

"If it makes him unhappy then why does he do it?" I asked, once Neo had settled, making my lap warm.

"Well, the weird thing about people," Polly said, "is, so very often, they'd rather feel important than feel happy."

I reached out and stroked the soft black fur of the cat.

"And they don't mind ruining other people's happiness in their quest to be important?" I added.

Polly tilted her head. "Bingo."

CHAPTER 39

Elijah: Hey, how are you doing? I can't stop thinking about you. A) because I'm worried of course, and want you to be OK, and B) other reasons x

Paige: I'm actually weirdly OK. Just very sleepy. Can't seem to get out of bed.
I can't stop thinking about you either.

Elijah: Well that's a relief. A) because I was worried, and B) other reasons x

Paige: Stop making me smile so much. It's confusing. And makes my face hurt x

I couldn't stop sleeping. I became a hibernating bear all weekend, though one who'd set their alarm clock to the wrong time of year. Outside Polly's window, children circled on bikes under pink snowflakes of blossom, savouring the sun on their face, and the ever-longer daylight hours. But I lay in a ball on my bed in the dark, curtains drawn, my body heavy. Twice a day, I dragged myself down to Polly's conservatory to obediently eat the food she'd made while the cats headbutted my ankles. She'd also feed me tiny pieces of information about my new life. My parents were happy for me to stay long-term, to "support Polly through her breakdown". She rang Adam and explained the real story and cover story to him too. He messaged, saying *Well done 4 getting out,* but didn't actually bother calling. Then, filled with food and life-changing decisions, I'd return to bed and reread all the lovely, kind, patient messages Elijah had sent, grinning and brushing my fingers over my lips where he'd kissed me.

Other than that, I slept to escape reality. I'd wake up, confused about where I was, my head swimming with questions about what was going to happen next, how much worse Dad would be without me there, and how to navigate the rest of my whole life with two parents who didn't want me around. So I slept and slept. I slept all through Monday – missing school. Polly stayed home too and let me. "Though you have to go tomorrow," she said. "They'll be giving you important revision stuff to do. It's just the final few days."

* * *

On Monday afternoon, I was woken by Polly's cool hand on my forehead. "You've got a visitor, Paige," she said, smiling down at me. "Waiting downstairs. An Elijah shaped one. Can I let him up?"

I struggled to drag myself out of sleep. "Elijah's here?"

I hadn't washed since before the ball. Hadn't brushed my hair. Hadn't worn anything apart from this stinky pair of pyjamas.

"You look fine." Polly guessed my thoughts. "And, I get the vibe that you could be wiped in excrement and he'd still want to come up."

"Polly!"

She laughed. "She's awake," she called down. "Come on up."

I only had time to run my hands through one side of my hair before Elijah's earnest, wonderful face appeared in my bedroom doorway. I broke into a fully body blush, and he did too. Polly smiled again, before standing.

"I'll leave you two to it. Don't be too long. She needs to rest." She mock waggled her fingers at Elijah before closing the door behind her. I scrambled up in my covers with my mad hair. We were alone. In a bedroom. These two facts set something off in me, made my blood turn to sherbet.

"How are you?" Elijah said.

"Sleepy. But better. You can sit down." I gestured to the end of my bed and he perched nervously. The kisses we'd shared hung between us, making everything strange and beautiful and scary.

"I, er…I got you something." He rummaged in his bag and produced a gift-wrapped, flat rectangle. "I just felt so useless about how to cheer you up, so I thought consumerism might be the answer."

I touched my heart with one hand as I reached for the box. "Thank you. Um…I'll unwrap it now, shall I?"

"If you want."

"Thank you."

"It's not much. It's just…well…open it."

I pushed my finger under the wrapping paper, which he'd clearly nicked from his mum, and opened it up to reveal a pen. A proper ink one, that needs cartridges. In a luscious deep red colour. "Oh my God."

"It's a pen," Elijah said unnecessarily.

"I can see that." I lifted it out of its box and found an engraving catching the light. The world *Sifter* was ornately etched into its side. Inside the box there were also several red ink cartridges. "I can't believe you've got me a…pen?"

He shrugged, blushing as he watched my delight. "Well, I was thinking about that notebook you got for Christmas and I've not once seen you actually write in it. Unless you're using it as a diary to write about how much you fancy me of course…"

I spluttered with embarrassment. "Elijah!"

He went redder at his own joke. "What? So you haven't been writing in your diary about me? Fine. In that case, use this pen. Use the notepad. Start writing something."

I ran the pen against my lips, grinning. "Like what?"

I thought about that notebook and how I'd only written one thing on the first page – otherwise it was empty. Blank. Patiently awaiting a story to be told.

"I don't know. Anything. The truth. In whatever form you want to tell it," he said.

I sat up and pulled him towards me and we toppled backwards onto my bed and kissed, and kissed, and kissed.

"Shall I tell you the truth?" I asked him, when we broke apart to stare at one another in wonder.

"Yes."

I reached down into the very depths of my courage. "I think I love you."

The second I'd said it, I felt more vulnerable and terrified than I'd ever felt in my life. Like I'd ripped off my skin and exposed myself to the elements. An awful two seconds passed while I watched Elijah's face digest what I'd said. They stretched out for hours.

After two years of two seconds, he replied. "Well thank God you said that, because I love you too. I don't even think it. I know it." Gold swirled through me, sparklers lit up on my skin. My heart swelled with complete euphoria. "I have done for ages but couldn't figure you out. Whenever we got close, you sort of clamped up. I didn't want to be one of those guys who can't be mates with a girl. And I've been worried it will just come hurtling out inappropriately for months now."

I giggled into his mouth, shutting him up with a kiss. "You love me?" I had to check. I'd have to check a lot.

"Paige, I bought you a pen. A pen?! Like a grandma. I had to google where on earth you even buy a pen from. This is what you've done to me."

"I love the pen."

"Good."

"And I love you. I always have, I think. Since that first message I found. Mr Red Pen."

We fell into kissing again and all thoughts of sadness evaporated. All sense of time evaporated too. There was only warmth in my heart, my stomach. Happiness shining through everything. The sense of being alive, and how gorgeous being alive could be – even if it is only for snatches.

Polly's voice came from the landing.

"Okay, guys, in three seconds I'm going to do a loud, dramatic cough to interrupt whatever's happening in here," she called from outside, interrupting us. "Are you ready? On the count of three. One, two...three!"

Elijah and I scrambled upwards as Polly hacked her lungs out. He leaped back to his end of the bed and we looked vaguely respectable when she entered with both hands over her eyes.

"Please have clothes on, please," she joked.

"Polly!"

She laughed and dramatically withdrew her hands. "A-ha! Brilliant. Oh no. Bollocks. Are you guys not actually a couple, and now I've totally mortified you both? Or WORSE, you're THINKING about becoming a couple, but you've not done anything yet, and now I've ruined it for ever and I'm the worst aunty in the WORLD."

"POLLY!"

Thankfully, Elijah was laughing. The cats, lured by the drama, all appeared in the doorway too. The ludicrousness of it sent me over the edge and I started laughing too, and Polly joined in.

"Polly, please stop being so embarrassing." I checked with him that I was right and he nodded. A stab of joy pierced my heart. "But, yes, Elijah and I...we're together."

"I thought so. Phew." She mock-swept her eyebrow. "Well, if I'm going to try and be a parent, I guess I should say you two need to leave the door open or something?"

"Polly!"

"I have no idea what I'm doing. I need to google it. Anyway, Elijah, you'd better be nice to her. We're having a bit of a time as a family, as you probably know."

"I promise."

Polly's face lit up. "Good. Well, anyone who can make Paige laugh right now is a winner in my book. But, umm, Paige? I did just call your mum, when I was downstairs."

The happiness in the room slid out through a trapdoor and I wiggled so I was completely upright and felt my stomach go back to how it always was.

"Yeah?"

Polly looked at Elijah, weighing up whether to tell me in front of him. I nodded.

"It's not a big thing..." she lied. "Just, you may have to go into school a bit late tomorrow. Your mum said she'll be out in the morning at yoga. She suggested it would be a good time for you to pick up your stuff."

Pick up my stuff.

Pick up what was left of my old life.

With my parents out. So they didn't even have to see me do it. So they could erase me from their lives without even having to witness the erasing.

"Is that okay? I can give myself the morning off work to come with you."

Of course it wasn't okay. Nothing about it was okay. It hurt. And would hurt for a very long time. Maybe even for ever.

Elijah reached out, took my hand and squeezed it. Polly was looking at me with so much guilt that she was the messenger, delivering such awful, painful news. Two people who didn't have to care about me. Who didn't have to love me and notice me, but had *chosen* to care about me, and love me, and notice me. That was beautiful. And the beauty of it gave me some strength. Maybe not enough. But a starting point to build some more.

I nodded.

"That's fine."

CHAPTER 40

School seemed smaller the morning I moved out of my house. I stood outside the gates, looking up at the building which would soon only be a memory. It was quiet and dormant at eleven a.m. All the chaos and drama suppressed as lessons went on – holding its breath and waiting for lunchtime to reignite.

My house that morning had also felt smaller. Polly and I knocked to double-check no one was home before letting ourselves in. We'd both cried as we quickly packed my stuff. There was no note. No goodbye. No marking of what had happened. The living room was spotless, no china dust left in the carpet. As Polly stuffed clothes into binbags and promised me we could go shopping for more, I picked up my personal items. My Christmas notepad, almost entirely clean and fresh. The books Elijah had given me, with all their red scribbles in them. My Alexa. And, finally, my notepads of all the horrid things from school. I shoved these into my rucksack when Polly wasn't looking and put everything else in a box to take to hers.

I walked around the rooms of my home one final time. There was no trace of me on the walls or the mantelpiece. I'd lived here for sixteen years and left no mark at all. I knew I would carry the pain of that my entire life. Part of my story would always be defined by the years I'd spent not-existing within these walls.

And, as I stood outside school, the years I'd spent not-existing there too sewed themselves into my story. Blossom fell into my hair as I realized you can't protect yourself from life. From people. From harm. I'd thought hiding myself away would shield me and yet not being noticed was just as damaging as drawing attention to myself might have been. If not more so.

I only had two weeks of school left. That wasn't enough time to leave a mark now but, as I took a breath and pushed through the gates, I realized the experience had left a mark on me at least. One that hurt, and that pain had taught me something. It taught me that I *wanted* to leave a mark. Telling my story was worth it, taking up space was worth it. Because not mattering hurt worse than anything else.

I lugged my bag onto my back and made my way to maths. Mr Sanders's face changed when he saw me. His eyes went all puppy-sympathetic.

"Paige, hello, sit down." He gestured to my chair. "We're just going through the revision timetables." His voice was overly bright and overly cheerful. Polly had rung the school to explain my family situation and ask for time off, and I'd laughed when she told me. "Polly, they probably had to look up in some database to figure out who the hell I was," I'd said. "Nobody would've noticed me missing apart from Ms Gordon."

I managed to pick up on the stale gossip from the Leavers' Ball. Grace and Sam had obviously won Prom Queen and King and obviously gotten together. It turns out it wasn't a night to remember – just school merely continuing, but at night-time, and with punch and cocktail dresses. I was due to meet Elijah for lunch, but needed to renew some revision books first. I sent him a message saying I'd be five minutes late, and rushed through the packed corridors and into the library.

"Paige! I was hoping I'd run into you."

Ms Gordon also had her super-kind face on. It matched her outfit of burned orange sundress with yellow accessories. I prepared for sympathy as I took my books up to the desk.

"Can I renew these? It wouldn't let me do it online."

"Yes, yes. Are you okay? I heard…"

"I'm fine. Thanks, miss."

"Okay, well." She didn't push further, which I appreciated. She took the books, bleeping them with her library gun. "I was about to come look for you actually. I know it's your lunch break, but I was hoping you could help me? You see, the girls are adding in the ball photos this lunchtime and then we can send the yearbook off to the printers."

She handed the books back. "It needs to go to print tomorrow to be delivered in time for the Leavers' Assembly. It's a tight deadline. They're only going to arrive the morning of your last day as it is."

"So, how can I help?"

"Well, I feel bad asking, especially with everything you're...well... It's just, Paige, you're our best proofreader, and I need a final pair of eyes on it. I went through it all last night, and it's fine. No typos that I could see. But could you give it a final look before we send it off? It should be super quick. We've all read it ten million times before."

I looked up at the clock and made calculations. I felt so *tired* of this yearbook. "I'm not sure I can fit it in this lunch break."

"After school then? I can give you the remote log-in? Then all you have to do is convert it to a PDF and email it to the printers. You've done it dozens of times before for the newspaper."

I suppressed a sigh. The yearbook. The stupid yearbook. I couldn't think of anything I cared about less. I was so tempted to say no.

"Yeah, fine. As long as you give me the world's best reference to get me into college."

She smiled in her burned orange ensemble. "Oh, Paige, you're going to go to the college? How exciting! I'll miss you of course, but, still, what an adventure."

I nodded. "Yes. I'm sending my application this week. I want...a new story. A fresh start. So, you'll give me a nice reference if I do this?"

"I'll do that anyway. But thank you. You're a life saver. Hang on, I'll come with you to the newsroom, show you the log-in you need." She called over to the library assistant who was restacking some *Catcher in the Ryes* and I grinned, thinking of Elijah's decorated copy hidden in the stack somewhere. "Jessie? Could you cover me for ten minutes?"

I sent Elijah a message as we walked across campus, Ms Gordon's novelty banana earrings playing a symphony on her shoulders.

Paige: Been dragged into doing the proofread for yearbook :(Sorry! Will probably miss you at lunch. Meet after school?

Elijah: Can't believe it. I've been puckering up for you all morning, waiting.

He sent a selfie of him pulling a ridiculous kissy face.

Elijah: But I'll live. See you after school. Love you xx

I almost stopped in the busy corridor. It was the first time he'd written it down and seeing it on my screen made the whole universe smile. I clutched my phone to my heart, like it was a love letter delivered by trusty steed or something.

He loves me, he loves me, he loves me.

He doesn't have to, but he does.

I was in such a state of blissful delight, I forgot I was entering a snakepit, until we got into the newsroom and found Grace and her merry bunch of sociopaths huddled over the computer, giggling.

"Girls!" Ms Gordon boomed and they all jumped away from their screen.

I noticed them frantically click onto a different page. They all looked guilty before plastering fake smiles on their faces. Lots of people might've missed it, but I certainly didn't. My suspicion sense started firing, and I narrowed my eyes.

"Are you almost done?" asked Ms Gordon.

"We're totally done." Grace smiled so sweetly I was surprised she didn't have more cavities. "It's all ready to send to the printer's."

Amelia started laughing behind her, trying to muffle it with her sleeve. This started a cascade of giggles between them. Further evidence.

"What's so funny, girls?"

"Oh, nothing," Grace said. "Just, I've been taking the piss out of Cara because she wore the same dress as Katie."

"Be nice to each other." Ms Gordon leaned over to check their ball page and, curious, I looked over her shoulder, wondering if I'd just imagined them hiding something. "Oh, this is lovely, girls. What great photos. Worth the last-minute rush, I say."

I took in the double-page ball spread and it was very much the final jewel in the populars' propaganda crown. A photo of Grace's victory was giant, front and centre, and at least forty per cent of the other photos were pictures of their group.

"It's all ready to send off now." Grace's voice was an octave higher than usual and I wondered how Ms Gordon didn't notice. Though, I'd been quietly monitoring people my whole life and, instinctively, it became very clear to me that the girls shouldn't know why I was there.

"Ms Gordon," I said, turning away to show how uninterested I was. "Can I use the photocopier?"

"What? Yes. Hang on, girls, let me just check the wording on this final page."

She didn't notice them glance at each other nervously, but I did. I played indifferent though. I took myself into the photocopying corner, my spidey senses tingling, and busied myself with taking out a lot of papers I didn't actually need copying. I utilized my very best wall-blending abilities, acting like I was lost in the fascinating world of photocopying maths coursework.

Please, hurry up and leave. Please. I kept my head down as they chatted final fonts with the librarian. And my invisibility cloak worked, as, once Ms Gordon gave them the thumbs up, they picked up their stuff and left, seeming to have forgotten me in the corner.

I hadn't forgotten them.

I picked up my warm batch of paper and made my way over to the computer. "So it's all done," I said, pointing to

Grace's perfect digital smile. She wore a tiara that probably only cost a few pounds from a fancy-dress shop but its social collateral was priceless.

Ms Gordon let out a deep sigh. "All done. Another year gone by. Another yearbook created. I don't know where time goes, Paige. I just keep getting older and older."

I didn't really know what to say to that.

"Sorry, I shouldn't go on. It just all passes so quickly. I really think this is one of the best yearbooks we've ever made though, Paige." She gave me a giant, sympathetic grin. "Which, of course, is so much down to you."

I squirmed. "You don't have to be nice to me just because of what's been going on at home."

"I…I…wasn't. Sorry. Don't think that. I mean, I'm sorry you're having a rough time but…you are a remarkable student, Paige. Truly. One of the best I've had on the paper. Sorry if I've pushed you out of your comfort zone with the yearbook sometimes. I only do it because I think you're so good."

The compliment landed happily in my heart. She was okay, Ms Gordon. A bit clueless, but she believed in me, and school would've been so much worse without her. "Thanks, miss."

"It's true. Anyway, let me show you how to log in remotely. As I said, one quick read-through. Shouldn't take more than an hour." She showed me around the back end of the document. "It should hopefully look the same on your home computer. I mean, wherever you proof it. Then, once it's done, you just download to PDF by clicking here – do you see?" I nodded, scanning the pages as she flicked through them. Nothing seemed different. Maybe I was thinking the worst? My instincts ravaged by the week's dramas. "If there *are* any typos – which there really shouldn't be – just correct them. Then let me know what you've changed so I can double-check before send-off. But, if not, just email it over to them. They know you. The printers are doing a rush job on it anyway because the deadline is so tight. They've made it very clear they can't proofread it for us, but I've gone through it three times. It should be clean. Thank you, Paige." She looked up at the clock and shuddered. "I've got ten minutes to grab some lunch. You've got my email if you spot a mistake."

I waved her away. "Have a good sandwich."

"At this time of lunch hour? No chance. There'll only be egg and cress left. I'll stink out the library."

She left in a bundle of orange, leaving just me and the yearbook. A year's effort. A year of lies that would sit on the shelves of every student here indefinitely.

I stretched out, cracked my knuckles, and clicked through the pages again. There wasn't really any point proofreading now, as ten minutes wasn't enough time to concentrate. I scanned through each beautifully laid out page. Everything looked like it should. Well, not what it *should* be, but you know what I mean. Maybe I'd imagined the Awfuls' guilty behaviour? I was just clicking through the *Most Likely to*… page, when a name caught my eye.

No.

It couldn't be?

Lily Welsh's name was on there. The very quiet, very big girl who hid in the library as often as I did. She spoke even less than I did. But that was strange. Lily hadn't been nominated in any of the *Most Likely to…* categories. My breath caught as I followed her name with my finger to see which category she'd accidentally won. Which didn't make sense if Ms Gordon had already checked this…but…

"No way."

There, in front of Lily's name, in exactly the same font, so it would take some time to notice it…there it was.

A new category and a new winner.

Most likely to eat their way through the entire school canteen…*Lily Welsh*

They couldn't have.

No.

Both of my hands clasped my mouth as I searched the page we'd laid out and finalized weeks ago. Some were still the same. Grace was still most likely to be a supermodel, of course. And Joe was still most likely to be a football manager. But they'd scattered in new ones. Awful ones. Truly, *what-the-actual-hell-is-wrong-with-people?* ones.

Most likely to end up homeless… *Chad Finnigan*

Chad came from the really rough part of town. Was in foster care. Sponsored by the church to be here. A nice boy. Really harmless. He ran to the canteen every lunchtime to get his free school dinner so nobody would notice and wore second-hand uniform that didn't quite fit, hoping nobody would notice. They had noticed, it seemed.

Most likely to be a crazy cat lady…
Laura Goddard

Most likely to end up accidentally pregnant…
Lisa Heartly

I mean, of course. How dare she get pretty and dismiss them?

Most likely to end up in a mental hospital…
Charlie Shaw

One final blow for the boy who had done nothing.

There were more. Each as cruel as the last. Hidden amongst the approved ones. The girls had obviously deleted the categories they deemed too boring, and held their own parliament. The senseless brutality of it all, the utter sociopathic shamelessness of it…it didn't make sense. It was so pointlessly, needlessly cruel. Why? They'd been crowned royalty – wasn't that enough? Surely they'd get suspended for this. But they obviously didn't care at all. Tears stung my eyes from rage. I closed them for a second, shaking all over, alone in the newsroom, and pictured how this would unfold. What would happen if I didn't do something?

Yearbooks delivered right before the Leavers' Assembly next week.

Unboxed by Grace and the girls. "*We don't mind doing it, Ms Gordon. We're happy to help.*"

Students standing in line to pick them up on their very last day of school. Their shirts covered in marker-penned farewell messages. Feeling good about themselves. Proud of themselves for getting through it. Already nostalgic, maybe, for "*the good old days*". Excited to pick up their yearbook. To see what it looked like. Trying to gather the courage to get the person they fancied to sign it before they left. Taking off the plastic. Marvelling at the front cover. This was their yearbook. Their keepsake. Finding a space to stand in the excitable, crowded hallway to flick through it. To have this moment with their history. Looking for their face, their section, their legacy. How they'd be remembered.

Getting to the *Most Likely to...* page.

And then...

Imagine being Lily Welsh and finding that.

Imagine being Chad and seeing that.

I opened my eyes and yelled into the empty newsroom. The pain this would cause. Instant searing pain. Unimaginable humiliation and confusion. Everyone you'd grown up with would see this. Everyone had this page in their own yearbook. *This* was your legacy. This was how they had decided you would be remembered…

They…

The bell rang and I jumped up, rage squealing through me. Noises of lunch-being-over echoed under the door as everyone rushed to their afternoon lessons.

Why?

Why had they done this?

I could never understand.

Or maybe I could.

To feel important.

The bell rang again. Somehow five minutes had already passed in this dark room with this dark discovery.

I was late.

And I only had that evening to decide what the hell to do.

CHAPTER 41

"I feel like I'm in a *Choose Your Own Adventure* book," I told Elijah that evening, in his bedroom. Pacing up and down, vibrating with angry energy. "But I don't want to choose my own ending. I just want to set the book on fire. The whole thing. Burn it all. Burn the stupid yearbook."

I'd just about made it through the afternoon without eroding with emotion. My guts felt like they'd been glued together, and I'd randomly yelled "*What the hell are you looking at?*" to some Year Seven in the toilets. That page of *Most Likely to…* was imprinted on my brain and swarmed into my consciousness whenever I blinked. I sent an SOS message to Elijah and he met me at the gate after school, looking concerned. I'd collapsed into his arms.

"I hate them, I hate them," I couldn't stop saying into his warm shoulder. "*What's wrong with people? What the actual hell is wrong with people?*"

"Shh, shh. It's okay. Well maybe it isn't. What's happened? Tell me and we can try to fix it."

I'd filled him in as we walked to his, with his arm over my shoulder, steering me there, like the stable captain steadying a wayward ship. When I explained what I'd found, his face registered actual shock for the first time since I'd known him.

"Christ," he said. "That's dark."

"I know."

"That's really, really dark."

"I know."

"Like, I'm in disbelief."

"I know. Well, I'm not. And I only have tonight to decide what to do. What the hell do I do?"

An hour of pacing Elijah's room later, and I was none the wiser. I kept thinking of poor, oblivious Lily Welsh, walking home from school, totally unaware of what was coming her way. Of Chad, laughing with his friends as he tried to make one milkshake last all afternoon in McDonald's, blissfully ignorant. It hurt me to think about it. All my emotions were too strong, undiluted, burning.

"Okay, so I have three options," I told Elijah, turning on my heel as he watched me from the bed. "One, I could just leave it. Behave like a freaking…nature documentary maker where you have to just stand back and let the baby elephant die that's stuck in the mud pit, otherwise you're interfering." I counted it off on my finger. "Two, tell Ms Gordon and dob them in. They'll get in trouble, but the school will hush it up. That, I guess, is the right thing to do."

Elijah turned over onto his stomach. "*Right?*"

"Well, the proper thing to do."

Elijah wrinkled his nose. "And when has the proper thing to do ever been the *proper* thing to do? If you know what I mean?"

He smiled his knowing smile and it did things to my stomach – loosened some of its iron grip. I leaned over to kiss him, so thankful to have him there to help me un-mess this mess.

"Okay, three." I leaped up, and continued where I'd left off. "I could just change it back to how it was? Nobody would know apart from me and them… I'm leaving school anyway so they can't really come after me. That way, nobody gets hurt."

Elijah made a steeple with his hands and leaned his chin on them. "You could do that, yes. I guess those are your only three options…"

Some cogs began whirring in my mind. The first two would get the girls some kind of comeuppance. They were clearly too inflated with their own self-importance to believe their little prank would get them suspended… though school was basically over. Was that enough though? And it wasn't just this cruel thing, it was all the cruel things they'd done. Unpunished.

"Or…" I said.

Elijah smiled again. "Or?"

"I could…" The cogs whirred faster. Clicking things into

place. Getting in touch with the part of myself that wasn't passive any more. That didn't just let things happen and say nothing. I had never stood up to these people, not really. I'd been too scared, but I was getting braver every day, and this was just too awful. People needed to know how evil they were. "I could tell the truth?" I said slowly. "About what they've done. But not just tell Ms Gordon. Tell everyone?"

Because I couldn't stop thinking about Lily Welsh opening that book and how that would feel. That pain rippling through her life. Because school matters, I'd realized. It wasn't just something you could beige your way through. What happens to you, the stories people tell about you, it all matters. If you do unforgivable things when you're sixteen, they're still unforgivable. The stain of what you've left on people still blemishes the fabric of their life story. I had a chance to tell the truth. I had a chance to alter the legacy. To make it reflect what actually happened, instead of what the more powerful decided to tell us. But was I brave enough?

I sat back down on the edge of Elijah's bed and put my face into my clammy hands. "What do I do?"

"You know I can't tell you." He trusted me to choose my own adventure, to narrate my own life. He peeled a hand off my face and kissed it. "I guess a good question to always ask yourself in life is...*what would you regret more?*"

"Regret?..."

The word unleashed more whirring cogs. That word... where had I heard it before?

No space of regret can make amends for one life's opportunity misused.

The sentence I'd found in *A Christmas Carol*. How much I regretted all the years I hid away because I was scared of the stories people would tell about me. Then I'd found the red pen, and followed it, and got out my own red pen, and found love, and courage, and myself again. Elijah had taught me to challenge other people's stories – even the stories of people I loved. He taught me I could argue back with the world. That I had my own unique view, based on the intricate, original story of my own life, and I should tell the truth about what it meant to be me. People could argue back. People could take out their own red pen and scribble all over my story – but at least I'd told it.

Should I take out my red pen now, and scribble over these people's stories? Tell the truth from the margins?

"What if the truth hurts people?" I asked Elijah, still on the edge of the cliff, not sure I had the guts to jump.

"What do you mean?"

"I mean, isn't it cruel? To expose people? Grace and co?"

"I don't think they were worried about cruelty when they changed that page."

"Yeah, but if I meddle with this, if I expose it – won't I be as bad as them? I don't want to be cruel," I said, leaning my face into his hand. "But I also don't want people to get away with being cruel either."

I thought of all the notebooks, heavy in my bag. Chock to the brim with terrible things I'd let pass. I'd lurked in the margins but never been able to fill them. Not once had anyone red-penned these people. Until now…

I let go of Elijah and took a long, hard look at the ceiling. There were only hours left until the print deadline. If I was going to do what I thought I was going to do, it was going to be a long night.

Tell the truth, the ceiling whispered.

Tell the truth, my heart urged me.

I closed my eyes and jumped, holding my nose as I plunged, because it would take time to resurface into these waters of the new me. Or maybe it wasn't a new me. Maybe this part of me had always been there. The me who made notes, who'd been on the school newspaper, spent my lunchtimes in the library, who noticed everything and refused to forget what I'd seen. Maybe I was finally ready to accept who I was, and who I wanted to be, and what I wanted to stand for.

"Elijah?"

"Yes."

"I'm going to need your help."

"I'm here." God, the way Elijah looked at me.

"In my rucksack. There's a pile of notebooks. Do you mind getting them out?"

We worked until it got dark outside. Rifling through the pages of all my notebooks from over the years – working out how and where to blend them into the yearbook. Elijah's mum came home from the lab – tired and wilting and surprised to find me still there. We told her we were busy revising and she ordered us a pizza in a burst of unusual motherly care. I messaged Polly to say I'd be home late and, with mozzarella hanging from our mouths, and a feverish air of scared anticipation, I rewrote the yearbook.

I added things to the *Do You Remember?* pages to add balance. I wrote a foreword and an afterword. Elijah fed me pizza, whispered words of encouragement, kissed my shoulder, and told me how proud he was. I leaned over and kissed him.

"What was that for?"

"For everything."

"I've not done anything, Paige. You've done it all. You."

It was almost eleven by the time I came to the *Most Likely to…* page. Polly had rung twice to remind me it was a school night, giving me a warm feeling of being cared about and worried over. Elijah's mum pointedly told us she was going to bed and suggested, firmly, we do the same.

"Almost done, sorry. One final philosophy question," he said. "We'll be quiet."

Tired and nervous, I clicked onto the most important page. "Final page," I said, taking his hand. "Are you ready?"

"Are you?"

"No, but yes."

"Crystal clear you are, Paige."

I laughed but my tummy felt tight.

I zoomed in on the *Most Likely to…* page. There it was,

in all its awful, bullying glory. Elijah, seeing it in person for the first time, let out a low whistle.

"God, it's real," he said. "I can't believe anyone thought this was funny."

As I scanned it afresh, the anger reignited, pulsing through me, reassuring me this action was worth the consequences. I took screen grabs to keep as evidence, before I checked the tracked changes, to remind myself of who actually won what, and typed it all back in carefully. Making it how it was before. Erasing the pain, erasing the humiliation. Saving the scars before they left their mark.

Then, when it was restored, I stared at the screen for a while. I clicked on the return button and added three more lines. Right at the top, so it was the first thing anyone would read on the page.

Most likely to rewrite this page before it went to print, inserting cruel made-up categories and winners, in a senseless act of bullying... (Luckily I found it in time and changed it back.)

Most likely to have no worries about the trauma this would cause...

Most likely to be needlessly, viciously cruel to people who have done nothing to deserve it...

Grace Langdon
Amelia Murry
Cara Williams

I read it back.

It wasn't a lie.

I didn't think even they could say this was a lie.

We proofread it one final time, so exhausted our eyelids kept twitching. I then hit *download* and waited for Elijah's computer to save it.

"I still can't believe I'm doing this," I said, my hand hovering over the laptop and an email to the printer.

"I can."

"I could still back out. I don't have to send this version over."

"You don't."

The *Most Likely to...* page was still up on his screen, feeding my anger.

"But I want to..."

Elijah smiled and took my hand. "I know you do."

As the download bar slugged along, I tried to imagine how the story of this would go next. I was not naive about the consequences. We would send it off and the printer would have no time to check it. I would email Ms Gordon to say there'd been no further typos. The yearbooks wouldn't arrive back until the day of the Leavers' Assembly. The Awfuls would offer to open the boxes and hand them out, so that Ms Gordon didn't catch onto their changes. Maybe the girls would have time to check them, and find out what I'd done, before the Leavers' Assembly. Maybe they wouldn't get a chance. Either way, it was going to be drama. But at least Lily Welsh wouldn't open the book and see herself winning that category. Instead she'd scan the pages and see her bullies held to account for the first time in five years. Some students would cheer at what I'd done, others would think I was pathetic. Many would have no idea of the humiliation I'd saved them from, and I never wanted them to know. I didn't need to be important in that way. And the popular gang would explode, of course. They'd be apoplectic with rage and deny any of it was true. Because everyone thinks they're the good guys in the story of their own lives, no matter how much they're the bad guys in other people's stories.

Me?

What would happen to me?

As my finger hovered over the mouse, I made peace with the fact I could very well be expelled. Though they might take my "family circumstances" into account. I'd be suspended at the very least. Would they even let me take my exams? I was leaving for college anyway but still... Would my classmates get to see this yearbook before the teachers stopped it? Or would it get out? Become legend?

From that point on, I wouldn't be able to control the story. I'd started writing one, but it was up to other people to help write the ending. All I'd done was throw a final plot twist into the tiny nothingness of my tiny year group's narrative, in our tiny school, in our tiny town. But I'd left a mark. I'd made an impact. I'd told a story. My story. My version of the truth. As true as I knew it.

Elijah's computer dinged. My yearbook was downloaded. I attached it to my email, my heart going mental. Elijah took my hand once more and squeezed it. And I knew the legacy of Elijah loving me would last throughout my life. When it came to the story of us, we were only at the start, with no idea how it would end. Maybe we'd last as long as our padlocks, weathering multiple storms on the banks of the Thames. I could only hope. But I knew his love had changed me. Every person on this earth deserves to have someone love them for precisely who they are. In fact, if more people felt loved for who they are, maybe they wouldn't feel so desperate to feel important at the expense of others.

"Are you ready?" Elijah asked. The boy who gave me a red pen, arming me to argue against the story of my own life.

I nodded, and hit send.

FINAL NOTE FROM THE EDITOR

Look, as I said, you didn't need to read this to be reminded what secondary school was like.

You were with me the whole way. You lived these pages with me. You have your memories now. That's all those years are now. A memory. After all of that.

I don't know if any of you will get to read this but, if you do, you may not agree with what I've done. You may not remember things happening the way I do. You may think my truth isn't the truth – it may certainly not be *your* truth. Or maybe it is, but accepting that hurts too much because it means you have to accept some truths about what you did, and what that means about who you are.

Just because I told this story doesn't mean you have to agree with it. In fact, I encourage you not to. I urge you to pick up a red pen and make this yearbook your own. Make your life your own. Make your story your own.

Pick up the pen. And tell the truth.

Paige Vickers

I hope people remember me as…

the girl who told the truth.

What would you like to tell your future self?

You did the best you could with what you had at the time.

My favourite thing about school was…

leaving it with my head held high.

Look who's MADE the news rather than writing the news??!! So proud. All my love, Elijah xxxx

---

St Benedict's Gazette

YEARBOOK DRAMA PROMPTS ANTI-BULLYING REVIEW

A school enquiry has been launched after the Year Eleven yearbook revealed details of systemic bullying by popular students.

A pupil on the yearbook committee discovered the *Most Likely to…* page had been rewritten with new categories and new winners to shame vulnerable members of the school community. Rather than alerting the teachers, the student decided to significantly rewrite the yearbook and expose the truth about the long-term bullying before it went to press.

The rewritten yearbooks were distributed at the Leavers' Assembly and "all hell broke loose" as students started reading them. Eyewitnesses said the school hall became pandemonium, with teachers struggling to contain the uproar. The three students who'd initially changed the *Most Likely to…* pages were escorted to the head teacher's office and suspended immediately. The student responsible for the significant rewrite was spared suspension, but is leaving the school at the end of term.

An anti-bullying review has been announced in light of the yearbook's revelations, however copies of the book are banned. Students were asked to return them immediately, but some are said to still be in circulation. The identities of the pupils shamed in the *Most Likely to...* pages have been kept secret, although the whistle-blower did send PDFs of the incriminating pages to the school as evidence of the scandal.

Head teacher Mr Steele said: "Nothing like this has ever happened in our school before and we take bullying extremely seriously. However, it appears some individuals have slipped under the net. We are reviewing our anti-bullying procedures to see what we can learn so this never happens again.

"However, I do urge any students harbouring these contraband yearbooks to hand them in immediately and allow the school to handle any in-school bullying professionally, rather than giving credence to this unacceptable act of vigilante justice."

The yearbook editor, who cannot be identified due to school rules, spoke to the paper only briefly to say this: "All I did was tell the truth. I highly recommend everyone does the same." ■

Exclusive content

HOLLY BOURNE'S TOP FIVE LIFE-CHANGING BOOKS

Paige and Elijah sift books for their best lines, words that can inspire and even change lives. For the best sifting material, try one of Holly's favourite life-changing books:

To Kill A Mockingbird by Harper Lee

Sorry to be THAT person, who tells you to read something that you have to study in school, but this book is a pure masterclass in teaching empathy. It's all about the innocence and joy of childhood, and exploring how part of that innocence is lost when you start seeing the world from other people's points of view, and realizing that adults often get it more wrong than children. It's also just funny and gorgeously written. Forget writing essays about it, just read it for the sheer joy of reading it.

Speak by Laurie Halse Anderson

This book is one of the most searingly beautiful books about high school ever written, combined with being one of the most searingly beautiful books about sexual violence ever written. It follows Melinda, a student who chooses to stop speaking after a party goes horribly wrong. The book haunts you and revives you as she starts to regain her voice and her power. Plus, as a bonus, there's a graphic novel version of it too.

Me And White Supremacy by Layla Saad

You may have heard a lot about the anti-racism movement on the news, and may think it doesn't apply to you. This book very gently points out that it does, and asks you to take on a 28-day guided challenge to unlearn harmful assumptions you may've internalized about race. This book won't just change your life, it could change the world.

How To Do The Work by Dr Nicole LePera

When I was researching one of my novels, I went to a mental health conference that changed everything. It was about having a more trauma-informed understanding of mental illness, how it's often a totally legitimate response to the life someone has had, rather than a sickness inside a person. *How To Do The Work* is a wonderful self-help book that explains this new way of seeing our mental anguish, as well as sharing daily rituals we can do to help regulate ourselves when our brains are wreaking havoc. A complete game-changer.

Angus, Thongs And Full-Frontal Snogging by Louise Rennison

Never has a book changed my life more, and never have I laughed as hard while my life changed. The diaries of Georgia Nicolson were basically my religion growing up, and have influenced my writing so much. It was totally revelatory to teenage-me that girls were allowed to be funny. Not even funny, but funnier than the boys around them. This series of books totally celebrated the giddy deliriousness of teen girls and the mayhem they get up to when away from the male gaze.

Happy sifting!

Holly x

If you have been affected by the issues raised in this book, the following organizations can help:

SAMARITANS

Samaritans are available round the clock, every single day of the year. You can talk to them any time you like, and in your own way, about whatever's getting to you.

Call, free, any time, on 116 123

Or email jo@samaritans.org

Visit – find your nearest branch on samaritans.org

THE MIX

Essential support for under 25s

The Mix is here to help under 25s get to grips with any challenge they face. Anywhere and anytime, online, over the phone or via social media.

Helpline: 0808 808 4994

themix.org.uk

THE YEARBOOK

SCHOLA EST HORRIBILIS

Most likely to...
keep you turning
the pages

#THEYEARBOOK

@hollybourneYA
@UsborneYA

@holly_bourneYA

@Holly.BourneYA